Gentlemen of a Company

Gentlemen of a Company

*English Players in
Central and Eastern Europe, 1590–1660*

Jerzy Limon

The right of the
University of Cambridge
to print and sell
all manner of books
was granted by
Henry VIII in 1534.
The University has printed
and published continuously
since 1584.

Cambridge University Press

Cambridge

*London   New York   New Rochelle
Melbourne   Sydney*

Published by the Press Syndicate of the University of Cambridge
The Pitt Building, Trumpington Street, Cambridge CB2 1RP
32 East 57th Street, New York, NY 10022, USA
10 Stamford Road, Oakleigh, Melbourne 3166, Australia

First published 1985

Printed in Great Britain at the University Press, Cambridge

Library of Congress catalogue card number: 84–28592

British Library cataloguing in publication data
Limon, Jerzy
Gentlemen of a company: English players in
central and Eastern Europe, c. 1590–c. 1600.
1. Actors – Europe, Eastern – History 2. Actors
– Central Europe – History
I. Title
792'.028'0922 PN2570
ISBN 0 521 26304 2

Contents

Illustrations

Illustrations 2–3, 5, 6, 8–12 are reproduced by permission of PAN
Library in Gdańsk.

Preface

SINCE E.K. Chambers devoted one of the chapters in his notable *The Elizabethan Stage* (1923) to the activity of professional English actors on the Continent in the sixteenth and the seventeenth centuries, not much has been written on the subject in English. The meagre list of publications includes a dozen or so articles scattered in specialized periodicals, and perhaps several chapters, or even paragraphs, in sundry books dealing with the acting profession in general. No matter how one looks at it, for some reason this intriguing phenomenon in European theatrical history has attracted little attention from English-speaking scholars, and this field of studies has, in fact, become a Continental speciality. Since about the middle of the nineteenth century, generations of scholars in Europe have been searching through archives and libraries, uncovering hundreds of pieces of evidence, which – when put together as if in a jigsaw puzzle – present to us a picture of English players' Continental activity of surprising scale and intensity.

However, if we stick to the jigsaw-puzzle metaphor, we may say that the picture is – as we look at it today – not complete, and although at first sight one would be able to recognize its significance, a closer analysis would reveal that a number of pieces are missing, which in consequence creates serious obstacles for any attempt to describe the picture in minute detail. The blank spaces may, of course, be filled with imagination, conjectures and hypotheses which might or might not be confirmed in the course of time. Thus, any newly discovered piece of evidence, however insignificant it may seem to an uninitiated person, becomes of major importance in this particular field of studies, for it fills the gap and at times may help to clarify significant sections of the whole picture.

Because the geography of Europe today is to a large extent coloured by the political situation and is, consequently, topsy-turvy (with Finland, for instance, belonging to the 'West', whereas the German Democratic Republic and Czechoslovakia belong to the 'East'), the title of this book needs some explanation. I have used the notion of 'Central and Eastern' Europe in its traditional geographical sense, without taking into account the politics of today. If on the other hand a scrupulous reader wanted to insist on the political situation in the sixteenth and the seventeenth centuries, it may be recalled that Prague, the capital of the Kingdom of Bohemia, had also for several centuries been the capital of the Holy Roman Empire of the German nation and, undoubtedly, for contemporaries this was the very centre and the heart of Europe. With this in mind, we are fully justified in labelling the neighbouring countries and provinces as Central European.

Almost all the major English acting companies performing on the Continent in the period under discussion may be traced in Central Europe. Their activity there was not restricted to a certain phase, or period, and, as the pieces of evidence provided and discussed below attempt to prove, this activity was not coincidental. On the contrary, Central Europe was clearly one of several distinct centres, where English acting companies found permanent employment and the noble patronage of the Kings of Poland and the Dukes of Brandenburg enabled a number of players to survive the Thirty Years War. This provides valid grounds for treating Central Europe as a distinct region in the history of English players' activity on the Continent, a fact generally neglected in this field of scholarship. For many scholars, English players' presence on the Continent was confined to Germany. This is reflected, among other things, by the most recurrent title of their works: 'Shakespeare in Germany' or the like. In point of fact, a title of this sort is misleading for at least two reasons: one, English theatrical activity on the Continent was neither dominated by Shakespeare as an actor, nor by Shakespeare the playwright (Shakespeare never went to Europe himself and the only link he had with the strolling players was that he knew some of them personally and that they included some of his plays in their repertory); and two, the activity of the English on the Continent was by no means confined to Germany, something which I hope to make clear.

Because more than sixty years have passed since E.K. Chambers published *The Elizabethan Stage*, mentioned above, and during that period no larger work on English strolling companies in general has appeared in English, I thought it reasonable and worthwhile to expand the Introduction to cover a somewhat wider field than the chapters which follow. This will provide the reader with rudimentary information about the origin, particularities and phases of English players' activity as a whole, and I hope that the Introduction in itself will prove useful to all students and scholars of both English and Continental theatrical history.

Parts of this book have already been published, or are in press. Thus, the Introduction incorporates a paper presented at the International Elizabethan Theatre Conference held in Waterloo, Ontario in June 1981. The chapter on Gdańsk is based on my Ph.D. dissertation to be published by the Gdańsk Learned Society. The chapter on Warsaw is an altered and enlarged version of my article published in Polish in *Pamiętnik Teatralny*. And the chapter devoted to the Gdańsk public theatre is based partly on my essay published in *Shakespeare Survey* 32 and on a paper presented at the annual meeting of the Shakespeare Association of America, held in San Francisco in 1979. The notes will provide the reader with bibliographical details.

Most of the archival materials used in this book have already been published. Because in a number of cases the originals were either lost or destroyed during the World Wars, I have been unable to verify the validity of their printed transcriptions. This is, for instance, the case with the archives in Stettin and Elbing. However, in most of the cases when the original documents have been preserved, it was possible to make sure that their printed form was properly transcribed. Such is the case in particular with the most valuable documents connected with the region – those from Gdańsk and Königsberg. In the State Archives in Gdańsk there is one of the largest collections of English players' original applications for leave to play, and the ducal archives of Königsberg have been fortunately preserved in Göttingen in West Germany. Some of these documents have been translated into English by other authors, and I have used these extensively, especially the ones translated by A. Cohn. Unless otherwise stated all the remaining translations of the originals are my own. These have been checked and revised by Dr Jeremy Adler of Westfield College, whose contribution to the last stages of this book cannot be over-estimated. In so far as they are modernized renderings, they are not sufficiently literal for academic purposes; however, specialists will find reference to the origins in the notes.

I wish to express my gratitude to all the people who encouraged and helped me to complete this book. This includes a number of scholars, archivists and librarians of many nationalities, a truly international family of people of good will, who provided me with invaluable pieces of information and critical remarks all of which contributed to the final shape of this book. They are too many to be mentioned by name and the only exception to this rule is Mr Neil Jones, who has generously devoted his precious time to smoothing the roughness of my English.

1. Towns visited by English players in Central and Eastern Europe

Introduction

THE PRESENCE of English players on the Continent was first recorded as early as 1417. An unidentified company of presumably amateur actors accompanied English bishops to the Council at Constance, and performed before the gathered nobles there. A contemporary account tells us that

The English are proud, among other things, of a new spectacle, or at least of one hitherto not known in Germany. This is a religious drama which the English bishops presented before the Emperor on Sunday 31 January, about the Nativity, the three Magi, and the slaughter of the Innocents. They had ordered the same play to be shown several days earlier in the presence of the magistrates of Constance and numerous other men of distinction, so that the players might act their roles better before the Emperor.[1]

The above description, interesting in itself, is an isolated one, and there is no doubt that the visit and performances in 1417 were unique events, unconnected with any sort of regular activity on the Continent. It is to the last quarter of the sixteenth century – or strictly speaking, to the last decade of the century – that we may trace the origins of one of the most fascinating and intriguing phenomena in English theatrical history: the age of the 'Englische Komödianten', as the English players were labelled by their contemporaries on the Continent.

When Fynes Moryson, the well-known Elizabethan traveller, visited Frankfurt during the annual fair in September 1592, he saw a public performance given by a company of English players. In his 'Itinerary' he left us his account of the performance, which is one of the earliest and most authoritative pieces of written evidence for the early phase of the English actors' activity on the Continent. This is how he recalls the event:

Germany hath some fewe wandering Comeydians, more deseruing pity then prayse, for the serious parts are dully penned, and worse acted, and the mirth they make is ridiculous, and nothing less then witty . . . So as I remember that when some of our cast despised Stage players came out of England into Germany, and played at Franckford in the tyme of the Mart, hauing nether a complete number of Actours, nor any good Apparell, nor any ornament of the Stage, yet the Germans, not vnderstanding a worde they sayde, both men and women, flocked wonderfully to see theire gesture and Action, rather than heare them, speaking English which they vnderstand not.[2]

Several points need particular attention here. First, Moryson labels the players 'our cast despised Stage players' who 'came out of England into Germany', which indicates that by 1592 there were already English strolling companies active on the Continent, and that they were composed of actors who found no employment at home. Secondly, the company described had neither a 'complete number of Actours, nor any good Apparell, nor any ornament of the Stage', all of which detracted from the quality of the performance. And thirdly, the language used on stage was English, and although the spectators could not understand a word they 'flocked wonderfully' – to Moryson's surprise – 'to see theire gesture and Action', which implies that the non-verbal acting devices used by the English were interesting enough to attract the attention of the audience. In other words, the skills and talents of the English surpassed those of their Continental rivals. Moryson confirms this in another passage of his 'Itinerary':

For Commedians [i.e. the Continental players], they little practise that Arte, and are the poorest Actours that can be imagined, as my self did see when the Citty of Getrudenberg being taken by them from the Spanyards, they made bonsfyers and publikely at Leyden represented that action in a play, so rudely as the poore Artizans of England would haue both penned and acted it much better. So as at the same tyme when some cast despised players of England came into those partes, the people not vnderstanding what they sayd, only for theere action followed them with wonderfull concorse, yea many young virgines fell in loue with some of the players, and followed them from citty to citty till the magistrates were forced to forbid them to play any more.[3]

Thus in Moryson's opinion it was the quality of 'action' rather than anything else that constituted the chief attraction to Continental spectators and ensured the success of the English players, all in spite of the incomprehensibility of the dramatic text. Far more important for our present purpose than the broken hearts of a number of virgins, is the fact that the described company travelled from one place to another, and that the players needed permission to play from the local authorities, which was not always granted.

With a few possible reservations all Moryson's remarks about the English players may be treated as true and even characteristic of the English dramatic companies that started to tour Europe at the close of the sixteenth century, particularly in the early, or 'reconnaissance' phase of their activity there. The surviving evidence leaves no doubt that the first companies to arrive on the Continent were indeed small, poorly equipped with costumes and stage properties, that the language used was English, and that they had to travel from one place to another in hope of financial gain. However, most of this was certainly not true of the companies that flooded Europe later on, in the first half of the seventeenth century. One of the last famous strollers, George Jolly, in his supplication to the Council of Basle, dated 1654, offered to delight all who love plays 'with his well-practised company, not only by means of good instructive stories, but also with repeated changes of expensive costumes, and a theatre decorated in the Italian manner, with beautiful English music and skilful women';[4] and of course the performances were given in German. These quoted sources illustrate clearly the development that the English companies had undergone.

It has to be stressed, however, that the company Fynes Moryson saw in 1592 was by no means the first English troupe to visit the Continent in the period under discussion. In 1579/80 a company of English 'instrumentalists' – Johann Krafftt, Johann Personn, Johann Kirck or Kirckmann, and Thomas Bull – was recorded at the Danish court, but nothing more is known of their stay there.[5] Interestingly, Denmark seems to have been the first important destination for the English players. In 1585 an unidentified English troupe is said to have played in the courtyard of the town hall at Elsinore, the performances evoking tremendous interest among local people who – to use Moryson's expression – 'flocked [so] wonderfully' that they broke down the wall.[6] These may have been the same players who visited Leipzig during the same year and were paid 5 thalers for their 'play with leaping' ('Spiel mit Springen').[7] In 1586 the Earl of Leicester's men visited again, and acted at, the court of the King of Denmark at Elsinore, whence they travelled as far south as Dresden.[8] From extant pieces of evidence it appears that the then King of Denmark Frederick II (1559–88) kept the players 'for a long time', and subsequently recommended them to the Elector of Saxony Christian I (1586–91). The Dresden appointment of the company includes the following names: Thomas King, Thomas Stephens, George Bryan, Thomas Pope, and Rupert Persten (Percy?), and the preserved Danish list adds William Kempe and 'his youth' Daniel Jones.[9] The same company may have visited Gdańsk in the following year.[10] One or two other companies are recorded in various countries in or before 1592. For instance Robert Browne, who is one of the most famous strollers, made his first Continental tour in 1590, when he was paid 15 guilder for performances at Leyden,[11] and a company of English 'instrumentalists' was recorded at Nyköping in Sweden in 1591/2.[12]

However, Fynes Moryson is mistaken when he contemptuously labels the actors 'cast despised Stage players', and, in another place, 'stragling broken Companyes'. Although the frequent failure of contemporary records to note the names of individual actors makes it extremely difficult to identify these companies and trace their precise routes, a sufficient amount of documentary evidence has been gathered to support the opinion that many of these actors were members of notable London companies, who, for various reasons, were forced to seek their fortunes 'beyond the seas'. Thus, among the numerous names of actors known to have been active on the Continent even in the reconnaissance phase of their regular visits, many may be found in London records. The names of Robert Browne, Richard Jones, William Kempe, Thomas Pope and Thomas Sackville may serve as examples. For instance, all the players mentioned in a passport granting permission to leave England for a Continental tour, issued on 10 February 1592 by Charles Howard the Lord High Admiral, were members of the notable Lord Admiral's company. The names given in the document are as follows: Robert Browne, John Bradstreet, Thomas Sackville and Richard Jones.[13] The question immediately suggests itself: why should such experienced and well-known actors as Browne and Jones[14] venture a risky journey overseas? To use Hamlet's words – 'How chances it they travel? Their residence, both in reputation and profit, was better both ways.' Were it an isolated case in English theatrical history, we would not really have to bother to give a convincing and conclusive answer. But these players were followed by dozens of others, who dominated the Continental theatrical scene for many decades. It would be naïve to assert that this was a conscious cultural enterprise, stemming from a desire to propagate and spread English drama on a wider scale. The reasons for this unprecedented exodus of players from England at the close of the sixteenth century are to be sought, above all, in the unstable economic conditions in London, and in the tremendous success the companies enjoyed on the Continent. For at times acting in London was unprofitable or even impossible, and, without the resource of going abroad or into the country, even the best of the city companies could hardly have survived. The conditions that forced the London actors to travel are well known and the three usually mentioned are the Puritan opposition, the ravages of the plague, which led to temporary inhibitions of acting, and growing competition among the companies. Not all of these factors contributed equally and it was the last of them that seems to have been chiefly responsible. This can be seen particularly clearly after the re-opening of London theatres in 1594, following a two-year inhibition due to the plague. The reconstructed organizations of players in 1594 had no continuity with those in existence up to 1592. Of the numerous companies active in London in the preceding period only two, the Lord Chamberlain's and the Lord Admiral's, now dominated the city's theatrical life. A sort of monopoly was established, which was confirmed by a letter from the Privy Council to the Master of the Revels, dated 19 February 1598:

Whereas licence hath bin graunted unto two companies of stage players retayned unto us, the Lord Admyral and Lord Chamberlain, to use and practise stage playes . . . and whereas there is also a third company who of late . . . have by waie of intrusion used likewise to play . . . Wee have therefore thought good to require you . . . to take order that the aforesaid third company may be supressed and none suffered heereafter to plaie but those two formerlie named belonging to us.[15]

Even if a contemporary account mentioning two hundred actors living in London is exaggerated,[16] there is little doubt that in and shortly after 1594 a number of players found themselves unemployed, facing not only poverty, but severe punishment under the law. By the Statutes of 1572 and 1598 unlicensed players were threatened with branding as 'rogues, vagabonds and sturdy beggars'.[17] And although the monopoly of the two companies mentioned above had broken down by 1602, when in March the Earl of Worcester's company received a licence[18] to perform in London, the competition between particular companies remained ruthless, and frequently the fortunes of particular players and even of whole companies depended on such base men as the London theatre entrepreneur Philip Henslowe. How effectively he waged war on rival troupes may be judged, among other things, by a complaint of Lady Elizabeth's men in 1615, who claimed that Henslowe 'in 3 yeares hee hath broken and dissmembred fiue Companies'.[19]

An additional serious menace to the prosperity of adult companies was the sudden and surprising popularity around the year 1600 of children's companies. An immediate echo of this 'war of the theatres' may be found in Shakespeare's *Hamlet*. When the Prince asks about the reasons that forced the 'tragedians of the city' to travel, he is answered that

there is, sir, an aery of children, little eyases, that cry out on the top of question, and are most tyranically clapp'd for't. These are now the fashion, and so berattle the common stages – so they call them – that many wearing rapiers are afraid of goose-quills and dare scarce come thither. (II, ii, 339–44)

This is even more precisely stated in the 'bad' quarto of *Hamlet*:

Yfaith my Lord, noueltie carries it away,
For the principall publike audience that
Come to them, are turned to private plays,
And to the humour of children.

Both the quotations illustrate how the children's companies were drawing audiences away from the public playhouses, where the adult players performed, to the private ones, which at that time were occupied by boys' companies. Another important reference to the boys may be found in Ben Jonson's *The Poetaster*, where the winter of 1600/1 is referred to in the following terms from a public player's point of view: 'for this winter ha's made vs all poorer, then so many staru'd snakes: No bodie comes at vs'. This of course had a disastrous effect on the players' income and it is not surprising that at least some of them found themselves in a desperate situation. There is further contemporary evidence of the misery and hopelessness of their plight, including Thomas Dekker's significant statement: 'We can be bancrupts (say the players) on this side and gentlemen of a company beyond the sea.'[20] As E.K. Chambers put it:

Certainly all the players did not grow rich, even in London. Some of them to the end, perhaps the majority, remained threadbare companions enough; in and out of debt, spongers upon their fellows, frequenters of pawnshops, acquainted with prison. Those who had to do with the stage were not all such riff-raff as a hasty reading of the Puritan literature might suggest.[21]

Thus the prospects of a better life abroad must have been tempting to London players. The sporadic Continental tours of small companies before 1594, exploratory in character, were followed by regular visits which were eventually to develop into a permanent presence of English players on the Continent until well after the Restoration.[22]

Of course, the situation at home was only the stimulus, the driving force which made the actors seek their fortunes abroad, and the fact that their expectations of financial gain were, in most cases, fulfilled on the Continent was entirely dependent on other factors, the most important being the patronage of Continental nobility and the steadily improving quality of performances. In spite of the fact that the English actors active on the Continent are traditionally labelled 'strolling', 'wandering', or 'travelling' players, one has to remember that most of the major companies found service at noblemen's, ducal, or even royal courts, where they stayed for many years, undertaking only occasional travels or none at all. It should also be added that in most towns public performances were prohibited throughout almost the whole year, and the actors were given permission to play only on special occasions, local celebrations, during feasts and fairs.

For example, traditional fairs were held at Leyden in summer and autumn; there was also an autumn fair at Amsterdam, and a summer fair at Utrecht; the Frankfurt fairs were held twice yearly in spring and autumn, and Gdańsk had a St Dominic's Fair in August and St Martin's Fair in the autumn. Permission to play was usually granted to the English players for a strictly limited period of time, on average for about two weeks excluding Sundays. This depended largely on the duration of a fair in a given town. Obviously, this was a long-awaited occasion that brought many people from the country, other towns, and in the case of larger towns, like Frankfurt, fairs were held on an international scale. Visitors to fair towns were naturally eager to see 'the tragedians of the city' and they were ready to pay for their entertainment, and in many cases it was these visitors in fact who were the major source of players' income. Had it not been for the fairs, it would often have been entirely unprofitable to give public performances in relatively small towns like Berlin or Elbing. At times, the total number of spectators at performances given for two or three weeks was comparable to the number of inhabitants of a given town. For example, when in 1628 an English company performed at Nuremberg in a newly opened public theatre there, the eight performances given by the players were attended by almost thirteen thousand spectators![23] On the other hand, when in July 1611 John Spencer was allowed to perform with his company for two weeks out of season in Gdańsk, the players gave up acting after a few days, owing to the very small number of spectators. They decided to leave the town and return during the traditional St Dominic's Fair, opening on 5 August. The company played with great success during the fair, and the popularity of performances was such that Spencer complained that a 'crowd broke secretly into the theatre'.

Thus, travelling was generally limited to the period between spring and autumn, and ceased almost entirely in winter. There were, of course, exceptions, and in some regions of Europe, the strolling companies were at times active throughout the whole year. This was particularly the case in the

Netherlands – a densely populated area, with numerous wealthy towns at a close distance to one another. On the other hand, the severe climate made winter travelling entirely impossible in Central and Eastern Europe, not to mention the fact that distances between towns were far greater than in the western part of the Continent. Occasionally, however, some English companies braved all difficulties to travel in winter to the remote corners of Europe, sometimes getting themselves into serious trouble. This desperate application was made by an audacious group of players who reached Riga in Livonia in winter 1647/8:

although we have received a good deal of money, we have . . . not yet recovered our expenses, and even less have we earned a penny to subsist on for a further journey . . . we cannot properly go anywhere else. It is impossible to go by water, and to travel by land . . . is . . . not worth either the trouble, or the expense. Nor is it the custom in any town to welcome us at this time of year.

For these reasons, finding service at court was a blessing and a guarantee of survival, because apart from permanent residence and a more or less stable income, the players were granted patents and licences, which enabled them to travel safely as servants of a given nobleman. As early as 1586, the King of Denmark had an English company in his service for several months. The same company played at the Elector of Saxony's court for an even longer period. More conspicuous was the case of the English players who entered the service of the Landgrave Maurice of Hesse-Kassel, the Learned, who, incidentally, had a private theatre, named the *Ottoneum*, built at Kassel between 1604 and 1605, in which the English performed until 1613.[24] The vogue for keeping English players at court must have been prevalent among the Continental aristocracy, since the Prince of Poland felt a capricious and costly need to bring a whole company direct from London to Warsaw in 1617. The vogue originated and spread on a wider scale towards the close of the sixteenth century and was of prime importance for the future fortunes of the English players on the Continent and, indirectly, for the quality and variety of their staging of plays, and consequently for their popularity among the common people.

It is one of the arguments of this book that the activity of the English players on the Continent could not have developed to the extent that it did without the existence of numerous large and petty courts that facilitated the players' attempts to make a living. The vogue for employing English actors and musicians at court spread among the Continental nobility as early as the 1590s. That noble patronage was widespread and lucrative for the players was generally acknowledged by contemporaries. One, Erhard Cellius, the German author of *Eques Auratus Anglo-Wirtembergicus* (1605), left us with the following account:

England thus produces numerous and outstanding musicians, and tragedians most experienced in histrionic art, among whom some formed congregations and for some time left their homes and went abroad, and they used to present and exhibit their art above all at ducal courts. Several years ago, the English musicians came to our Germany . . . and having stayed for some time at the courts of great princes, they gained – through their musical and histrionic art – so much favour that they returned home generously rewarded and loaded with gold and silver.[25]

Many other sources, some of which will be discussed below, support the view that the players were often accompanied by musicians, as was the case with John Dowland, the most famous English composer of the period, who emerged on the Continent in c. 1594, and was also present at Kassel, where the Landgrave Maurice the Learned had a company of English players in his service.[26] Dowland left us an account of his Continental adventures, painting a picture of the success all the strolling 'instrumentalists' must have dreamt of:

When I came to the Duke of Brunswick he used me kindly and gave me a rich chain of gold, £23 in money, with velvet and satin and gold lace to make apparell, with promise that if I would serve him he would give me as much as any prince in the world. From thence I went to the Lantgrave of Hessen, who gave me the greatest welcome that might be for one of my quality, who sent a ring into England to my wife, valued at £20 sterling, and gave me a great standing cup with a cover gilt, full of dollars, with many great offers for my service.[27]

And in November 1598 Dowland was appointed lutenist to Christian IV of Denmark at the salary of 500 thalers per annum, a very large sum indeed, and stayed in Denmark for eight years.[28]

It may be noted that the names of patrons given in Dowland's account were not accidental: these nobles not only hired individual artists to perform at their courts, but also had whole companies of English players and musicians in their service for many years. The best known and most prominent case is that of the Landgrave Maurice of Hesse-Kassel. As early as 1594 some English players were mentioned as his comedians, and the company, although changing its cast frequently, remained active at Kassel until about 1613.[29] The court of Duke Henry Julius of Brunswick-Wolfenbüttel was one of the first visited by Robert Browne in 1592,[30] and Christian IV's father, Frederick II, had a company of English players in his service as early as 1586. The same company that visited Elsinore in 1586 emerged thereafter at the court of the Elector of Saxony, Christian I, at Dresden, and from that year Dresden became one of the centres of the English players' activities.[31] Christian's two sons, Christian II and John George I continued their father's patronage and on many occasions employed the English. John George I was such an admirer of music and theatre that even the Thirty Years War did not prevent him spending substantial sums of money to keep an English company at his court. Despite contemporary sources, which record that John George's mania was drinking and hunting, he seems to have been, as C.V. Wedgwood put it 'not without culture'[32] and took an intelligent interest in fine arts and above all in music and theatre.

In Central Europe, there were three major noble families whose patronage enabled the English players to develop their activities there. These were the Hohenzollerns, i.e. the Electors of Brandenburg, the Royal line of the Vasas in Poland, and the Habsburgs in Bohemia and Austria. These will be discussed in greater detail in further chapters of this book. It may be noted here, however, that through family connections and relations all of the above houses helped significantly to smooth the way for English players elsewhere on the Continent. By the early seventeenth century it had become customary among the members of aristocratic families to recommend, and even 'lend' English acting companies to one another, and also to town councils. Early examples may be found in the last decade of the sixteenth century, but more conspicuous ones after 1600. Thus, in 1604 an English company was recommended to the councillors of Nuremberg by Duke John Frederick of Würtemberg.[33] In the same year, John Spencer's men submitted a letter of recommendation from the Elector of Brandenburg to the councillors at Leyden.[34] Spencer was again recommended by the Elector in 1609, this time to the Elector of Saxony's court at Dresden.[35] The Landgrave Maurice of Hesse lent his English comedians for a couple of weeks in 1610 to the Elector of Brandenburg on the occasion of the Elector's brother's wedding celebrations,[36] and the same happened in 1612, when the Landgrave lent his comedians to the city of Frankfurt-am-Main on the occasion of the coronation of the Archduke Mathias of Austria as Emperor.[37] In 1609 the Duke of Stettin recommended English players to the Elector of Brandenburg, and the latter recommended John Spencer again to the Elector of Saxony in 1613.[38] When Robert Archer came to Gdańsk in 1615, he carried a patent from the Elector of Brandenburg and two 'testimonials' from the Duke of Stettin and the Bishop of Köslin.[39] In 1617 John Green's company received a letter of recommendation from the Royal court at Warsaw to the Archduke Charles of Austria, the then Bishop of Breslau, who – in turn – recommended the same company to Cardinal von Dietrichstein. And Richard Jones' men were recommended in 1619 by the King of Poland to the councillors of Gdańsk. At times, the players accompanied their patrons in their travels. In 1611 there was a company of English players and musicians with the Elector of Brandenburg at Ortelsburg in the Duchy of Prussia, accompanying the Elector to Warsaw. The Landgrave Maurice may have been accompanied by his actors when he visited Prague in 1610, and the Elector of Saxony took his company to Torgau, where on 1 April 1627 the marriage was celebrated between the Princess Sophia and the Landgrave George of Hesse-Darmstadt.[40] The list, of course, could be made much longer.[41] Noble patronage extended far beyond the court of a given aristocrat, was essential to the fortunes of the English players and was an important contribution to the dissemination of the art of theatre in various parts of the Continent.

Thus by the early seventeenth century, English players had a number of friendly courts at their disposal, and when necessary they could plan their travels in detail beforehand to take in neighbouring towns during the theatrical season, or perform in towns or villages on the way from one court to another. At times the companies travelled hundreds of miles to reach their destination. For example, in 1607 John Green's troupe went from Gdańsk on the Baltic coast to Graz in southern Austria. The same players left Graz early in 1608 and travelled straight to Brussels, presumably recommended to another Habsburg there, the Archduke Charles. This last example may serve as an additional illustration of how the noble patronage extended and spread through family connections. Thomas Heywood in his *Apology for Actors*, published in 1612, but written in or about 1607, mentioned that 'the Cardinall of Bruxels, hath at this time in pay a company of our English comedians'.[42] This 'Cardinall of Bruxels' has been identified as the Archduke Charles (a Habsburg, of course), Governor-General of the Spanish Netherlands from 1598 to his death in 1621. A recently discovered passport, dated 13 February 1607, reveals that indeed there was a company of English players, seventeen in number, enjoying the Archduke's patronage at about the time Heywood wrote his *Apology*.[43] This may in fact have been John Green's troupe.

One of the first privileges deriving from a nobleman's patronage was the possibility of increasing the number of actors in a company. That the company Fynes Moryson saw at Frankfurt in 1592 did not have a 'complete number of Actours' is by no means surprising. The few companies recorded on the Continent around that period were small indeed, five or six players being the average strength. It seems natural that the managers of travelling companies tried to limit expenses by keeping down the number of actors. The same tendency may be observed in England whenever the London companies toured the country.[44] The growing number of both actors and companies is noticeable almost immediately after 1594, a year which seems to mark the beginning of their regular activity on the Continent, and becomes even more apparent after 1600. It seems, however, that the companies formed *ad hoc* in England were relatively small, and that they grew in strength after they had reached the Continent. Sometimes they joined forces, and sometimes particular companies were supplemented with Continental actors. The custom of hiring foreign players may be observed almost from the very beginning of the English theatrical impact on the Continent. A company of eighteen 'instrumentalists' performing in 1591 at Nyköping in Sweden was composed of twelve Englishmen and six Swedes.[45] In 1600 George Webster, John Hill and Richard Machin, obviously English players, were accompanied by an actor, Bernard Sandt, who was apparently German,[46] and in 1604 we encounter a company styling itself as 'English and Cologne comedians'.[47] Among John Spencer's men in 1615 there was one German and one Dutch player.[48] About the same time Robert Archer and the Peadle brothers were associated in a company with two German players, Behrendt Holzhew and August Pflugbeil.[49] In 1617/18 the Elector of Brandenburg had a company of players in his service who were labelled 'comedians from England and the Netherlands' ('eine Compagnie aus England und den Niederlanden').[50] In 1620 John Spencer asked the Elector for the reimbursement of his expenses connected with bringing foreign actors to his company,[51] and three years later he was accompanied by a German player Thomas Sebastian Schadleutner.[52] And a German, Jacob of Hesse was a member of John Green's company in 1627.[53] The tendency to employ Continental players in English companies became even more evident during and after the Thirty Years War. An English actor, John Payne, was active with some Dutch players in one company in the 1630s; and in 1646 Payne signed a partnership agreement, by which he and William Roe, together with a number of Dutch players, were to form a company for the duration of one year.[54] A company that visited Gdańsk in 1647 was composed of English, Dutch and German actors. The abundance of evidence for the presence of foreign players in English companies leads to the conclusion that most of the troupes active in the seventeenth century were, in fact, mixed, but the English alone were the managers and leading players. The further we look into the seventeenth century, the fewer English actors we find in companies which were still styling themselves 'Englische Komödianten'. For example, a company of this sort visited Dresden in 1671 composed of the following players: Gideon Gellius, J.J. Mülder, Charles du Mesniel, Johan Thorian, Johan Bartholomeus Buhler, Christian Starke, Johan Christian Dorsch, Gottfried Pistorius, Siegmund Biehner, Johan Georg Encke, Johan Baptist Waydt.[55] These names hardly sound English, and in fact only one of the players may be identified with all certainty as an Englishman: the last on the above list is the well known veteran actor, John Wayde, who was first recorded on the Continent in 1617!

Regardless of the nationality of particular players, it is clear that after 1600 the number of actors in English companies active on the Continent increased rapidly. Thus, there were 12 actors in 1596 at Strasburg, 10 in 1597 at Tübingen, 12 in 1600 at Cologne, 15 in 1602 at Nuremberg, 14 in 1604 at Nördlingen, 18 in 1605 at Frankfurt, 19 players accompanied by 16 musicians in 1611 at Königsberg, 24 in 1615 at Cologne, and so on.[56] These examples illustrate that early in the seventeenth century 'Continental' troupes reached the size of a typical London company,[57] which, in turn, enabled them to stage unabridged texts of plays.

This brings to us a whole set of questions connected with the quality and development of staging techniques as used by the English on the Continent. The companies in question were composed of highly skilled professional actors experienced in complex productions of plays which were the highest achievements of the period; however, playing with less than a full company would have made it difficult for them to show all their skills. Another problem was the language barrier. There is no doubt that the early Continental performances were given in English. We may recall Moryson's account again here, with the last recorded instance of this practice in 1606 at Loitz in Pomerania. In the case of private, or court performances an interpreter may have occasionally been hired, who simply translated the text simultaneously.[58] This practice, however, was not possible at all in the case of outdoor public performances. Acting before an audience who did not understand a word of what was being said on stage naturally would have affected the staging of plays. It would obviously have been risky to present a full-length play in such circumstances, and it seems more likely that the stress was put on the non-verbal elements of the performance. Perhaps the favourite form was a jig,[59] although contemporary accounts refer to plays presented as histories, comedies and tragedies. Thus, in 1590 Robert Browne was paid 15 guilder at Leyden for 'having acted and played divers comedies and histories, besides for having made divers leaps'.[60] In the following year, the same actor was given a passport to go abroad to perform among other things 'games of comedies, tragedies and histories'.[61] In 1597, at the court of the Landgrave Maurice of Hesse at Kassel the English were paid for presenting a 'comedy'.[62] In 1605 Richard Machin and his fifteen companions offered twenty-four beautiful 'comedies, tragedies and pastorals' to the citizens of Strasburg,[63] and William Roe's company had 'chronicles, histories and comedies' in its repertory when acting at Cologne in 1648.[64] On the other hand, it is generally acknowledged that the distinction between particular genres was not very precise in those times and, for example, the word 'comedy' had basically two meanings: first, it was a general term equivalent to today's 'play' or 'drama'; and secondly, it was used in its modern meaning to denote anything 'funny', including the vaultings of the clowns.

There is little doubt that before the substitution of German for English, which took place at the turn of the century, the texts of presented plays must have been abridged, and it was actually music and clowning that constituted chief attraction. As E.K. Chambers put it: 'That in a land of alien speech, even more so than at home, the strict arts of comedy and tragedy had to be eked out with music and buffoonery and acrobatics goes without saying.'[65] This general statement finds partial confirmation in the Continental sources; 'partial' because it may be fully applied only to the early phase of the English players' activity on the Continent, and to the public performances rather than to the ones given at court. Thus, a humorous German poem printed at Frankfurt in 1597 gives us an account of an English clown's doings:

> For so distort his face he can,
> He looks no longer like a man.
> And many a clownish trick he knows,
> Wears shoes that don't much pinch his toes.

His breeches would hold two or more,
And have a monstrous flap before.
His jacket makes him look a fool
With all the blows he takes so cool.[66]

The clownish tricks and pranks often mentioned in sources as commonly used by the English players, apart from evoking cheap applause[67] were frequently the cause of serious trouble from severe authorities. The English were often prohibited from further performances for the indecencies they showed or said on stage. 'Heard you the English and other strangers sing? / Saw you their jolly dance, their lusty spring?' – a passage from a contemporary Dutch drama expresses the frequently repeated opinion.[68] In the Frankfurt poem of 1597 we find the following lines:

The tumbler also did us please,
He sprang high in the air with ease . ...
His hose they fitted him so tight,
His codpiece was a lovely sight.
Nubile maids and lecherous dames
He kindled into lustful flames . . .
For, know that those who paid their fee
To witness a bright comedy,
Or hear the tunes of fine musicians
Were more entranced by the additions
Of bawdy jests and comic strokes,
Of antics and salacious jokes,
And what, with his tight-fitting hose
The well-bred tumbler did disclose.[69]

The abundance of bawdy elements in performances should not be surprising in view of the fact that the Puritan attacks against theatres in London usually stress the immoral and lascivious elements of staging.[70] And it seems obvious that at least in the early phase of the English players' activity on the Continent bawdy elements played a considerable role in their staging practices. With an audience not understanding the language on stage, this was the easiest device to attract the attention of spectators and cause laughter. As in London, the 'immorality' of productions was compounded by the fact that women's parts were played by youths. To my knowledge, no evidence is extant to suggest that in the first half of the seventeenth century there were actresses in English companies overseas. We know for certain that wives of actors did sometimes go along. There were wives accompanying Thomas Sackville, Robert Bradstreet and Jacob Peadle at Frankfurt in 1597.[71] Richard Jones and George Vincent were thus accompanied in Poland for several years from 1618. John Spencer's wife collected entrance money at Rothenburg in 1613,[72] and Robert Reynolds' wife was given a pension by none other than the King of Poland, Vladislaus IV, after her husband died shortly after 1640. But it is 'Jungen' i.e. boy actors that are mentioned in various records. As we have seen William Kempe was accompanied by 'his youth' at Elsinore in 1586; there were two 'Jungen' in Browne's company at Strasburg in 1618, and four in Robert Reynolds' troupe at Torgau in 1626.[73] The first record of actresses in English companies 'beyond the seas' appears in 1654 in George Jolly's company, i.e. towards the close of English activity there.

The 'Englische Komödianten' must have become associated with bawdry as early as the late 1590s because the companies that were to follow, having in their repertory serious plays in German prose translations, were at pains to convince city or town authorities that, in spite of the fact that they were English, there was nothing immoral or irreligious in what they wanted to present. This of course does not mean that the bawdry disappeared from English productions on the Continent, but that when the players switched from English to German, they simply had more to offer even to less sophisticated audiences. Thus, an English company that visited Elbing (Polish, 'Elbląg') in August 1605, was prohibited from further performances for having shown 'disgraceful things' in the comedy. At Cologne the English were warned not to present anything 'indecent and scandalous', and the same admonition was repeated at Ulm in 1606. In the same year, the councillors at Frankfurt complained about the bawdy songs of the English.[74] Little wonder that the pious Archduchess Maria Magdalena of Austria expressed her delight, because in the plays presented in 1608 by John Green's men at Graz there was 'not the least little bit of love-making'. And in 1611, again at Cologne, the players were asked to refrain from 'scandalous' things in their plays.[75] When in 1615 John Green applied for leave to play to the City Council in Gdańsk, he was answered that a permit would be granted after the councillors had seen the rehearsal of the play to be shown. In numerous instances consent is given to the English to play on condition that nothing indecent will be presented, which by itself indicates that the reputation of the English companies was, justly or not, rather tarnished. For instance, in 1650 an English troupe was granted a patent by the Emperor himself on the condition that the players 'should entirely refrain thereby from all improprieties in their words as in their actions'. All this, however, seems to have had little effect on the insubordinate players, and even as late as 1659, George Jolly's performances shocked the Viennese, who complained that his company's comedies were 'spiced with the most scandalous obscenities'.[76]

Interestingly enough, because their presentations might give offence, the custom arose early in the seventeenth century that the English players, on arriving at a Continental town to give public performances invited, first of all, the local authorities, with families and friends, for a special show with admission free of charge. Very often, as was the case with Green's company in Gdańsk, this performance was of prime importance to the players, since it determined the censorious councillors' decision as to whether they should be allowed to perform or not. This may also be interpreted as an early example of preventive theatre censorship on the Continent. For instance, in 1600 George Webster's men offered their 'histories' to the councillors at Nuremberg as a 'preview' show,[77] and a couple of years before the English had been ordered to give a free sample presentation there.[78] The captious councillors at Ulm ordered English companies to give previews in 1602, 1603 and again in 1614.[79] The première of a new play was occasionally a pretext for a grand performance restricted to the elite only. The custom of inviting local men of distinction to special performances given in their honour had, however, its analogy in England, where touring companies gave similar performances before the authorities of provincial towns. This was described, for example, by one R. Willis, the author of a half-autobiographical, half-religious treatise entitled *Mount Tabor*, published in 1639:

when Players of Enterludes come to towne, they first attend the Mayor, to enforce him what noblemans servants they are, and so to get license for their publike playing; and if the Mayor like the Actors, or would shew respect to their Lord and Master, he appoints them to play their first play before himselfe, and the Aldermen and common Counsell of the City; and what is called the Mayors play, where every one that will comes in without money, the Mayor giving the players a reward as hee thinkes fit, to shew respect unto them.[80]

This may also describe the Continental custom. There seems to have developed yet another tradition on the Continent: that of a farewell performance. In an application for leave to play, dated 30 August 1619, a company of English actors performing in Gdańsk refer to this practice:

Because we have had no opportunity to bid farewell to our spectators from this noble public administration and the citizens of the town, as we have not (contrary to our customs) given a farewell performance, it may not only be interpreted as mere impoliteness. For, if this piece of news reaches our spectators in other places, it will be understood as if we had departed as unwelcome guests, as if we were banished for wrongdoing, and had thus made a bad name for ourselves.

Therefore, we humbly submit our final request to your Noble Lordships: May the Noble and High Council graciously permit us to play next Sunday as a farewell to the true and Faithful citizens and to present a delightful comedy, so that we may leave with honour intact and with a good name.[81]

Sometimes, a grand performance was given in honour of the town authorities as an expression of gratefulness for the favour shown, as was the case with an English company acting in Gdańsk in August 1619:

For our company has hitherto observed the common custom of putting on a particularly fine performance to honour the Noble Council as a sign of gratitude for all favour and kindness received, albeit not as this would fully deserve, but as thanks for the effort.[82]

And towards the close of English activity on the Continent, in August 1652 a company performing at Basle offered in honour of the High Council 'to hold a curious comedy, if we were informed of a day and the time'.[83]

This of course may have been one of the numerous cunning tricks that the players used to obtain consent for additional performances, or to receive 'testimonials' of their good behaviour and the high quality of their plays. It is beyond dispute that, apart from the noble patents, which naturally were not so easy to obtain, nor available to all companies, the letters of recommendation from town councillors were indispensable to the players, particularly during the summer theatrical season. This was the time of strolling, and it is likely that the players also visited towns enjoying by no means friendly relations with their patrons. For example, in 1619 John Spencer was refused leave to play in Gdańsk in spite of the fact that he was the Elector of Brandenburg's servant: this may be accounted for by the Elector's sudden conversion to Calvinism, which outraged Lutheran Gdańsk. To avoid pitfalls of this kind, the players sought appropriate letters from local authorities, and obtained them, provided they behaved properly and did not stage anything indecent. When in 1606 an English company emerged at Rostock, in their application to the councillors there the players made a significant request:

but as in other towns, where we had performed before, we used to receive a certificate of our demeanour under the common town's seal, we beg most humbly and respectfully . . . your honours and high worthies may extend their favour, until now shown to us, and give us a certificate of conduct under the common town's seal.[84]

And when towards the close of the English players' activity in Central Europe, George Jolly's company visited Gdańsk, the players invited the High Council to a special performance in its honour, so that they would receive a letter of recommendation. Another example comes from Osnabrück, where an English company performed during the Congress for the negotiations between the parties at war in 1644, and the town councillors gave them a testimonial stating that they had acted plays to the satisfaction of spectators.[85]

The players' popularity, concomitant with noble patronage, subsequently enabled the actors not only to subsist abroad for the whole year, but also to strengthen companies with new players, and to become themselves naturalised to the extent of learning German. And, characteristically, clowns were the first to use German on stage, as we learn from a Münster chronicle of 1599. The same source brings us to yet another significant feature of Continental staging, namely, music and dance, which seem to have played a far more important role there than they did in England:

On the 26th of November 1599 there arrived here eleven Englishmen, all young and lively fellows, with the exception of one, a rather elderly man, who had everything under his management. They acted on five successive days five different comedies in their own English tongue. They carried with them various musical instruments, such as lutes, cithern, fiddles, fifes, and such like: they danced many new and foreign dances (not usual in this country) at the beginning and at the end of their comedies. They were accompanied by a clown, who, when a new act had to commence and when they had to change costumes, made many antics and pranks in German during the performance, by which he amused the audience.[86]

It should be stressed that in the early years, as well as facing the language barrier, English players were often performing before audiences not accustomed to theatre at all, and still less to the sophisticated staging techniques and conventions that had been developed in London. For this reason many strolling companies labelled themselves 'comedians and instrumentalists', and were composed of both actors and musicians, some of the latter highly praised in the history of English music: John Dowland may serve as an example. When required to do so, a dramatic company of this type could easily transform itself into a musical entertainment, giving concerts accompanied by dances.

In numerous Continental accounts of actual performances given by the English it is stressed that it was music and dance that attracted the attention of spectators and won their praise and admiration. In fact English music and English musicians had been known and admired before the acting companies emerged there. For instance, between 1556 and 1584 English fiddlers, trumpeters and pipers were recorded at Königsberg in Prussia.[87] This of course is not surprising, because it was during the reign of Elizabeth I and James I that English music reached perhaps its greatest heights, and English composers and instrumentalists attained eminence without parallel in all Europe. Characteristically, the same performance that Fynes Moryson saw at Frankfurt in 1592 was described in different terms by a German. It was not the poor apparel and lack of 'ornament' on stage that struck him, but the 'excellent music' and 'perfect dances' such as he 'had not seen or heard before'.[88] As we learn from the Münster chronicle, music and dances were performed before and after the show and additionally during the intermission between the acts of a play. The dance by way of an afterpiece was a regular and enduring custom in the London theatres, developed into a special form called the jig.[89] And we know that in the London private theatres at least music was also played before the dramatic performance. When Philip Julius, Duke of Wolgast visited one of these in 1602, we learn from his secretary's diary that instrumental and vocal music went on for an hour before the actual performance began. The convention of playing music during the intermission was also described by Michael Praetorius among others, one of the major contemporary writers on music:

So it is also done in comedies, where sweet and lovely Musica instrumentalis is performed between the acts, with cornets, fiddles, and other similar instruments, varied sometimes with vocal music . . . in order that the personatae personae might be enabled to change their costume, to prepare themselves for the next acts and to recreate themselves.[90]

This staging convention must have been developed in the 1590s and, interestingly enough, was not abandoned when the English players started using German on stage.

Throughout the period under discussion music and dance remained an element in the staging of plays by the English players. As early as 1596, Peter Philips, an English composer and organist, appeared for the first time on the Continent and was described as the organist of the Archduke Albert and Archduchess Isabella. Philips seems to have stayed at Brussels until his death sometime between 1633 and 1640.[91] There were twelve English 'comedians and instrumentalists' at Cologne in 1600.[92] In 1606 several pious citizens of Loitz complained that the English had desecrated the castle chapel and had turned the latter into a 'Spielhaus' and a 'Tantzplatz'. The Landgrave Maurice of Hesse aroused criticism for having hired English players who devoted their time to idle activities like acting, leaping, dancing and playing music.[93] In 1607 a company of English 'comedians and musicians' performed at Königsberg and were paid for the show, which among other things included music and dances. When John Sigismund, the Elector of Brandenburg and the Duke designate of Prussia went to Warsaw in 1611 for the purpose of receiving the investiture of the Duchy, he was accompanied by an English company of nineteen actors and sixteen musicians. In the following year, the Landgrave Maurice's men presented to the citizens of Nuremberg 'foreign' comedies and tragedies, and they played 'beautiful music' and danced various dances, in addition to 'leaps and many other unheard of tricks'.[94] In 1613 another English composer, organist and virginalist, John Bull, entered the Archduke Charles' service at Brussels. Bull's case is an interesting one, because it shows us that poverty and hopes of financial gain were not always the only reasons that induced players and musicians to travel outside England. After his departure from London, it was recorded there that: 'John Bull, Doctor of Musicke, went beyond the seas without license, and was admitted into the Archduke's service, and entered into paie there about Michaelmas.'[95] From a letter written on 30 May 1614 by a British minister at Brussels to James I we learn that Bull had claimed that he had been persecuted in England on religious grounds (by doing so, Bull presumably wanted to win favour of a Catholic Archduke). But the writer says in the letter that he had informed the Archduke

that it was notorious to all the world, the said Bull did not leave your Majesties service for any wrong done unto him, or for any matter of religion, under which fained pretext he now sought to wrong the reputation of your Majesties justice, but did in that dishonest manner steal out of England through the guilt of corrupt conscience, to escape the punishment, which notoriously he had deserved, and was designed to have been inflicted on him by the hand of justice, for his incontinence, fornication, adultery, and other grevious crimes.[96]

Whatever the case, John Bull found protection and employment at the Archduke's court, as did many other players and musicians well into the 1640s.[97]

English players had still more to offer than plays, music and dance. When

John Green came in 1615 with his company to Gdańsk, he recommended in his application to the City Council not only plays, but also 'music and other interesting things', and made clear that the language used would be 'pure German'.[98] These 'other interesting things' could mean leaping, and, perhaps, mime. In 1608 the authorities of the city of Leyden allowed William Peadle, senior (English dancer, acrobat and pantomimist) to give 'various beautiful and chaste performances with his body, without using any words'.[99] A company performing in Pomerania in 1606 was criticized for showing, among other things, 'dumb fantasies'. It should be added here that the dumb-show, such as that in Shakespeare's *Hamlet*, must have been another staging convention used by the English not only in the early period of their activity abroad. The scraps of evidence seem to suggest that this served as a brief summary of what was to follow, which was particularly important when playing before an audience having no knowledge of English. The dumb-show, however, became a stage convention and remained in use by the English long after they had started using German on stage. Thus, in 1644 and 1648 it was recorded at Berlin that in a performance given by the English every act was preceded by a dumb-show ('mit stummen Personen').[100] And in the same period, in 1646, an English company acted at Dresden and staged *The Prodigal Son*, and before every act a show with 'dumb persons' was presented.[101]

The available evidence seems to support Moryson's account of 1592 that the early performances on the Continent were given by small companies poorly equipped with costumes and stage properties. It is difficult to imagine that in this reconnaissance period the English players would take the risk of investing substantial means, even if they had any, to buy expensive costumes and stage properties, not to mention carriages and horses, and to take them abroad without any guarantee of financial gain and personal safety. This is why the first tours were usually short, and the actors, having performed in one or two towns and in villages on the way, returned to London. This was the case, for instance, with Robert Browne's first tour in 1590. It took some time before they got acquainted with local customs and traditions and were able to plan their tours beforehand without taking the risk of finding the city's gates closed to them. Here, again, noble patronage was indispensable, with a permanent residence being an obvious advantage. Even if the players were not lodged at court, they rented rooms in citizens' houses and the costs of accommodation were often covered by their patron (for example the company which visited Dresden in 1586, whose players received additional 40 thalers 'for house-rent, or for lodging-money',[102] and John Spencer's company in 1611/12, whose players stayed at Königsberg, their living expenses reimbursed by the Elector's treasury). An interesting record at Dresden tells us that in August 1617 a company of English players was paid 300 thalers, and

Besides this, what they had consumed at their landlord's, before they had been supplied with their meals at Court, and whatever else they had required and used in the way of rooms, closets, and beds, amounting to 120 florins, which is also paid by the treasury.[103]

Moreover, this patronage enabled the players to acquire costumes and other items necessary for the production at little or no cost at all. And the Münster chronicle, quoted above, tells us that in 1599 the English actors changed costumes during their performance, which marks a significant contrast to the destitute players Fynes Moryson saw in 1592 at Frankfurt.

Even earlier than that, in 1586, the Elector of Saxony had costumes made for the English company that stayed at his court for several months. In addition, the actors were promised one coat a year, and a free table at court.[104] In 1597 in the list of expenses of the court of the Landgrave Maurice of Hesse, we find items like 'white clothes for the clown', 'a pair of shoes for the fool', and 'six ells of white woolen cloth', which are necessary for the English to present their 'comedy'.[105] Thomas Sackville was given in 1608 three pieces of flesh-coloured, and three pieces of blue silk ribbon, as payment for performances at Brunswick.[106] And when John Dowland appeared at the same court, he was given, in addition to money, 'velvet and satin and gold lace to make me apparell'. The often quoted undated letter which Richard Jones, who went to the Continent in the troupe of 1592 and may have therefore been at Frankfurt at the time of Moryson's visit, wrote to Edward Alleyn, shows what must have been the common condition of the actors going abroad:

I am to go over beyond the seas w^t Mr Browne and the company . . . now, good Sir, as you have ever byne my worthie frend, so helpe me nowe. I have a sute of clothe and a cloke at pane fo^r three pound, and if it shall pleas you to lend me so much to release them, I shall be bound to pray fo^r you so longe as I leve; for if I go over, and have no clothes, I shall not be esteemed of.[107]

This letter leaves no doubt about the importance of rich costumes: Jones was convinced that he would not 'be esteemed of' if he went on the Continent without one. Considering the surprisingly high cost of clothes in those times, we may see that once again noble patronage and bounty were absolutely indispensable in this respect. Examples may readily be provided in corroboration of this statement. Thus, in 1611, the Elector of Brandenburg ordered suits of clothes to be made for the entire English company of nineteen players and sixteen musicians. The Landgrave Maurice of Hesse-Kassel aroused criticism because he kept a great number of English players at his court and 'he fed them generously, offered drink and clothes and gave them other things . . . so that the steward was often left with no supplies'.[108] The same nobleman contributed substantially to the actual performance of plays, by providing the actors with various items necessary for the production. One of his orders connected with stage matters has been preserved, and we learn from it that 'On your kind request we have ordered that old apparell, weapons, armour and clothes that are in our possession should be graciously dispatched for the performance of a comedy about ancient potentates.'[109] In 1606, two English players, Peadle and Archer, were paid 100 Polish guilder at Berlin, in addition to free table at court and two suits of clothes.[110] Sometimes players' travel expenses were also covered, as was the case with George Webster who was paid 20 thalers in 1598 for going from Kassel to Heidelberg,[111] or an unidentified company that was paid for the journey from Warsaw to Vienna in 1639.

After the English players had established themselves on the Continent permanently, it was their rich costumes that were often admired and described. When John Spencer's company performed at Nuremberg in 1613, it was recorded that the show was not only given in good German language, but also with 'rich masquerade and costumes' ('in köstlicher Mascarada vnd Kleidungen').[112] And one of the well-known writers of the period, John Sommer, in one of his works reflected on the luxury of his contemporaries, comparing them with the English: 'Their collars must be set with pearls, and such a display of finery is indulged in, that they strut along like the English comedians in the theatre.'[113] It is worth mentioning that one of the original costumes used by the English players on the Continent, now lost, used to be in the collection of the 'Prussia' Society at Königsberg and was shown in a theatre exhibition in Vienna in 1891.[114]

All of this, and the replacement of English by German, contributed to the high quality and splendour of staging in both temporary and permanent court theatres, and consequently increased the quality of public performances as well. Even the temporary court arrangements for production were akin to those of the English stage. An example of such an arrangement may be found at Königsberg, where, in the autumn of 1611, an English company under John Spencer gave a memorable performance on the occasion of the Elector's investiture. This is discussed in detail in Chapter 3 below; it will suffice to mention that a 'theatrum' was arranged *ad hoc*, and at high cost, in the 'old grand hall', which was covered with red cloth, and the city of Constantinople was erected for the actors who presented *The Destruction of Constantinople*. The costumes were rich and costly, as were the stage properties. The scenery even included painted clouds, and in the extant list of expenses we find, among others, the following items: blue, red and white cloth, fringes, gold border, 70 ells of red silk, 50 ells of red cord, monks' dresses, 18 large and 17 long plumes, a sword with a gilt hilt, a wooden shield, four death's heads, carved work and turned work, and so on. There is little doubt that in such ideal conditions, before sophisticated audiences and using the German language, performances must have approached, if not matched, the standard of London productions.

The Continental repertory of the English players seems in most cases where it has proved possible to identify plays from their German titles to have included plays staged previously in the London playhouses. For example, one of the earliest repertory lists of John Green's company, dated 1608, included among others *The Proud Woman of Antwerp*, *The Jew*, *Doctor Faustus*, *Fortunatus*, and *The Turkish Mahomet and Hiren the Fair Greek*, all of which were in the repertory of the former Lord Admiral's company in London.[115] It seems natural that those players of the London companies who had decided to seek fortune overseas, made sure before their planned departure to collect a supply of play texts either in print or in manuscript.

The first anthology of English drama in German prose translations was published as early as 1620, followed by an enlarged edition in 1624.[116] Altogether about thirty English plays were published at that time, including eight plays by Shakespeare, and several by other major dramatists such as Marlowe, Dekker, Greene, Peele and Kyd.[117] Naturally, in later periods further plays were added to the English repertory. For instance, the same John Green's repertory in 1626 included, among others, the following pieces: *Romeo and Juliet*, *Julius Caesar*, *Nobody and Somebody*, *Hamlet*, *Orlando Furioso*, *The King of England and the King of Scotland*, *The Spanish Tragedy*, *Doctor Faustus*, *Fortunatus*, *The Jew of Malta*, *King Lear* and *The Prodigal Son*. In the course of time, some German plays were also added. The experience of travelling must have influenced the repertory. In the early phase of the English presence on the Continent the dramatic texts had, for reasons discussed above, to be abridged. Later, when the players started to use German on stage, some of the plays reveal a local 'colouring', as if they were written for a company's star performer, or for a special occasion – to please the noble spectators, or even the 'groundlings' by alluding to contemporary events and to people known to everyone in the region. For instance, a number of short plays were written for Robert Reynolds, alias 'Pickleherring', undoubtedly the greatest comedian of Continental companies; these were even labelled 'Pickleherring-Spiele'. An example of an 'occasional' play may be that performed by John Green in 1608 at the Graz court of the Habsburgs, recorded as 'a play about a Duke of Florence who fell in love with a nobleman's daughter'. Although the play itself does not survive, we may suspect that the drama was connected with contemporary events, if not directly, then by analogy: the Archduchess Maria Magdalena of Austria, who was present at Graz during Green's visit there, and left us a meticulous description of it, had just been betrothed to the Duke of Florence, Cosimo Medici, and the plot of the play could have been a variation on this theme.

The repertory of the English companies has been scrutinized satisfactorily by other authors,[118] and there is no need to go into details here. According to the available evidence, in both court and public performances a different play was staged on each consecutive day. For instance, in 1605 Richard Machin's and Ralph Reeve's company offered twenty-four different 'comedies, tragedies and pastorals' to the citizens of Strasburg. The company that performed at Dresden in 1626 had twenty-nine plays in its repertory, and John Green's troupe when it appeared at the Graz court in 1608 presented ten different plays there. The Münster chronicle already quoted states clearly that the English players 'acted on five successive days five different comedies'. It has to be stressed once again that the very selection of plays, of which sample titles have been mentioned above, imposed technical constraints upon the actors, who were at pains to suit their staging to the demands of the dramatic text. This was particularly difficult in the case of public performances, which, until the first public theatres were built on the Continent, were in most instances held in rather primitive conditions. The number of different physical stage conditions no doubt demanded a variety of staging techniques, and the same play performed by the same company might have been presented in quite different ways for performance in a village inn, or in a town market place, or in a rich merchant's house, or in a public theatre equipped with a large stage, trapdoors, and machinery.

The variety of places in which performances took place may be illustrated by the following examples. In 1586 it was the courtyard of the town hall at Elsinore. George Webster, John Hill, Bernard Sandt and Richard Machin were mentioned in 1600 as having given performances in an 'Augustiner closter'.[119] In January 1605 John Spencer's company was permitted to act in the 'great hall under the library' at Leyden.[120] A year later a castle chapel was used for the same purpose at Loitz, and William Peadle performed in a church at Leyden. In 1603 the English gave performances in a market place at Leipzig,[121] and in 1610 the castle courtyard was used by them for this purpose at Jägerndorf (Krnov) in Silesia. Court performances at Dresden were given in 'the room near the chapel', called 'the Marble Hall',[122] and at Königsberg it was 'the old grand hall' that was used for this purpose. In Gdańsk, the English performed first in St George's Hall, then in a public theatre which was also a fencing-school; in the same city they were forbidden to act by the city gates which they had apparently been doing, and were forced to build 'something' (i.e., a stage) on the nearby Bishop's Hill. Arthur's Hall was used by the English companies at Elbing, where the players were also permitted to give private performances in merchants' houses. And in 1629 a tennis-court was assigned to the use of an English company at The Hague.[123] From a contemporary account we learn that in 1613, John Spencer had a 'theatre' built at Regensburg, at the considerable cost of 135 guilder:

The English comedian John Spencer built a large stage, and a theatre on that stage, where with various musical instruments he played in more than ten sundry ways, and above the theatre-stage one more stage, 30 feet high, on 6 big columns, above which a roof was built, and below it a quadrangular platform, where he represented beautiful actions.[124]

In the period under discussion, the English players had two permanent court theatres at their disposal: first at Kassel, where they used the *Ottoneum* until about 1613, and then at Warsaw, where in 1635 the King of Poland had a permanent theatre built in the Royal Castle.

These examples demonstrate that it is difficult if not impossible to give a simple account of how performances on the Continent were staged. However, there seems to have been a general trend among the English companies towards improving the quality of their performances, public performances in particular, until they rivalled both court productions and those back in London. The attempts to achieve this were undoubtedly connected with, and stimulated by, the strong rivalry between particular companies, and also by the growing demands of more sophisticated audiences.

In their endeavours to increase the quality of and add splendour to their productions, the players were to a large extent supported by their rich patrons, who provided them with costumes, with some of the stage properties, and occasionally even with means of transportation. This latter problem was of prime importance to the players. As the companies grew larger and began presenting unabridged texts of plays requiring at least some basic stage properties, it is difficult to imagine the actors covering longer distances without appropriate means of transportation. This was not difficult to secure, provided the actors were enjoying noble patronage. They could simply rent a waggon or two, and several horses or mules from their patron's stables, to carry their goods and chattels. A waggon of course served the additional function of a mobile home, a caravan. We know that as early as 1586, the English players were given a 'carriage-waggon' by the Elector of Saxony, to use as a vehicle on their journey. In 1598 the Landgrave Maurice gave the following order:

Let the comedians travel day and night with eight horses, of which they should harness four to a coach, and the other four to the cart on which they carry their instruments and other things, so that they are neither obstructed not hindered.[125]

A company of English players was provided with three carriage-waggons when in 1607 they travelled from Loitz to Wolgast in Pomerania. Towards the close of the English activity in Europe, in 1650, one company was given a patent by the Emperor himself, by which 'English comedians together with their people, horses and effects' were allowed to 'pass and repass at all places, by water and land, freely'.[126]

The players were partly supported by their noble patrons; they also tried to manage on their own. In the numerous supplications to town authorities that have been preserved in Continental archives, it is the high costs of production that the English players mention most frequently in their appeals to prolong the time given them to play. Thus, in July 1615, the Elector of Brandenburg's company complained to the City Council in Gdańsk that their 'theatre had suffered much from rain and storm'.[127] It seems likely that in this case the word 'theatre' means scenery, elements of which were apparently left on stage overnight and had been damaged by rain and wind. In the same supplication rehearsals and 'other preparations' that lasted for four days are mentioned. This implies that, in addition to rehearsing before the first performance, the actors had been busy ordering, buying and arranging various items necessary for the production. Several years earlier, in 1611, when John Spencer's company visited Gdańsk, the actors mention in their application the 'silk merchants' and 'other craftsmen' to whom they owe money, and ask the City Council to grant them a permit for additional performances so that they can leave the city without any debts.[128] Similarly, John Green's company paid in 1615 in Gdańsk 100 marks to have 'galleries, benches, and other things' made by local craftsmen.[129] This was a large sum of money indeed, equivalent perhaps to 20 English pounds,[130] and may serve as evidence of the actors' efforts to prepare a superb production, or at least the best they could afford. At the Frankfurt Easter fair of 1605, English actors paid 10 florins for erecting and as much for taking down their 'scaffolding', i.e. the stage.[131] These pieces of evidence seem to lead to the ultimate conclusion that whenever it was possible, or when the rewards justified it, the English players tried to add splendour to their productions and did not hesitate to invest money both in costumes and stage design. The splendour they sought after depended, of course, largely on their hopes of financial gain, the conditions on which they were permitted to play, and the duration of their stay, i.e., the number of performances. The latter, in the case of public performances, varied from a couple of days to two months of daily shows, as was the case with one English company visiting Gdańsk in 1643.

Noble patronage guaranteed a permanent income to the players. We know for certain that special contracts were signed, and the actors received annual salaries, in addition to occasional extra fees. For example, in 1612 John Spencer received 600 thalers at 36 groschen which was due to him 'on the contract made with his Electoral Grace'. It is not known, however, whether a definite number of court performances was prescribed in a contract of this sort. Presumably the players simply had to stay on hand at the court, always ready to perform on demand, and were allowed to leave the court temporarily only during the theatrical season. For instance, when in 1586 a company of English players was hired for one year at Dresden, their appointment included several conditions:

we have appointed and received the same [i.e. the English players] into our service at our Court . . . that they may be trusty and obliging and dutiful, to demean themselves well at our Court, and when we travel to follow us always at our command, and when we hold a banquet to play as often as the same is ordered them, and attend with their fiddles and instruments belonging thereto, and play music, and amuse and entertain us also with their art in leaping and other graceful things that they have learned.[132]

In a number of cases the English companies were hired for special occasions only, and this seems to have been very profitable indeed. For instance, the English were paid 300 florins for seven shows at Tübingen in May 1597. When in August 1617 the same John Spencer performed at Dresden on the occasion of the Emperor's visit there, he received 300 thalers from the Electress, in addition to board and lodging, and 100 florins from the Emperor. For the often-mentioned performances at Graz in 1608 John Green received 400 thalers. Sometimes the players were hired for only one or two performances, as was the case with the company that performed at Dresden in 1600 and received 75 florins for the trouble. Similarly, the English were paid 30 florins for one comedy and 40 florins for its repetition at Munich in 1597; and the players who 'acted and danced twice' at Königsberg in October 1605 were paid 75 marks. For a single performance before the Emperor Mathias in September 1613, Robert Archer's company received 20 florins.[133]

It is not easy to determine the relative value of Continental currency to English money. With the multiplicity of local mints, a 'thaler' had one value at Lübeck, and a different one, say, in Gdańsk. And the exchange rates naturally varied as they do today, according to economic conditions and the shifting value of gold and silver with respect to one another.[134] Attempts have been made to establish the relative value of Continental currency in order to calculate players' income in terms of English money, but none of these seem fully satisfactory.[135] The companies, it should be remembered, covered enormous distances, and in every place where they stopped for performances, they were paid in local money: 'Reichsthalers', 'guilder', 'marks' or 'Polish guilder' and 'florins' to mention a few. Only certain relations between various coins in circulation were stable; for instance, 1 'batzen' = 2 'albus' = 4 'kreutzers' = 16 'pfennigs' (see Appendix 2). It was the 'groschen' that were a common basis of reckoning currency's real value. For example, at the time of Moryson's visit to the Continent, a silver 'thaler' passed for 24 groschens, whereas in about 1610 it was valued at 36 groschen, and during the Thirty Years War its value doubled. Therefore, it is not surprising that in numerous extant records, the actual sums of money paid to the English players are accompanied by the currency's value given in groschen. Accepting the conclusions of specialist works on the subject, it may be conjectured that an English pound was worth about $4\frac{1}{2}$ thalers in the period under discussion.[136] The purchasing power of a thaler differed of course from one place to another, for prices also varied. When Fynes Moryson stayed at Hamburg and Lübeck, his board and lodging amounted to a trifle more than a thaler a week, which indicates that he could live at a reasonable standard for less than a pound a month.

The amounts paid to the English players and musicians by their noble patrons were very high indeed. Spencer's annual salary of 600 thalers at the Königsberg court equalled approximately 130 English pounds. We cannot be certain, however, whether Spencer could keep all the money for himself, or whether he had to divide it between all the members of his company. Of English companies' internal financial agreements almost nothing is known. Taking into account the fact that the players' living expenses were also covered by the court treasury, we can see that such contracts were very lucrative and sought after by the players, and that at least some of them 'returned home generously rewarded and loaded with gold and silver' – as one of the above quoted accounts indicated. But salaries, of course, were not the players' only source of income. It should be remembered that in the summer theatrical season players retained by noble courts were allowed to visit other places. This was not always possible, especially during perilous times of war, but the very fact that a number of companies under noble patronage were eager to leave their patron's court in the summer indicates that the players considered touring the country as worth the trouble and risk.

In the case of public performances, the players' profits depended on three main factors – the number of spectators; the admission fee; and tax: with the latter two usually determined by the local authorities. We know from Moryson's description of the performance he saw at Frankfurt in 1592 that people 'flocked wonderfully', but it is by no means easy to establish precise, or even average, figures for the number of spectators in various towns. The lowest attendance mentioned in the sources, and one which indeed is difficult to challenge, occurred at Brunswick, where on a certain occasion in 1614, an unidentified English player had no spectators at all and was given an indemnity of one thaler by the council.[137] The other extreme is to be found at Nuremberg, where on the grand opening of the public theatre there, on 15 June 1628, an English company, under the patronage of the Elector of Saxony, performed before an audience of almost three thousand spectators; and after seven further performances, the total number of spectators amounted to 12,765, as a meticulous record of the event informs us.[138] On the opening day the box office had an income of 266.28 florins, of which the players received 131.8 florins; in two weeks, during which eight performances were given, the company earned about 470 florins.[139] Another example of astonishingly high profits comes from Regensburg, where in 1613 John Spencer performed and on the first day had an income – if we are to believe a contemporary source – of 500 guilder.[140]

The period during which performances were allowed varied from one town to another. Two examples will suffice here. At Cologne, the English were allowed to perform for 14 days in April 1602, for 8 days in July 1603, and for 14 days in July 1604.[141] And in Gdańsk, John Spencer was allowed to play for 14 days in July 1611, and this was extended for the whole of August; John Green was permitted to act for eight days in August 1616, and for 14 days in 1619. Another English company performing in Gdańsk was granted leave to play for four weeks in 1643, a period which was extended for another week, and for three weeks in 1647. Records from other towns support the conclusion that on average the English were allowed to play for two weeks, excluding Sundays, with a tendency in the later period for runs to become longer. For instance, an English company performed for nine weeks at

Hamburg in 1648,[142] and George Jolly performed for five weeks in Gdańsk in 1650. The various conditions on which these permits were granted often included councillors' attempts to keep down the price of admission to public performances. Appendix 2 shows examples that have been recorded in various towns.[143]

The councillors' decision regarding the size of the entrance fee was often accompanied by the imposition of a tax. This, too, varied, as the following examples show. In 1605 at Leyden, the English were ordered to pay 12 guilder for the poor of the city; in 1613, at Regensburg, Spencer had to pay 22 florins a week; in 1618 the English were ordered to pay 2 thalers daily to a guild; in April 1629, the magistrates of The Hague granted leave to play to an English company, for which privilege the players had to pay 30 guilder to the orphanage.[144] Robert Archer had to pay as much as 1,000 guilder on behalf of St James' church in Gdańsk in 1636, and in the same city, in 1643, the English were ordered to support the city prison with 500 florins, and when the time given to play was extended for a week, the players had to pay 200 florins extra. In the last two examples, the tax imposed upon the players was exorbitant indeed. With the entrance fee at 9 groschen, the players would have to admit over three thousand spectators, before they started to earn anything for themselves, allowing for a tax of 1,000 guilder, valued at 30 groschen each. The fact that they agreed to such severe conditions demonstrates their conviction that it was possible to make a profit. And the Nuremberg example of 1628, mentioned above, shows us clearly that the players' hopes of financial gain were at times fulfilled. From a different source, however, we learn that sometimes companies employed dishonest means to avoid paying the tax, the players cheating the councillors and simply absconding from town.[145]

At any rate, having received leave to play, the players' major problem was to attract the attention of as many people as possible, so that they could amass their kreutzers, groschen, and albuses. In larger towns, public performances by the English players were usually announced by printed bills, of which several have been preserved.[146] From a Dutch document, dated October 1565, we learn that the English actors had posted handbills on the city gates with information about their plays.[147] However, all the preserved bills and references to such are of later date, i.e. after 1625.[148] In the earlier period of English activity on the Continent, it seems that there was a tradition of making a parade through a town, accompanied by drums and trumpets, a practice well known in England, especially in the provinces. Drums and trumpets were used as advertisements in London at any rate until 1587, and were in fact traditional in the provinces up to the middle of the eighteenth century.[149] In Shakespeare's *All's Well That Ends Well* we find Parolles telling us that Captain Dumain 'has led the drum before the English tragedians'. And Philip Henslowe, the well known London entrepreneur of the Lord Admiral's company, bought a drum and two trumpets for his players 'to go into the country' in February 1600.[150] That the English players used the same blatant methods to advertise their performances on the Continent may be seen in contemporary records. In 1610 they were forbidden to use their drum and to make music at Cologne.[151] In 1612 and in 1613, again at Cologne, the English were ordered not to make noise with their drum, and were forbidden to play.[152] A Nuremberg account tells us that in 1613 the English players paraded through the town with 'two drums and four trumpets'.[153] It seems that the frequent complaints of magistrates and common citizens led the players to abandon this practice. An English company that visited Lüneburg in 1648, boastfully declared that the players had *not* been using either drums or trumpets to announce their plays:

The Council is hereby officially informed that we shall publicly pass through the streets without drums and trumpets, and that a drum will be used only at the beginning and at the end of a play, and people will be informed about the comedy by means of bills publicly displayed.[154]

In most cases, public performances were held outdoors, during the hours of daylight, although there are several instances known when parts of municipal or private buildings were turned into temporary theatres with artificial lighting. And the latter must have been a rule in winter time. It is difficult to establish the length of a typical show, but two or three hours may have been the average. The author of a German satirical poem, dated 1615, is obviously exaggerating when he claims that

> Folk like to see the English play,
> Far more than hear a parson pray:
> Four hours rather stand and hear
> The play, than one in church appear.[155]

It appears possible to distinguish certain trends and phases in the development of companies and their staging practices on the Continent. An attempt to do so will also reveal the importance of Central Europe, Poland in particular, as a region where the English players found refuge and employment during the Thirty Years War. The available evidence leads us to the conclusion that first was the 'reconnaissance' phase of dramatic activity, which lasted for about ten years starting from the mid 1580s and was characterized by occasional tours by small companies, poorly equipped with costumes and stage properties. Performances were given in English, the dramatic texts abridged and the chief attractions clowning, as well as various non-verbal devices like leaping, pantomime, music and dances. It was such a company that Fynes Moryson described at Frankfurt in 1592.

Next was the period before the Thirty Years War, characterized by the increasing number of large companies protected and supported by noble patrons. This patronage enabled English companies to become permanently established on the Continent. The players stayed at their patron's court during winter, and travelled, carrying appropriate patents and letters of recommendation, during the theatrical season which lasted from spring to autumn. Numerous fairs provided the actors with the best opportunity of earning substantial sums of money. In pursuit of such rewards, companies covered enormous distances in order to reach a given town in time for the fair. Because of the growing competition (e.g., three English companies visited Gdańsk in the summer of 1619!) the players often tried to obtain leave to play before their arrival. Sometimes they wrote letters directly to the councillors of a given town; sometimes they tried to secure permission through the intervention and support of friendly citizens who applied to the Council in the name of a company. Several such cases will be discussed in the following chapters of this book. After the substitution of German for English, and with a sufficient number of actors, these well-equipped companies performed full-length plays; and in appropriate conditions their staging may have been similar to that of the London theatres.

During the Thirty Years War, a number of veteran players returned to England. This is illustrated by Appendix 4. Thus, Robert Browne was last seen in Germany in 1620, John Green disappeared from the records in 1627, John Spencer was last seen in 1623 and so was Richard Jones. Those who remained formed new companies, and sought safer regions for the continuation of their theatrical activity. However, in most regions of Europe, which were now turned into battle-fields, their activity ceased almost entirely. So it did in most of approximately sixty German towns, which had previously been visited by the English.[156] There is, for example, a sudden break in the visits by English players recorded in Strasburg in the period between 1628 and 1651; at Nuremberg it was between 1628 and 1649; at Cologne between 1631 and 1645; at Ulm between 1618 and 1650; at Frankfurt between 1631 and 1649; at Dresden between 1632 and 1651.[157] An account of 1631 tells us that when Germany 'was still in the state of prosperity . . . everybody liked to amuse himself with comedies and other representations, which is now no longer the case'.[158] It is in those countries in Central Europe that remained neutral during the War that the English found refuge: the Kingdom of Poland and the Duchy of Prussia. Finding permanent employment at the Royal court at Warsaw and the Electoral court at Königsberg enabled some of the notable players to endure the calamitous period, even though there was a war in progress between Poland and Sweden. This, however, ended before the Thirty Years War did, and so Poland and Prussia again became one of the important centres for both court and public performances by English players. For about ten years, between 1635 and 1645, this was in fact among the few safe regions on the Continent, and the intensity of English activity there is not matched elsewhere (Appendix 3). Two of the most important companies in that period, one led by Robert

Reynolds, the other by Robert Archer, found protection and support at the courts of Königsberg and Warsaw respectively. Besides all the privileges deriving from noble patronage, the companies gave public performances after the peace treaty between Poland and Sweden had been signed in 1635, much earlier than in most towns of the Empire, where public shows and travel became possible only after the Thirty Years War had ended in 1648. And here, it seems, lies the importance of Central Europe, of Poland and Prussia in particular, in the history of the English players' activity on the Continent.

Then comes the final phase, which covers approximately the period until 1670. Only a few major companies, led by veteran actors, remain active on the Continent, temporarily supported by a fresh supply of players from England, as the result of the closing of the theatres in London. One such London company in exile was recorded in the Netherlands in 1644. In one of the extant documents we find the names of players: Jeremy Kite, William Cooke, Thomas Loveday, Edward Shatterell, Nathan Peet and his son.[159] The Prince of Wales' company of English players sought fortune in Paris in 1646, but the troupe was reported dissolved for want of pay.[160] Some new players from London were also incorporated into Roe-Wayde's company in 1647.[161] In the last years, as was the case with George Jolly's company, the staging of plays was evidently influenced by new theatre trends coming from Italy. And one has to agree with Leslie Hotson that Jolly

knew that the popular taste was turning toward music, decorations, and machines of the Italian opera, and he had made up his mind to meet and even anticipate the demand . . . For English theatrical history Jolly is even more important, since his development of music, scenery, and the use of actresses preceded Davenant's opera by several years. Jolly is in reality the first English producer to use the modern stage.[162]

Only the last statement may be objected to: Jolly was not the first English manager to use the modern stage. At the Royal theatre in Warsaw English players had an opportunity to get acquainted with a theatre fashioned in the Italian manner. It had been built in 1637 by Italian architects, and was equipped with all the necessary machines for complex opera productions. In this theatre, long before Jolly's first encounter with the new trends in staging, an English company under Robert Archer, and later including also Reynolds, Roe, Wayde, Wedware and Pudsey, performed in the period between 1637 and 1645. This new theatrical experience may have helped the players to develop their staging practices in accordance with the new fashion and to prevent them from falling behind the times.

Bearing in mind all the obstacles, dangers and difficulties the English players had to face on the Continent, one must admire the scale and scope of their indefatigable travels after 1594. They flooded the Netherlands, both Catholic and Protestant countries of the Empire, paid frequent visits to Scandinavia, found permanent employment in Poland and Prussia, and even reached remote corners of Europe like Riga in Livonia. Apart from the frequently unfavourable conditions in London, several factors contributed to this unprecedented phenomenon. It is beyond dispute that the popularity and fame of the English players originated in the high quality of their staging. These actors were highly skilled professionals, whose art and talents surpassed the Continental average. They were generally acknowledged by their contemporaries to be the best in the profession. For instance, in the preface to the first edition of *Englische Comoedien und Tragedien* (1620) we read that 'in our times the English comedians, partly by their pretty inventions, partly by the gracefulness of their gestures, often also by their elegance in speaking, obtain great praise from persons of high and low condition'. One John Rhenamus, a physician who had travelled to England early in the seventeenth century, and the author of a comedy entitled *The Battle of the Senses* (1613), indicated in his preface that among the writers and performers of comedies the English maintained the first place. 'There is no doubt about it, they really are good actors', cried the Archduchess Maria Magdalena of Austria, after having seen in 1608 performances by the English players at Graz. And another German writer, Daniel von Wensin, stressed in his *Oratio contra Britanniam* (1613) that whereas in England most of the strolling artisans were of German descent, the English people were devoted to gluttony, voluptuousness and acting, which they had developed to such a level that 'now in Germany, the English players are most admired by everyone'.[163] Individual players were also highly praised and admired. Robert Reynolds – generally identified as 'Pickleherring'[164] – for instance, surprised the spectators, because he could so 'frame his face and countenance that to one half of the people on one side he would seem heartily to laugh and to those on the other side bitterly to weep and shed tears'.[165]

Given noble patronage and support, these players formed large, well-equipped companies, and having changed from playing in English to performing in German they presented their audiences not only with the great English drama of the times, but also with a standard of staging which in itself became a goal for their Continental rivals and successors. The name 'Englische Komödianten', at first associated with frivolity, later came to denote actors of high quality, and was even used by some German and Dutch companies long after the true English players had ceased their activity on the Continent.[166] Moreover, the stage-names of some of the actors, like Hans Stockfish and Pickleherring, have been incorporated into the history of Continental theatre. The most significant and characteristic feature of the English companies was undoubtedly their remarkable ability to adjust to any staging conditions and to any type of audience, and this flexibility is in itself a proof of their high standard. Finally, it has to be stressed once again that the

English players were responsible for the dissemination of theatre art in countries with little theatrical tradition, and their activity on the Continent constituted essentially the beginnings of professional theatre north of the Alps. They were, indeed, 'the abstracts and brief chronicles of the time'.

PART I
The Baltic Route

1 Gdańsk

E VEN in the partially preserved documents referring to theatrical matters in Gdańsk, we see that visits by English companies were surprisingly frequent; this is particularly the case in two periods: between about 1600 and 1619, and 1636 and 1654. The first troupe of English players may have come to Gdańsk as early as in 1587, although no direct evidence may be provided for this conjecture.[1] The company in question is the one that had visited Dresden and Elsinore a couple of months before. However, this first visit by the English players may have been treated as a sort of reconnaissance of this part of the Continent, and we can speak of regular performances given by them only after 1600.

That Gdańsk became one of the major centres of English theatrical activity on the Continent is not surprising. Being a wealthy and populous city,[2] an important trade centre on the Baltic (illustration 2), with a class of learned and open-minded burghers, Gdańsk welcomed the companies first with a measure of suspicion, but later with growing and unconcealed enthusiasm and appreciation. The evidence provided below will show that, in spite of the fact that in this relatively Puritan city the official 'dispensation' for public revelry was confined to the time of the traditional St Dominic's Fair, i.e., to two or three weeks in August, the English were often granted leave to play for much longer than the prescribed period. At times, of course, and much to their *chagrin*, the players were refused consent to play, but none the less they became an inseparable element of fair-time festivities, played a leading role in the dissemination of the art of theatre, and instilled an admiration of theatre into wide circles of Gdańsk society, giving also an impulse to local dramatic writing and productions.

In what follows, I propose to present in chronological order a commentary of all the evidence found to date connected with the English players' presence in Gdańsk. Because most of the documents taken into account have already been published by Johannes Bolte,[3] only excerpts from these, significant for our purposes, will be quoted. Full texts will be provided only in the case of yet unpublished records, with their original versions reproduced in Appendix 1.

In an application to the City Council, submitted on 23 August 1601 by an unidentified German company of players, we encounter the first record of actual English performances in Gdańsk. The Germans had arrived from Bergen in Norway, but apparently were not let into the city,[4] for their application includes a complaint that they had been waiting in vain for the

37

DANTISCVM.

Dantzig.

Council's reply to their previous epistle, whereas a rival company from England had been granted leave to play 'a long time ago'. The situation in which the German players found themselves must really have been hopeless, since all they asked for was permission to 'come near the city gates', so that everyone could see what the actors 'had learned'. They also indicated that the permit given to the English had been prolonged 'from day to day', which would seem to suggest that these latter had been favourably welcomed, and may also serve as an indication of the English players' instantaneous popularity. Apart from obvious envy, the German players' application is couched in bragging tones: they claim that if permission were given for performances, their company would prove not to be worse than the English one:

The English were permitted to perform here a long time ago, and they continue to play from day to day . . . We would also be delighted to perform one or two comedies and tragedies, or as many as Your Noble Graces desire. Since Your Noble Graces have seen the art of the English, You may wish to see that we Germans have also learned a thing or two, and just as well as the English.[5]

In his commentary on the above application, Johannes Bolte claims that the English players must have performed in Gdańsk during the St Dominic's Fair, i.e. for two or three weeks in August 1601.[6] However, the 'long time ago' ('so lange tidt') of the application could indicate that the players came even earlier than that. Although E. Herz, who agrees with Bolte as far as dating is concerned, classified, in his influential book,[7] the English company as unidentified, it may be assumed that this was Robert Browne with his men. Browne was not only the most mobile player in this period, courageously discovering 'new theatre lands' for his activity, but also when we follow his route in 1601, we notice a gap from June, when he performed at Strasburg, to October, when he emerged at Munich.[8] A period of three months between June and October would be sufficient to cover the distance to Gdańsk, to perform there, and to return to Germany. This identification remains of course conjectural and is based on indirect evidence and on the author's opinion that in that period it was Robert Browne rather than anyone else who would venture on travels to distant countries. It may be added that when in March 1601 Browne submitted a petition to the councillors at Frankfurt, he was accompanied by Robert Kingsman, Robert Ledbetter and Thomas Sackville. We know that Ledbetter was a former Lord Admiral's man, and Sackville went on the Continent together with Browne in 1592.[9]

Still another English company came to Gdańsk in the summer of 1605 and performed there during the St Dominic's Fair. An entry in the city accounts, dated 6 August, tells us that 'The Elector Christian of Brandenburg's comedians and musicians were paid 20 thalers = 37 marks.'[10] The entry is slightly misleading for Christian had never been the Elector of Brandenburg, and was, in fact, the Elector Joachim Frederick's brother. However, we know for certain that there was an English company attached to Christian's court at Halle from about 1603.[11] And we also know the names of the leading players: Richard Machin, George Webster and Ralph Reeve, former companions of Browne's.[12] The Elector, too, had an English company in his service, but this was managed by John Spencer.[13] Since the Margrave Christian's name is mentioned in the entry quoted, we may suppose that it was his company that visited Gdańsk in 1605. Nothing is known about the length of the visit or the players' repertory. Having performed in Gdańsk, the company travelled eastwards, and on 14 August was recorded at Elbing, and early in October in Königsberg.[14]

Even though little more is known about this company, the surviving bits of information contain an important implication, namely, that a new route had already been established by 1605, leading along the Baltic coast, from Gdańsk to Königsberg, with Elbing on the way. In addition, further towns will have been included in later years, marking a regular route covered by the English players along the Baltic coast, from Wolgast and Stettin in Pomerania, to Riga in Livonia. It is also worth noting that in the early phase of the English theatrical activities in Gdańsk the players were paid by the city. This seems to have resulted from the lack of professional theatre in Central Europe; all amateur performances were given to the general public free of charge and financed by the city or the guilds. In later periods, when the financial side of things became the company's sole responsibility, the players collected entrance fees themselves.

During the St Dominic's Fair of 1607 John Green appeared with his men, all or most of whom had been members of Browne's company. Browne was first accompanied by Green at Lille in 1603 and at Frankfurt in 1606,[15] where they were mentioned together with Robert Ledbetter. At that time among members of this company Richard Jones may also have been a leading player. Jones, whom Browne had known at least since the 1580s, was a well-known actor in the Lord Admiral's company until February 1602,[16] and had gone with Browne on the Continent in 1592. By spring 1607 Green had succeeded Browne in the leadership of the company, which held together for a while longer. Browne's name disappears from Continental records for a decade. All we know about him is that he was a member of the Queen's Revels syndicate in London in 1610 and he wrote a letter to the famous player Edward Alleyn on 11 April 1612.[17] Before coming to Gdańsk, Green's company visited Elbing, where the players had applied for leave to play on 16 July 1607; this being granted provided that the performance would take place in a private house.[18] We learn about Green's visit to Gdańsk from his application submitted to the councillors in July 1615, in which he indicated that it was the ninth year since he had visited the city for the first time. From Gdańsk, Green and his men went as far south as Graz in Austria. A list of plays presented by this company before the Habsburgs has been preserved, and is presented in

Chapter 8. Probably the same plays were staged in Gdańsk in August 1607.

Some scholars have surmised that John Spencer's company visited Gdańsk in 1609, but there is no direct evidence available supporting this view. Before their supposed visit to Gdańsk, the English players were recorded at Königsberg, where on 14 July they received the Elector of Brandenburg's letter of recommendation to the Elector of Saxony. It has been suggested that Spencer's company passed through and performed in Gdańsk on the way from Stettin (Polish, 'Szczecin'), where the players had stayed for some time, to Königsberg.[19]

John Spencer was certainly back in the Electoral service by 1611, for when he appeared in July 1611 in Gdańsk, he signed his two extant applications[20] as the Elector of Brandenburg's 'musician and comedian'. In the first of these, dated 15 July, we find several interesting pieces of information. For instance, the players were granted leave to play for a fortnight, which was a departure from the local tradition allowing public entertainment during the St Dominic's Fair only. However, having already given several performances (which, in turn, indicates that the company must have arrived at the beginning of July) Spencer was driven to the following conclusion:

. . . I note, however, that few spectators have been found to this time . . . Therefore, I have decided for the time being to perform here until the forthcoming Sunday and . . . to go to Königsberg and stay there, God willing, until the forthcoming St Dominic's Fair, when I will return here once again . . .[21]

In Spencer's second application, dated 29 August 1611, further complaints are added. The players had staged a première of a *New Comedy* in honour of the High Council, but an uninvited crowd broke into the theatre[22] without paying the entrance fee and consequently the company found itself in debt and had no money to pay the 'silk merchants and many other craftsmen'. The councillors showed some consideration and allowed Spencer to give two additional performances.

It is apparent from the above-mentioned application of 29 August that the players, having gone to their patron's court at Königsberg, returned, as planned, to Gdańsk for the St Dominic's Fair, which usually commenced on 5 August. Possibly, they stopped on the way and performed at Elbing.[23] The frequent complaints by the actors should not surprise us since this was the usual preface to asking for further privileges, especially from the time when finances had become the company's risk. However, it should also be remembered that production costs were increasing steadily, because the English players, whenever favourable conditions were provided, did not hesitate to invest substantial sums of money to add splendour to their performances. Hence Spencer's reference to 'silk merchants and many other craftsmen'. This expenditure, of course, reflected the competition growing up among the English and Continental companies and the increasing demands of audiences. In addition, when German was substituted for

English on stage, it became possible to stage unabridged texts of plays which made the productions far more complex and elaborate.

In an application to the City Council of 20 July 1615,[24] a company of 'Brandenburg' players asked for leave to play in the Fencing-School ('Fechtschullen'), in which their 'Antecessor vor dreyen Jahren' had also given performances, i.e. in 1612. One might have suspected that this was John Spencer's company again, because the players stayed for the whole winter 1611/12 at Königsberg,[25] and could have visited Gdańsk during the summer season. But on the basis of a hitherto unpublished record found in the Gdańsk State Archives, we may claim with all certainty that this was John Green's company, the fate of which, after performances in 1607/8 at Graz, has puzzled scholars. Having left Austria, Green emerges in the Spanish Netherlands in 1609 and 1610,[26] once again enjoying Habsburg patronage. Willem Schrickx has recently presented a new and convincing interpretation of one of the documents from Ghent. This is a letter written on 18 February 1610 by a local nobleman to the Ghent councillors, in which the 'English comedians' are recommended to the Council, and their good morals are praised. Schrickx has identified this company as John Green's[27] and there is no reason to disagree with him. This practice of obtaining letters of recommendation from local men of distinction appears characteristic of Green's endeavours to secure permission to play from occasionally reluctant councillors.

And this is precisely what he did in Gdańsk. In 1616 he asked one David Krüger, a local citizen, to write a letter to the City Council recommending John Green and his 'compagnia'. Krüger's letter is dated 11 July 1616, and includes a piece of information which leaves us in no doubt as to the identity of the company that performed in Gdańsk in 1612, for Krüger stated precisely that the troupe in question was the same one that had performed in Gdańsk four years before.

As Your Noble Lordships may certainly recall, four years ago you graciously permitted the English players to play freely here in this town, for which they again express their humblest gratitude. Because, Gracious Lords, the same players, that is John Green with a company under his management, are on the way and will soon arrive here, I have been informed by a letter and asked to submit in their name a supplication to Your Gracious Lordships.[28]

Thus, we may identify beyond doubt the company that visited Gdańsk in 1612 and was the first known troupe to perform in the newly built public theatre, the so-called Fencing-School (Illustrations 3 and 4). This piece of evidence also contributes substantially to our knowledge of Green's activities during this period. Nothing has hitherto been found in Continental archives to show what happened to the company between 1611 and 1613, when in November Green emerged at Utrecht.[29] But far more important is the fact that by 1612 a permanent public theatre had been opened in Gdańsk. The architectural similarity between the Gdańsk theatre and the London Fortune playhouse will be discussed elsewhere in this book. Nevertheless, it is worth noting now that among the actors who had visited Gdańsk before 1612, several were recorded in London after the Fortune had been built in 1600, and may have therefore been responsible for bringing the idea and architectural details to Gdańsk.

After a surprising three-year break in theatrical activity in Gdańsk, two rival companies appeared there roughly at the same time in summer 1615. One was an international, German–English troupe, presumably led by Robert Archer, the other was again John Green's. Both the applications to the City Council submitted by Archer's men, dated 20 July and 'July' 1615 respectively, are signed by otherwise unknown players, Johannes Fridericus Virnius and Bartholomeus Freyerbott.[30] Archer, in fact, is not mentioned in either of the documents, and his association with this company might be doubted, were it not for several pieces of information to be found there. One is that the actors claim to be the Elector of Brandenburg's men, a claim confirmed by the Elector's patent they enclosed (now lost).

Since Our Most Gracious Lord, His Electoral Grace of Brandenburg, whom we entertained with our comedies during the last winter (by the power of the enclosed patent graciously awarded by His Grace), has graciously allowed us to go to other places this summer and to present our plays there . . .[31]

According to the players' account, before coming to Gdańsk they had also performed in Pomerania.

Since c. 1604, the company attached for many years to the Elector of Brandenburg's court had been John Spencer's. However, the company may have fallen into disgrace, for John Sigismund dismissed the players in April 1613. Because of the Elector's recent conversion to Calvinism he had to leave Lutheran Prussia for some time, and at his court at Berlin he hired a new company, which included three Pedel (Peadle?) brothers, William, Abraham and August, Robert Archer, and two German players, Behrendt Holzhew and August Pflugbeil.[32] Archer's name recurs in the Electoral records until 1616, when in May he was paid 250 florins compensation.[33] The intriguing omission of Archer's name from the Gdańsk applications of the Brandenburg company may be accounted for by several possible explanations. One is simply that he was not the manager of the company at that time, and only the leading actors were usually mentioned in the records. The other possibility, perhaps less likely, is that the players, knowing that a rival English company would soon arrive in Gdańsk, decided to win the favour of the councillors by stressing the fact that they were German. In their first application the players further asked for leave to present fourteen comedies before the commencement of the St Dominic's Fair, and for permission to perform in the Fencing-School, where their 'predecessors had acted three years earlier'. Consent was granted for the presentation of seven comedies,

3. The Gdańsk Fencing-School

4. A conjectural reconstruction of the public theatre in Gdańsk

on the condition that the entrance fee would not exceed two groschen.

The company's second application,[34] includes numerous complaints by the players, whose work in Gdańsk appeared to have been a failure. First, they had had to rehearse and make all the necessary preparations, which lasted from Monday to Thursday. On Friday a tragicomedy had been presented, but without much success, and the players' income had not even covered expenses. In addition, their 'theatre' had suffered much from rain and storm, which indicates that the 'necessary preparations' mentioned, were connected with scenery or properties which had apparently been left on stage overnight and were damaged by bad weather. As though there were no end to their misfortunes, a rival company of English players had just arrived, and as with other 'foreign' troupes, this one – according to the authors of the application – specialised in lasciviousness, instead of presenting decent and chaste shows. For this reason, the players humbly begged the councillors to prevent the English from beginning their performances until the Brandenburg players had finished their own, including the requested three additional performances. However, they were not allowed to prolong their stay in Gdańsk. It is worth noting that in the second application, one play – *Lapsus Davidi cum Bathseba* – was recommended by the players as particularly worthy. Ironically, this play is also 'foreign', because it is a German version of George Peele's *The Love of King David and Fair Bethsabe*, in the repertory of the Earl of Worcester's men from 1602.[35]

The details extracted here from the two applications are revealing not only of the local theatrical customs and conditions, but also of certain characteristic features of the strolling companies in general. The fact that Robert Archer may have been among the Brandenburg players is of major significance to a close study of the English players' precise movements on the Continent. Another important fact is that the players arriving on 20 July 1615 asked for permission to present fourteen comedies before the beginning of the St Dominic's Fair, which indicates that they intended to stage a different play on each consecutive day, excluding Sundays (the fair traditionally opened on 5 August). Another significant piece of information is that it had taken them four days to prepare scenery, which was apparently destroyed by bad weather, which, in turn, suggests that the stage in the Fencing-School was not covered with any sort of 'roof' or 'heavens'. And in the second application, the size of the company is mentioned: it numbered eighteen players, a characteristic figure for the companies active in this period.

In the three applications left in 1615 by John Green and his men, several things deserve particular attention.[36] The first application, dated the end of July, has already helped us to identify the company that visited Gdańsk in 1607. Apart from their comedies and tragedies presented in 'pure German language' ('in reiner deutscher Sprache'), the players recommended music and 'other amusing things' ('andere kurzweilige sachen'). In reply, the councillors decided to see a rehearsal first, and take a final decision later. The apprehension of the City Council is understandable in view of the rather tarnished reputation that the English companies enjoyed. In this case the actors were fortunate, the rehearsal made a good impression on the severe magistrates, and the company was granted a consent to play, as we learn from the remaining two applications. Both of these, dated 7 and 25 August respectively, include a long list of complaints about expenses[37] and unsatisfactory returns, followed by a request for the prolongation of time given to play. We also learn that the company numbered eighteen players, and the next town they planned to visit was Wolfenbüttel, whence Green and his troupe had come to Gdańsk.[38]

Not much can be said about the remaining actors in Green's company, for no names are given in the sources. However, in the first application, in which the players indicated that it was the ninth year since their company had first performed in Gdańsk, a plural form is used throughout the whole text which is not signed by Green himself, but by the whole company of 'Englische Comoedianten'. This seems to indicate that at least the principal actors of the 1615 troupe must have been in Gdańsk, together with Green, in 1607. It is highly probable that Richard Jones was one of them. In an undated letter to Edward Alleyn he wrote: 'I am to go over beyond the seas w^t Mr Browne and the company, but not by his meanes, for he is put to half a shaer, and to stay hear, for they ar all against his goinge.'[39]

As mentioned above, before the next visit of Green's company to Gdańsk, on 11 July 1616, David Krüger submitted a letter of recommendation to the councillors there. Krüger may have been related to Peter Krüger, a learned Gdańsk astronomer and mathematician, and he was obviously a representative of the well-educated class of burghers and an admirer of theatre himself. His letter enables us to identify the company which was the first to perform in the newly built Fencing-School. It is strange, however, that in his letter Krüger refers to Green's performances of 1612, and not to those of 1615. Perhaps he wanted to stress the fact that in 1612 the players were given permission to play in the Fencing-School, whereas in 1615 for some reason such a permit was not granted.

In 1616 Green's company had arrived in Gdańsk from Denmark, and the players submitted their first application on 28 July.[40] This is signed by John Green and Robert Reynolds in the name of all the 'Englische Comoedianten'.

Now it is certain that the way of the world can not be more artfully depicted than in Comedies and Tragedies, which like a mirror represent and show all men's lives and natures, both good and evil, that everyone may see and recognize himself therein. This art was valued above all measure by the ancient Greeks and Romans, and will no doubt continue as long as the world exists. It is also loved and admired by all knowledgeable people in our own times, so that it now finds its way into and subsists in various tongues and manners . . .[41]

Little wonder that after such a bombastic introduction the learned councillors consented to let the players perform for eight days. There were, however, three conditions: one, that the entrance fee would not exceed 3 groschen; two, that nothing indecent would be presented; and three, that after eight days the players would unconditionally cease to play in Gdańsk.

To my knowledge, the above document is the first record of Reynolds' presence on the Continent. The fact that his name appears together with Green's suggests that he had already been recognised as the principal player in the company, by no means a 'freshman'. Before coming to Gdańsk, Reynolds was still in London in January 1616.[42] This indicates that he may have joined Green's company in Denmark, and travelled with his new companions to Gdańsk. He may have stayed on the Continent somewhat longer, possibly at the Royal court at Warsaw, where Green's men stayed for a couple of months after they had performed in Gdańsk, but he had certainly left the company by the time the players left Warsaw for Silesia in March 1617. Reynolds returned to London for a while, where he was recorded in March 1617, but he was soon back on the Continent and developed his matchless comical talents there. For it is Robert Reynolds who became one of the most important managers of English 'Continental' companies, and under the stage-name 'Pickleherring' has entered the history of Continental theatre as one of the notable personalities of the period. An account of 1631 tells us that: 'This Monsieur Pickelherring was first introduced into Germany by the English while it was still in a state of prosperity [i.e. before the Thirty Years War], and everybody liked to amuse himself with comedies and other representations.'[43]

Already in the first collection of German prose translations of English plays that appeared in 1620 under the title *Englische Comoedien und Tragedien*, Pickleherring is mentioned on the title page, and the collection itself includes two such 'Pickleherring plays'.[44] Interestingly, in one of these, entitled *A Merry Pickleherring Play About Beautiful Maria and Old Henry* ('Ein lustig Pickleherring Spiel von der schönen Maria und alten Hanrey'), the title character, Maria, happens to live in Gdańsk at the 'Long Market'. This very street is today still the heart of the picturesque Old Town of Gdańsk, and is called in Polish 'Długi Targ', which means exactly the same thing – a long market.[45] This is one of the few topographical allusions in the plays in the repertory of the English companies active on the Continent.

To return to the visit of Green and Reynolds to Gdańsk in 1616, it may be observed that after the time allotted for performance had expired, the players invited the councillors to a grand performance, for which they were given a gratuity of 30 marks, in addition to wine which cost another 15 marks and 24 shillings. The remaining two applications of the Green–Reynolds company, dated 19 and 25 August 1616, include the usual complaints about the players' financial difficulties, and the various obstacles they had to overcome. The number of actors is the same as in 1615 – eighteen men. In the last application, however, a new and interesting piece of information comes to light: that the players had been advised to get in touch with the King of Poland, and had in fact already written to him offering their services; they had decided to wait for the reply in Gdańsk, but having no means to make a living, they asked the councillors for an extension of the performance time. This was not granted, but the company did go on to the royal court at Warsaw.

The year of 1619 saw an abundance of visits by the English players, for no less than three companies came to Gdańsk during the summer. Of the six applications that have been preserved in the State Archives in Gdańsk, only one has not yet been published.[46] It is dated 7 June 1619, and is signed by 'Englische Comoedianten' with no players' names given. In spite of the fact that the councillors remained deaf to the company's appeal, this document is not without importance.

Since our company has for some time stayed at the court of His Royal Majesty in Poland and intends to return there again towards winter, we humbly ask for permission to visit this city and other towns in the region. We would like to present our meagre skills here during the forthcoming St Dominic's Fair.[47]

The fact that the players refer to performances in Warsaw, may lead us to the conclusion that it was John Green's company which spent the winter 1616/17 at the Royal Court at Warsaw, but this cannot be the case, because soon after this first company had left Gdańsk, Green emerged there in August and was given permission to act without any hindrance. We would be unable to identify this company, but for J.G. Riewald, who draws our attention to a hitherto neglected document among the records of the Privy Council in London.[48] This is dated 27 June 1617 and includes a list of players and musicians who were permitted to leave London for Warsaw on the request of the Prince of Poland. The details of this surprising theatrical enterprise are discussed elsewhere in this book. The very fact that this company had been brought to Warsaw directly from London suggests that the players were hired on a permanent basis, and only during the summer theatrical season were they allowed to leave Warsaw and visit other towns. The evidence is conclusive that this was the company that visited Gdańsk in June 1619 and was refused leave to play.

Next was the company under John Spencer, who had last been in Gdańsk in 1611. Since that year, Spencer's career seemed to have reached its peak, and although in 1613 he was dismissed from the Elector of Brandenburg's court, he gained international fame under the stage-name 'Hans Stockfish' and performed before the highest nobles in Central Europe, including the Emperor, and his name appears in various records in both Catholic and Protestant countries.[49] Spencer had been back in the Elector's service by 1618, and before his Gdańsk visit he was recorded in March at Elbing, and in June at Balga and Königsberg. In his Gdańsk application of 26 July 1619,[50] the

Elector's 'musician and comedian' indicated that the company was on its way to Berlin, and the players asked the councillors for leave to play 'comedies and tragedies' for fourteen days in the Fencing-School during the St Dominic's Fair. They also promised not to offend or outrage anyone but, in spite of all the company's fame, permission was not granted 'for numerous reasons'. This is the last recorded visit of Spencer's company to Gdańsk. Soon after the players reached Berlin their protector John Sigismund died in December 1619.[51] His successor, George William (1619–40), kept the company in his service for a while longer, and the last record of Spencer's presence on the Continent is found in 1623, when he was refused consent to act at Nuremberg.[52]

The identification of the third English company that came to Gdańsk in summer 1619 is particularly difficult, for in the players' four applications that have been preserved,[53] no names are given, apart from the usual 'Englische Comoedianten', and, moreover, no references are made either to previous performances in Gdańsk, or to towns the company had visited before coming to Gdańsk or was planning to visit. All we learn from the applications is that the players had undertaken 'a distant journey' to reach Gdańsk. In the first of these documents, dated 31 July 1619, a request is made for leave to play 'tragedies and comedies' for fourteen days in the Fencing-School during the St Dominic's Fair, which is accompanied by the customary promises not to offend anyone, the plays to be presented being 'chaste' and 'in good taste', and not to charge more than three groschen entrance fee. Permission was granted for eight days on two conditions: that nothing indecent would be presented and that not more than two groschen would be charged. On the request of the players, the consent was extended on 19 August until 'the end of this week'.

The only direct hint as to the company's repertoire comes from the players' penultimate application of 28 August, in which a new *Tragedy of Roman Lucrece* ('Tragoedia von der Römischen Lucretia') is mentioned. This may have been Thomas Heywood's *The Rape of Lucrece* (1608).[54] However, this will not help us much in solving the last problem, i.e., the identification of the company in question. Obviously, the two companies that had come to Gdańsk earlier have to be ruled out. Of the remaining English strollers active in this period, two may be taken into consideration, Robert Browne and John Green. If E.K. Chambers' conjecture is correct, namely, that both of these leading actors joined forces sometime in 1618,[55] it would appear highly probable that this amalgamated company came to Gdańsk in summer 1619. Since both Green and Browne were known in the city from their previous performances, this would provide a satisfactory explanation for the puzzling fact that only this particular company out of the three was given permission to play.[56]

If we accept this conjecture as true then it will not be difficult to ascertain the repertoire of this company, as just a year later a collection of English plays in German prose-translation was published in Leipzig. Apart from the two 'Pickleherring pieces', the 1620 edition included the following: *Esther and Haman*,[57] *The Prodigal Son, Fortunatus, A King's Son of England and a King's Daughter of Scotland, Nobody and Somebody*,[58] *Sidonia and Theagenes*,[59] *Julio and Hyppolita* and *Titus Andronicus*.[60] Of the above list five plays were still in Green's repertoire in 1626, and three had been so long before the Gdańsk visit.[61]

The year 1619 marks the end of the first period of English theatrical activity in Gdańsk. Of the companies that visited the city between 1601 and 1619, we have been able to identify several conclusively. These were the troupes of Robert Browne, John Green and Robert Reynolds, John Spencer, Richard Jones, and – presumably – companies led by Robert Archer, Richard Machin and Ralph Reeve. A number of these veteran players ended their Continental careers at about this period (see Appendix 4). Spencer's activities culminate in 1623, when he is last mentioned at Nuremberg; Browne's in 1620 at Prague; and Jones is last seen in 1624 at Wolgast in Pomerania; Green, who went with Browne to Prague in 1619/20, in the period following the outbreak of the Thirty Years War withdrew from these perilous regions and was recorded, among other places, at Cologne in April 1620 and then in the Netherlands in July 1620 and April 1624; his name was last recorded at Frankfurt in 1626.[62] The relatively short-lived company of Webster, Machin and Reeve was last mentioned at Frankfurt in 1613.[63] Only two of the actors recorded in Gdańsk in the period under discussion, Robert Archer and Robert Reynolds, remained active on the Continent, and both of them frequently visited Gdańsk after 1635.

There is no doubt that the Thirty Years War and the war between Poland and Sweden had an immediate effect on the fates of the English players in Central Europe. It forced companies to seek their fortunes in safer regions of the Continent, and frequently led to their dissolution. Thus between 1619 and 1635 (when a peace treaty was signed between Poland and Sweden) not a single English company was recorded in Gdańsk, with the possible exception of a troupe that emerged there in 1623, offering comedies, tragedies, ballet, masquerades and English dances. However, the application of this company, dated 26 July[64] is signed with three totally un-English names of otherwise unknown players: Paul Schultz, Michael Frantzosz and Johann Tiesz.[65]

The first English company that appeared in Gdańsk after the end of the Polish–Swedish war was Robert Archer's, who had been recorded in this city over twenty years before. Of the two extant applications of this company to the City Council,[66] the first is dated 28 July 1636, and is signed by 'Arend Ärschen'. This includes the following passage:

Following the death of King Sigismund the Third of blessed memory, whom we, the English comedians, had served for many years, our company has performed in Holland, before the King of Denmark, before the Duke of Holstein, and in this region at Königsberg. We are now awaiting a letter from His Majesty now reigning, from Vilnius, with decision as to where we should go to His Royal Highness' service – to Vilnius or to Warsaw. Therefore, because of the forthcoming St Dominic's Fair, we would be glad to make a living by presenting our comedies . . .[67]

Interestingly, in the application quoted, the players asked the councillors not to refuse their request 'this time', which indicates that the players had been refused leave to play some time before, presumably in 1635.[68]

Archer's troupe, of course, cannot be identified with that of Robert Reynolds, which acted in the Netherlands in the early 1630s. Even though these actors were companions in 1627, when they were recorded together at Torgau,[69] their troupe seems to have split up sometime between 1627 and 1628: Archer with some actors went to Warsaw, whereas Reynolds' presence was recorded in the Netherlands and in Germany about this time.[70] And they are still mentioned independently as leaders of two distinct companies in 1636: Archer in Gdańsk, and Reynolds together with Edward Pudsey in Amsterdam.[71]

At the players' request of July 1636, the company was granted leave to play in Gdańsk for three weeks on several conditions. One was the usual warning that the players should abstain from all obscenities in the plays to be shown. They were allowed to play in the Fencing-School, but forbidden to charge more than 9 groschen as the entrance fee, and they were ordered to pay some money for the rebuilding of St James' church.

The next application is dated 8 September 1636, and includes a request for an extension of the performance time for another 'week or two', and this is accompanied by an invitation to a performance in honour of the Council to be given on 'the forthcoming Thursday', i.e., 9 September. The plea, however, was rejected by the councillors on the grounds that the players had already given additional performances without the Council's consent. Nevertheless it seems that Archer's activity in Gdańsk was very successful in 1636, since having already performed there for over a month, he was still convinced in September that there would be more spectators willing to see plays.

With the scarcity of available evidence it is not possible to identify the remaining actors of this company. Scholars have assumed that Archer joined forces with Reynolds about this time.[72] However, on the basis of new pieces of evidence, hitherto unpublished, it appears possible to conclude that in the period between 1636 and 1640 there were two distinct companies active in the Gdańsk region. One of these, still under Archer, was recorded in 1638 and 1639. We learn about these visits from later applications made by an English company that came to Gdańsk in May 1640 and in July 1643. In the first of these we read the following:

Herr Burgomaster, Noble, Honourable, Famous and Wise, Praiseworthy Magnificences, you will graciously recall that during the last St Dominic's Fair we requested permission to perform our comedies before the inhabitants of this city, which had often been granted before. But Your Magnificences expressed objections because of the plague which was then rife and we did not want to have put ourselves to the expense of our journey in vain, and we were of necessity forced to erect something [i.e. a stage] on the Bishop's Hill, although this hardly covered our costs. Later we stayed with His Royal Majesty at Warsaw, where we served him according to his convenience and his desire; we received leave of absence from thence for some time, on the condition, however, that we should return again after a time. We now wish to express the highest praise for this, and as the danger of plague has disappeared from this city, and we would not like to be without employment in the interim before the date of our return to court, we accordingly submit our most humble request to your Magnificences, asking that you might bestow on us your great grace and favour, and permit us to hold our performances here around St John's day, so that we might thereby entertain the citizens: our entertainment will be so modest and polite that nobody will be offended by it; on the contrary, there will be all manner of instruction for everyday life to be gained, without, however, forgetting about bitter blows though always paying regard to what propriety can mitigate. As you will see from the enclosed recommendation of His Royal Highness, He would not be opposed to our performances in this place too. Thus we entertain the sincere expectation that Your Magnificences will graciously accede to and grant our humble request, for which we will always offer our praise and which we will repay with our most attentive services. Remaining the Council's debtors

Humbly
The English Comedians

[The Council's decision:]
English Comedians.
Read at the Senate on May 1640
The Council does not see how the petitioners' request could be met.[73]

The players' request was rejected presumably because the theatrical summer season in Gdańsk had not yet begun by May, which is also confirmed by the same company's application of 1643. The players' reference to their attachment to the Royal Court at Warsaw indicates that this may have been Robert Archer's company again. We last saw him in Gdańsk in 1636. On the basis of the above document, we may reach some positive conclusions, namely, that the same company's presence was recorded in Gdańsk in 1635(?), 1636, 1639 and 1640. Further information is provided by an application of July 1643, in which the players mentioned their previous performances in Gdańsk three and five years back, which would indicate 1640 and 1638.

Herr Burgomaster, Noble, Honourable, Famous and Wise, Praiseworthy Noble Lords. Noble Honourable Lords, and Noble and Honourable Council of this glorious and famous city of Gdańsk. We, the whole company of English comedians, would like to submit a request that disgrace be not shown to us, but wish to remind Your Noble Lordships of the consolation you offered us three years ago [i.e. in 1640], when we asked Your Honours for a place in the Fencing-School, but were refused. However, we were given the hope that if we came at some other time, the High Council might show us its favour and perhaps grant our request, since at that time three years ago, as also five years ago [i.e. in 1638], we had to make do with other patronage. Thus, we submit our most

53

humble request to the High Council to show us grace and to recall the hope you gave us, asking you to take into account the long journey we had to undertake in order to reach this glorious town, and not to make our request fruitless, but to show us your favour in this matter. For this we will oblige ourselves to pay a tax of 200 Reichsthalers for the poor. We shall acknowledge such great favour of the High Honourable [etc.] Council of this town with an honest heart and shall have all cause to praise it. In expectation of a positive answer,

Humbly
The whole company of
The English Comedians

[The Council's decision:]
Read at the Senate 16 July 1643. Comedians. The High Council has approved the request that they should perform their comedies for four weeks in the town (excluding Sundays), on condition that they would behave well and not involve themselves in any wrongdoing. If anything of this kind happens, they will lose their freedom forthwith. In addition, they will be obliged to pay at least 200 Reichsthalers towards the prison, insofar as more money should not be obtainable from them. They are not allowed to charge more than 9 florins for either upper or lower seats.[74]

This application helps to identify the company that visited Gdańsk almost every year in the period 1635–40. Some scholars have claimed that this was the same company that was in the service of the Elector of Brandenburg George William: Robert Reynolds, Robert Archer, William Roe, John Wayde, Edward Pudsey and William Wedware.[75] However, the dates do not fit:[76] we are in fact dealing with two distinct companies. On the basis of the available evidence we may claim that one of these, under Robert Archer, had been permanently attached to the court of Vladislaus IV at Warsaw from 1636 to spring 1640, undertaking occasional visits to Gdańsk, whereas the second company, under Robert Reynolds, found a different patron in the person of the Elector of Brandenburg, and on the way to Königsberg, the players may have stopped at Elbing, where 'Pickleherring' was recorded in 1638.[77] It seems very likely that the two companies joined forces after Archer's unsuccessful visit to Gdańsk in May 1640. Having joined forces, the players decided to leave the Elector's court, and went to Warsaw, where in fact they were expected, as is apparent from their Gdańsk application of May 1640. Thus, the company that came to Gdańsk in 1643 was presumably composed of players mentioned in the Electoral patent, with the exception of Robert Reynolds who had died in Warsaw by that time.[78]

The players were allowed to perform for four weeks on several conditions; of these the most interesting is the one that states that if the players did not pay the prescribed sum of money, they would be imprisoned, which indicates that in the past the English may have secretly left the town without paying any tax. On the basis of the second application of the company, now lost, Bolte noted that on 8 September the players asked the Council to prolong the performance time, complaining that due to bear-baiting they had not had an opportunity to perform every day.[79] A permit was granted for one week of additional performances, provided the players paid 200 florins. This indicates that the company acted in Gdańsk for two months, from 16 July to 15 September, and may serve as an example of the exceptional and growing popularity of theatre in the city.

That this particular company stayed in Gdańsk even longer is proved by another hitherto unpublished application of 15 January 1644:

Right Noble, Stern, Honourable, Praiseworthy, High and Wise Burgomaster and Council, our ever Respected and Gracious Lords and Mighty Benefactors,
After we had by your Noble [etc.] gracious leave performed here in Gdańsk during the St Dominic's Fair for some time, we wished to continue our journey to other places, but an unforeseen accident stopped us, so that we had to stay here for quite a long time and suffer great expenses (particularly myself who, as a citizen of this glorious city, had here a wife, children and servants); our situation is similar now, when winter makes our further journey anywhere impossible, either by sea, or overland. We therefore, in view of our expenditures, would like to earn a little money again. Thus we would now be inclined to give public performances for a time at shrovetide. Because nothing of this kind may take place without the permission and support of Your Gracious [etc.] Lordships, we therefore submit to Your Gracious [etc.] Lordships our humblest plea and request and ask Your Gracious [etc.] Lordships to grant us the greatly desired leave and allow us to put our plan into action by permitting us to give a week's time for three or four more performances, according to Your Gracious [etc.] Lordships' will. At the same time we would like to assure Your Gracious [etc.] Lordships that apart from eternal gratefulness for this kindness and favour, we shall be ready and willing to pay and hand over a quarter of our income. We shall also take great pains both to deserve this kindness and to repay the debt for the kindness shown to us, afterwards and at all times.

[The Council's decision]:
Comedians. The Council doubted the wisdom of meeting the petitioner's request. Read at the Senate 15 January [16]44.[80]

The above application explains a somewhat puzzling Polish source. This is a letter of a Polish nobleman, Krzysztof Ossoliński, to Krzysztof Opaliński:

The Bishop of Kujawy has written to me from Gdańsk that in his inn he had an English comedy staged for the Gdańsk citizens and their wives and children.[81]

Mikołaj Gniewosz was then the Bishop of Kujawy, and he often resided in Gdańsk. The 'inn' (Polish, 'gospoda') means here the Bishop's residence in Gdańsk. Since Shrovetide is referred to in the letter, the play must have been performed before 24 February 1644. It is not unlikely that the Bishop had seen the players in Warsaw.

It was undoubtedly the same company that sent an application to the City Council from Elbing, which was considered by the councillors on 29 July 1644. This application is reproduced here for the first time:

Noble, Honourable, Praiseworthy and Wise, Gracious Noble Lordships, we the English comedians, having performed our comedies this year at Riga and Königsberg, and having now reached Elbing, have further decided to visit the glorious city of Gdańsk. We are 18 in number and since our intention is to present something new for the particular

55

entertainment of your Noble [etc.] Lordships and the praiseworthy burghers, we submit our most humble petition and request to the High [etc.] Lordships to show us grace and to allow us to perform again during the St Dominic's Fair in the usual place in the Fencing-School, where we have performed before, and to allow this at a reasonable fee. We are ready to serve Your Most Praiseworthy [etc.] Lordships with all our talents and skills, and to be the Council's debtors, trusting in God's protection and awaiting a favourable decision.

> The humble servants of Your Noble [etc.] Lordships
> All the English comedians
> Stationed now at Elbing

[The Council's decision:]
Read at the Senate 29 July [16]44.
The High Council does not approve the request. They are accordingly sternly reminded that they should not dare to perform in the regal Arthurian Hall, nor fix any broadsheets or announcements to the gates, on pain of a severe penalty.[82]

The councillors' decision implies that in the past the English players must have neglected the Council's orders, and having been refused leave to play in the Fencing-School, gave performances in other places, such as King Arthur's Hall, mentioned above: a magnificent building, which was the centre of the city's mercantile life. Equally interesting is the mention of playbills fixed to the gates.

Having been refused leave to play in Gdańsk in 1644, the company went to the Netherlands. On 8 July 1645 William Roe and his company applied for leave to play during the annual fair at Utrecht.[83] After his visit to the Netherlands, Roe – who had succeeded Archer in the leadership of the company – emerged at Cologne, and in September 1646 at Dresden, and then in April 1647 once again at Cologne.[84] Interestingly, in March 1646 William Roe and a number of Dutch players signed a partnership agreement with another English player, John Payne, who was first recorded on the Continent in 1639.[85] This shows us clearly the changes that the English companies had undergone during the Thirty Years War. Because there were relatively few new actors coming from England, the veteran players began to form international companies, which traditionally labelled themselves 'Englische Comoedianten', even though only the leading players were in fact English. Such a company, composed of players from various countries visited Gdańsk in August 1647:

Herr ruling Burgomaster [etc.] Praiseworthy [etc.] Lords, we are offering our most humble services and will not conceal our following supplication from the Honourable [etc.] Council. We and our companions from England, the Netherlands and German Hanseatic towns, have come to this very famous place, to the Royal City of Gdańsk (after an exhausting sea-voyage) with hopes to delight the Wise Council and dear burghers with our plays during the St Dominic's Fair, according to our profession; that is with new comedies never hitherto acted.

Because it is known from all histories that many comedies (which seek through useful teaching and stories to show how one can avoid all number of sins, and which, on the other hand, encourage the young to exercise honour in their daily lives) it would be commendable – both for their art and for the sake of the young – to present them [i.e. the comedies] in public; not to mention others, like Terence, Plautus, Seneca, Aeschylus etc.

We therefore submit to Your Honours [etc.] our most humble request to show us magnanimity and allow us to play here during the time of the St Dominic's Fair, when everyone likes to seek pleasure and diversion; we wish to perform good and useful comedies, which are pleasant at the same time, in a place that the High Council may be gracious enough to allot us. This could be the Fencing-School, or the city Weighing House, or St George's Shooting Garden, or elsewhere. For our part, we will endeavour not only to live to serve you . . . but to pay an appropriate tax. Commending Your Lordships to the especial protection of the Almighty, for a peaceful and happy rule,

> Your most Noble
> And Just Masters'
> Humblest servants
> John Wayde
> and
> William Roe

for themselves and in the name of their comrades

[The Council's decision:]
Request [of the] English Comedians.
Read at the Senate on 5 August 1647
The Most Wise Council has decided that the English players should be permitted to act for three weeks in the Fencing-School, in respect of which they should pay a certain amount for the prison. At the same time they are ordered to refrain entirely from improper *dictis et factis*, and to observe honour in all things. In the event of the opposite, performances will be prohibited, and they will be expelled from the country. The permit does not include Sundays.[86]

The outbreak of the Civil War in England and the closing of the London theatres must have driven at least some actors to the Continent. Some of these may have joined Wayde–Roe's company, contributing new plays to the troupe's repertoire – hence the new comedies 'never hitherto acted' that are mentioned in the application. Another piece of evidence is perhaps more persuasive. Before their Gdańsk visit, the players were recorded in April in Cologne, where Roe declared that the company had arrived 'at high cost' from England,[87] which indicates that either Roe and Wayde went home for a while to organise a new troupe, or they were joined on the Continent by some London players.

After their visit to Gdańsk, the players went to Königsberg and further east to Riga, where the company was recorded in January 1648. In the Riga application to the Town Council, the only play mentioned is *The Tragedy of Dorothea the Martyr*, which seems to mean Philip Massinger's *The Virgin Martyr* (1620). And this play, among others, may have been staged in Gdańsk in 1647. A supplementary list may be provided from the repertoire of this company from Dresden, where the players had performed a year before. This included the following: *Tragedy of Romeo and Juliet*; *Tragedy of the Rich*

Man and Lazarus; *Comedy of the Prodigal Son*; in addition to several plays which I have been unable to identify, such as *The Tragedy of Lorenz* (*The Spanish Tragedy?*); *Comedy of a Young and Proud Ernesto*; *Comedy of the Creation of the World, with a Puppet Show*, and so on.[88] The changes of individual players in particular companies and the parallel rise of professional Continental players were accompanied by changes in the repertories which started to include plays written by Continental dramatists, plays which were often styled as 'English'.

Yet another company of English actors that came to Gdańsk in 1649 is worth particular attention. In their application to the City Council, dated 29 October 1649, these unnamed players mentioned that before arriving in Gdańsk they had performed 'for some time' at the court of the Archduke Leopold at Brussels. This application sheds new light on the activities of English players in other regions on the Continent, and solves several controversial issues.

High Honourable, Respectable, Praiseworthy, Highly Learned Lords, Herr Burgomaster and the Council,
Particularly Praiseworthy, Gracious and Ruling Lords, our company of comedians has for some time stayed at the court of His Highness the Archduke Leopold at Brussels in the Netherlands, at which there were numerous servants to His Royal Highness the King of England of gracious memory. However, we have never been here in Gdańsk before, since we did not have time and opportunity to come here for the previous St Dominic's Fair; but, we did not wish to neglect to visit this famous and praiseworthy city during St Martin's Fair, and to present our plays to the High Council according to its will. This is why we have submitted this most humble request to the Council, and ask it for the great honour of graciously allowing us to play here in Gdańsk for a time: for we are experienced players, most of whom have been trained as actors since their youth, who will not present any vices or condemnable tricks; only things appropriate to decency will be presented, in addition to charming and pleasant English music and excellent ballets, which will the better increase the pleasure of the spectators and listeners. Accordingly, we hope that the High [etc.] Council will not refuse our earnest and humble request, but will most graciously allow and permit us to engage in our theatrical performances. Forever grateful,
[Your] Humblest servants
and
Comedians

[The Council's decision:]
Read at the Senate on October 29, 1649
It is agreed that at present time it is not possible to approve the application, but some of the plays may happily be presented and accepted at the next St Dominic's Fair [i.e. in August 1650].[89]

Since the Archduke Leopold William of Austria, a Habsburg, took office as the governor-general of the Spanish Netherlands in April 1647, this unidentified company must have performed in Brussels sometime between April 1647 and October 1649. Fortunately, an account book of the

Archduke's household expenses has been preserved in the General Archives at Brussels; its first entry relating to the English players is dated 8 February 1648.[90] The evidence found in Gdańsk supports and confirms Hotson's view that the company in question was led by George Jolly.[91] The only other possibility is that this was one of the London companies, or one arranged *ad hoc* by the London players after the closing of the theatres. There was in fact one company of this sort recorded in Paris in 1646: this was the Prince of Wales' company.[92] And Jolly was mentioned, together with Mathew Smith, as Prince Charles' man in 1640.[93] The company recorded in Paris is said to have been dissolved for want of money in November 1646,[94] and it seems likely that Jolly stayed on the Continent with some of the players.

George Jolly's stormy activities on the Continent in the period between 1648 and 1660 have attracted much attention on the part of scholars, because Jolly was the only well-known player of the strolling companies to become an important personality of the theatrical scene back in London.[95] It is not possible to trace the fortunes of the company after the players had left Gdańsk in October 1649. Presumably it split up soon after. The peculiar features of Jolly's personality did not further harmonious co-operation among the players. From the available body of evidence concerning Jolly, we get a picture of a brutal, rapacious and unscrupulous actor–manager who often did not refrain from fisticuffs. Thus, one Johann Janicke was beaten up by Jolly at Nuremberg, and the same thing happened to Christoph Blümels – ironically, one of Jolly's leading players.[96] It is therefore hardly surprising that when he returned to Gdańsk in 1650, his company was composed of different players from those he had with him in 1649.

Before Jolly's arrival, one of the Gdańsk citizens, a certain Johan Roszawen, submitted an application, dated 1 August 1650, to the City Council asking the councillors to treat the players kindly and to grant them leave to play.

I have recently received a letter from a company of English players, in which I was notified that they are on their way to Gdańsk in order to perform during the St Dominic's Fair, and to stage for the enjoyment of the citizens beautiful comedies and tragedies . . . Since this company, excepting one or two persons, has never played in this place, and was one of the foremost companies of the late King [Vladislaus IV?] and was also at Her Royal Majesty's Court in Sweden, and has gained the favour and high praise of noble Lords . . .[97]

This is the second surviving example of a Gdańsk citizen's written support for the English players, the first being David Krüger's application. The document leaves no doubt that among the members of this company there were one or two players from the former Reynolds–Archer troupe, who over the previous decade had often visited Gdańsk. Besides, the reference to the 'late King' almost certainly means Vladislaus IV, who died in 1648, and we know that that company was attached to the Royal Court in Warsaw. We also know that when Wayde and Roe were recorded at Riga in January 1648, they indicated that they had planned to go to Sweden, which apparently they did.

This is confirmed by Swedish sources. Some English players were recorded in Stockholm in 1648, when in July they were paid for performances at court and again in 1649 when they performed in the guildhall there.[98] And George Jolly's name appears in a Swedish document, dated 14 December 1649.[99] On the basis of these pieces of evidence we may conclude that after his first unsuccessful visit to Gdańsk in October 1649, Jolly went to Sweden, and, having met some of the former Wayde–Roe's men, formed a new company, with which he returned to Gdańsk for the St Dominic's Fair of 1650.

The Council's reply to Roszawen's request was favourable. In accordance with its former promise, the Council permitted the players to perform during the St Dominic's Fair, with the usual provisos. And they were ordered to pay 1,500 florins for the city prison, as we learn from Jolly's two applications, dated 12 and 29 August 1650.[100] The tax imposed upon the players was surprisingly high, even though the entrance fee was higher than in the previous years – 12 groschen, of which the actors received only half. Both the applications are written in an extremely polite manner, which may serve as an example of how Jolly's notorious rudeness could at times be tempered, especially when it was necessary to propitiate the councillors. Traditionally, they include recurrent complaints about low income and requests for prolongation of time given to play.

On 29 August the Senate 'unanimously' agreed to additional performances, which may serve as proof of Jolly's indisputable success in Gdańsk. The company performed there for over a month. The evidence allows us to form a fairly convincing theory as to the origin of this company. However, apart from Jolly, we cannot be certain of any other actor's name, and can only conclude that this company was presumably short-lived, owing to Jolly's choleric temperament.

In 1653 a company of players arrived in Gdańsk, styling themselves the Archduke Leopold's comedians. They may in fact have been English, for an English company performing in December 1651 in Prague claimed to have acted before the Archduke. Leopold's company was first recorded in September 1649,[101] and it is very likely that these were the same players who had previously enjoyed the patronage of the King of Poland, Vladislaus IV; after Vladislaus' death in 1648, they simply found a new patron.

In the following year, the same company, or what was left of it, came to Gdańsk again, this time under independent leadership of William Roe (which indicates that he had split up with his old companion, John Wayde). The players' application, dated 30 July 1654, is reproduced here for the first time:

Herr Burgomaster,
High Honourable, Stern, Noble, Praiseworthy, Most Wise and Especially Respected Lords,
Since the time approaches when the St Dominic's Fair will be held again, at which time all manner of amusements are permitted, we have come here in a rather large company of 24 persons in the hope that it may be permitted us to present sundry religious and secular plays to be watched and listened to, both comedies and tragedies, most of which are new and ingenious and yet noble at the same time. This is what we have humbly and appropriately seen fit to beg Your Magnificences, namely to show us grace not only by granting us permission to play, but also by assigning the Fencing-School to us, as being a very suitable place. We for our part will gladly make an appropriate payment. Besides this, we will behave in such a way that everyone will take pleasure in watching us. In expectation of your gracious and favourable response, we remain

> Your True
> Humble
> I, William Roe in the name
> of the whole company

[The Council's decision:]
The humble request of the English comedian.
The Council has allowed the supplicants to present their comedies in the Fencing-School, but on the condition that they perform nothing dishonourable or which could offend against decency. In addition they should contribute an appropriate amount to the prison and in this matter Mr Adrian Engelke should be contacted, which by this decree they are exhorted to do.[102]

The application and response support the previous conjecture that the company performing in Gdańsk in 1653 was English. The word 'again' used in this document leaves little doubt that the players had their previous visit in mind. We may also suspect that in 1653 the permission to play was revoked because of indecencies shown on stage. William Roe's application of 30 July was followed by another one, dated 14 [August?] 1654.

Herr Burgomaster, Noble, Honourable, Famous, Wise and Generous [etc.] Masters: We begin by wishing you a successful rule and all good health, from God the All-High, and thank you Noble [etc.] Masters most humbly for having graciously consented to let us act and perform all manner of plays at the Fencing-School for a certain time, to refresh melancholy spirits; by this, our wish is partly fulfilled, in that we had selected this widely renowned town before other towns, to wait on it according to its wishes with our services, and by this means to earn us a small piece of bread. We had come quite a long way here, and since we are a rather large number of persons, this cost us much money. However, as is well known, the weather did not suit us at all the time of St Dominic's, as it usually rained down on us, and also dashed our hopes. However, we comfort ourselves with the following thought, since it is well known that You Noble [etc.] Masters, according to your good custom, have never desired harm to anyone, but rather have assisted in one and another way. You will therefore not wish this our loss, which we incurred because of the wet weather, and the long journey, and the building of the stage at the Fencing-School which cost us much money. We therefore submit to You Noble [etc.] Masters our most lowly and humble request, to allow us to remain a little time more, according to your pleasure, and to allow us to perform, so that we can again make some money. We would appreciate this great grace and favour with grateful hearts, and would know how to praise it in foreign courts. Besides this, we would take You [etc.] Noble Masters and this widely renowned town up into our prayers, and call always upon Almighty God for you. We commend you to God's protection and await a favourable response.

Most humbly
The whole company of Comedians.

[The Council's decision:]
Comedians. Lect: 14 [August?] 1654. The Council permits the petitioners to perform their comedies until the end of the month, if it be to the profit of the prison; upon the condition that they do indeed pay their dues to the prison.[103]

This company's visit to Gdańsk marks the end of regular English activity in the region. A war between Sweden and Poland followed in 1655, known as 'the Flood', and made any theatrical activities impossible for a number of years. An isolated visit by George Bentley's company in 1670[104] is the very last record of the English presence in Gdańsk. This does not mean of course that no trace of them was left in the city. During the fifty years of their regular visits to Gdańsk, the English players had established what we may call a theatrical tradition, and they had managed to implant a love and understanding of theatre in the broad mass of society there. Through the presentation of the highest achievements of dramatic art they set standards in taste and in levels of theatrical skill for their successors to emulate. This remains their permanent contribution to the culture of the city in the period of its highest development.

2 Elbing

I N the beginning of the seventeenth century Elbing (Polish, 'Elbląg') was an important trade centre rivalling both Gdańsk and Königsberg (Illustration 5), and had for some years been the home of the English Eastland Company, something not without relevance to the activities of the English players there. In addition to the fact that a large English colony resided at Elbing, the town lay on the route from Gdańsk to Königsberg, and in fact it may be assumed that whenever the English companies travelled between the two cities, they must have stopped on the way and performed – if allowed to do so – at Elbing. Unfortunately, the town was captured several times during the perilous wars between Poland and Sweden in the seventeenth century, which culminated in 'the Flood' (1655–60). Whole libraries and archival collections were then looted from Poland, and some of these may still be found today, scattered in Swedish collections.[1] As was the case with Warsaw, most of the scanty pieces of evidence referring to English theatrical activity in Elbing come from records found in other places, particularly in Gdańsk and Königsberg.

The presence of the English players was first recorded at Elbing in 1605, when on 14 September they were prohibited from giving further performances because of 'disgraceful things' presented in a play staged the previous day. The town Council's decree tells us further that the players were paid 20 thalers for their troubles, for a previous performance, which had in fact amused the councillors.

In consideration of what the English comedians acted the day before yesterday for the pleasure of the Honourable Council, it is hereby resolved to award them 20 thalers as an honorarium. Further, it is decreed that they shall forthwith cease to perform in view of the fact that they yesterday enacted scandalous things in their comedy.[2]

It seems possible to identify this company as the one which, before coming to Elbing, had been recorded during the St Dominic's Fair in Gdańsk. The Gdańsk archival entry refers to the players as the Elector of Brandenburg's 'Comedianten und Musikanten'. This was a company led by George Webster, Richard Machin and Ralph Reeve. Having been prohibited from further acting at Elbing, the players went to Königsberg where they were recorded in October of the same year.

It is important to note that Elbing was one of the few towns in Central Europe for which there is clear evidence that in the period under discussion performances were given in public.[3] There was no nobleman's court there, and the town was administered solely by the Council. By 1605 the English

A. Die Pfarr Kirch
B. Wannliche Kirch
C. Reü Städte Kirch
D. Reffor baan Kirch
E. Alt Städtisch Rathhauß
F. Neüstädtisch Rathhauß

G. Hospital
H. Collegium
I. Marcken Thor
K. Schmied Thor
L. Burg Thor
M. Die Wage

N. Fischer Thor
O. Brücken Thor
P. Daß Schieß hauß
Q. Der Zimmer Hoff
R. Die Nachstuben
S. Die Speicher

T. Der Grüppenhagen oder Hamblsgarten
V. Mühlen Damm
W. Königs berg Lam̄
X. Der Badim
Y. Die Wilke

Elbing Fl

5 A view of Elbing

players had established a route leading from Gdańsk to Königsberg via Elbing – a route they would exploit until the middle of the century.

Still another company came to Elbing in 1607, and on 16 July the players submitted an application for leave to play, which was supported by one 'Deputy Brakel'. Although the document itself has not survived, the Council's decision, dated 16 July, has been preserved:

English comedians urgently entreat, etiam intercedente Brakel deputato, that they may be permitted to present their plays. But because this means tax upon the burghers, which is not possible in the present miserable state of affairs, the High Council has decided to refuse their request. However, should the Deputy Brakel or anyone else wish them to perform privately in his house, they have permission to do so.[4]

We can be almost certain that this was the same company that visited Gdańsk in summer 1607, which has been identified as John Green's. It is also worth noting that – as was customary in other towns – one of Elbing's citizens supported the players' application. And the reference to private performances in burghers' houses is of particular importance, for it implies that there may have developed a tradition of this sort among the wealthy merchants of Elbing.

At present it is not possible to determine with any certainty where in Elbing the public performances took place. However, it seems that in the early phase of English theatrical activity on the Continent the players were paid an agreed fee irrespective of the number of spectators. Thus, the plays may have been staged outdoors on stages arranged *ad hoc* in town marketplaces, or any other convenient site, and everybody who wished could see a play at no cost. Additional sums of money may have been collected after the performance. The above entry, however, suggests that, at least at Elbing, there may have been a custom of collecting a 'revels' tax for such enterprises from the citizens. It was only when the finances became the company's responsibility that it appeared necessary to charge an admission fee, and to find an appropriate, enclosed place where the fees could be collected and the admission of spectators controlled. In a contemporary source, we find a passage telling us that at Elbing 'comedies and other plays' were presented in a merchant-hall, called King Arthur's Hall, located in the Old Town marketplace. This piece of information was found by Bruno Th. Satori-Neumann[5] in a book written by the then Mayor of Elbing, Israel Hoppe, entitled *Typus rei publicae Elbigensis*, where Arthur's Hall is described as the place where wedding ceremonies took place, and where also 'comedies and other plays' were presented at the time of fairs.[6] The same Israel Hoppe informs us in his book that in Arthur's Hall there was a special hall ('Saal') called the 'Music Choir' ('Musikchor'), built in 1603, in which concerts were customarily held.[7] It is, therefore, possible that the English companies of 'comedians and instrumentalists' used this 'Music Choir' for their performances.

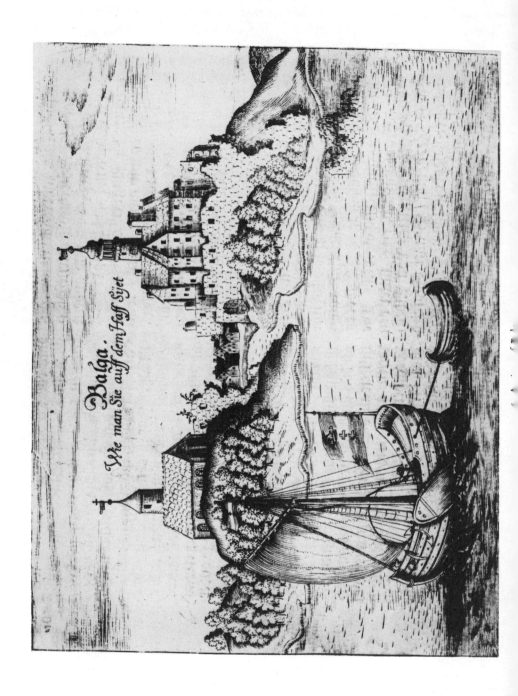

Balga.
Ihre man Sie auff dem Hoff Sijet

It is not until 1618 that we find evidence of the English players performing at Elbing; in 1609 and 1611 companies passed through Elbing, but there is no evidence of their playing. An entry in the Electoral book of expenses, dated 17 March 1618 at Königsberg, tells us that one 'Stockfish' (Spencer's stage-name) was paid 90 marks for bringing his comedians from Elbing to Königsberg: '90 marks at the gracious command of His Electoral Grace, being 50 thalers at 36 groschen, given to one Stockfish, whom His Electoral Grace sent to Elbing to bring from thence the English comedians, paid 17 March'.[8] The players stayed at John Sigismund's court, undertaking occasional travels, until June 1619. We learn about this from the Elector's decree:

To the High Councillors of the Duchy of Prussia. We, John Sigismund, by the Grace of God etc. have granted, once for all, two hundred Polish florins[9] to the players for their trouble, who, as is well known to you, have at different times at our gracious command, acted in our apartments at Königsberg and Balga [Illustration 7], and hereby graciously order you accordingly to pay them the said 200 guilder out of our treasury. Dated Elbing, 20 June 1619.[10]

In the Electoral book of expenses there is another entry referring to the performances of Spencer's company for which the players were paid on 22 June 1619, that is two days after the above decree was announced. We may thus assume that this was either a back payment for some past performances, or for plays presented before the Elector at Elbing, before the company's return to Königsberg on 22 June 1619: '150 marks to 18 English comedians who acted several comedies before his Electoral Grace, paid 22 June'.[11]

After 1619 there was a long break in the activities of the English companies in Regal Prussia, caused by the Polish–Swedish conflict. The warlike King of Sweden Gustav Adolf attacked first the Polish province of Livonia, and on 25 September captured Riga.[12] In a new campaign of 1626, Swedish forces captured a number of towns in Regal Prussia, including Elbing, which surrendered on 13 July. Elbing remained in Swedish hands until the peace treaty was signed in May 1635.[13] The perilous time of war made any travel hazardous, and as evidenced elsewhere in this book, the theatrical activity of the English outside the courts of their patrons in Central Europe ceased almost entirely within the period 1619 and 1635. In spite of this, some amateur performances were recorded at Elbing. For instance, in March 1628 some Scottish and German soldiers garrisoned there staged several 'comedies'.[14]

Although little evidence is available, we may assume that the English companies who visited Gdańsk from the mid-thirties until the middle of the century performed also at Elbing. In July 1644, the Reynolds–Archer troupe submitted an application to the City Council at Gdańsk, and the players stated that 'having performed our comedies this year at Riga and at Königsberg, and having now reached Elbing, we have further decided to visit the glorious city of Gdańsk'.[15] From the same application we learn that the company numbered eighteen players. On 29 July their plea was rejected by the reluctant Gdańsk councillors, and this brief reference remains the last available record of English theatrical activity at Elbing.

3 Königsberg

S INCE the political status of Prussia in the first half of the seventeenth century and her relations with Poland and Germany are not very well known in the English-speaking world, it may help to briefly review the rather complex situation.[1] The legal basis of the division of Prussia into two parts, Ducal Prussia and Regal Prussia was the peace treaty ending the war between Poland and the Knights of the Teutonic Order, signed on 19 November 1466. According to its provisions, Poland regained Gdańsk Pomerania (i.e. the so-called Pomeralia) and areas along the lower Vistula, including the former capital of the Teutonic Knights: Marienburg (Polish 'Malbork'). This newly acquired land was divided into three voivodeships, and remained in Polish hands until the partitions in the late eighteenth century.

That there were, in fact, two parts of Prussia was generally acknowledged in Europe. Among others, one Dr Bruce, Queen Elizabeth's agent in Poland, described Prussia in his *Relation of the State of Polonia and the United Provinces of that Crown Anno 1598*:

Prussia is the most riche and populous province of the Crowne of Polonia, 1658 Germane or Polonish myle longe and 50 braade . . . To returne to the other parte of Prussia called Regalis, as being immediately subject to the Crowne (thys distinction rising uppon the former accord), it hath for heade Marienburg, sometymes the seate of the Order . . . This Prussia hath 3 Palatinates, Culme (wherein is Torumna on the Vistula), Marienburg (wherein is Elbing) and Pomerania Citerior, whose Metropolis is Dantzig.

When Albrecht Hohenzollern, the last Grand Master of the Teutonic Order (with its new capital at Königsberg) decided to secularise his country in 1525, he reached an agreement with his uncle, the King of Poland Sigismund I, and on 8 April signed the Treaty of Cracow, which gave legal status to and recognition of the important changes. The Teutonic Order was dissolved, and in its place a secular Duchy was established, with Albrecht being awarded the title of 'Dux in Prussia'. The fact that he became a Duke in Prussia, and not the Duke of Prussia, was of vital importance, considering that the other part of Prussia (i.e. Regal Prussia) was a Polish province. Ducal Prussia became Poland's fief, and on 10 April 1525 the first ceremony of the oath of allegiance took place in Cracow. Moreover, the Duke was obliged to participate in military actions of Polish kings, and became a Crown Senator. In case of felony, the King had a right to retrieve the fief from the Duke. The title and right to rule in the Duchy were hereditary, although restricted to Albrecht's male line, which included his three brothers. It is also worth noting that on 6 July 1525, Albrecht officially announced his conversion to Lutheranism, and thus Prussia became the first Lutheran state in Europe.

It is important to note that the Treaty of Cracow did not allow the Brandenburg line of the Hohenzollerns to have any legal hereditary rights to the succession in the Duchy. Rights of succession were acknowledged only for the Anspach line of the family, which died out in 1618. Had the articles of the Treaty of Cracow been then observed, the Duchy should have been incorporated into Poland. This, however, did not happen, owing to the short-sighted policy of Polish kings. As early as 1563 the King of Poland, Sigismund Augustus, seeking support from the Brandenburgs for his foreign policies, granted succession rights to this branch of the Hohenzollerns. This, however, was not ratified by the Polish Diet, and after the death of Albrecht, the rule in the Duchy remained in the hands of the last male successor of the Anspach line, George Frederick. Another reason for this was that Albrecht's only son and heir, Albrecht Frederick, was slightly insane and was not able to govern alone, even though he kept the title of the Duke in Prussia. The situation became even more complicated after the death of George Frederick in April 1603. The Brandenburg court at Berlin claimed its rights to succession on the basis of the 1563 agreement with Sigismund Augustus. In the beginning of the seventeenth century the newly elected King of Poland Sigismund III Vasa, was engaged in a war with Sweden over his rights to the Swedish throne and for this reason he sought support for his actions from the Brandenburgs. Consequently, in 1605 Sigismund III decided to postpone the final decision concerning the succession in the Duchy, and for the time being granted a wardship over the Duchy to the Elector of Brandenburg, Joachim Frederick. This decision, again, was not ratified by the Polish Diet. The wardship, however, was hedged about with various restrictions: the Elector had no right, for instance, to visit Prussia personally without the King's permission, and – more important – the wardship was not hereditary. The latter fact had further consequences, because after Joachim Frederick's death in 1608, the new Elector, John Sigismund, had to request the wardship again. This was granted in 1609 and the official ceremony of receiving the investiture of the Duchy took place in Warsaw in November 1611. After the death of the Duke Albrecht Frederick in 1618, the status of the Electors of Brandenburg became even greater, and owing to the weakening of Poland in the course of constant wars, a new treaty was signed in November 1657 between the Elector Frederick William and the King of Poland John Casimir, which recognised the Elector's sovereignty in the Duchy, and practically meant the incorporation of the latter into Brandenburg, in spite of strong opposition on the part of the Estates.

During the period under discussion, Königsberg was not only Prussia's capital, an important sea-port and a trade centre, but with its population exceeding thirty thousand inhabitants, it was one of the largest towns in

Central Europe and one of the important artistic and educational centres, with the University founded as early as 1544. Not surprisingly, the Electors of Brandenburg preferred to reside at their Castle at Königsberg rather than in small and provincial Berlin. Although practically all records concerning the visits by English players there refer to court performances, the wealthy and learned burghers formed a potential audience, and it is likely that public performances also took place.

The English players were first recorded at Königsberg in 1605, when they performed at the court. The only piece of evidence for their presence at Königsberg may be found in the court register of expenses: '75 Marks at the desire of my gracious Princess and Lady etc. Duchess of Prussia, to some English comedians, who acted, danced twice, and performed delightful music before her Princely Grace, paid 3 October.'[2] A conjectural identification of this company can be made from records that have been preserved in other towns. Before coming to Königsberg, the players had been labelled 'the Elector Christian von Brandenburg's comedians and musicians' when they performed in Gdańsk and were paid for their trouble on 6 August 1605.

The same company was recorded in September at Elbing, and may perhaps be identical with the one that emerged earlier at Leyden, for when in January John Spencer's troupe appeared there, the players submitted to the Leyden councillors a letter of recommendation, dated 10 August 1604, and signed by the Elector of Brandenburg.[3] However, the Gdańsk entry is slightly confusing, for Christian had never been the Elector of Brandenburg, and the title belonged to Joachim Frederick who was the Elector from 1598 to 1608. Thus, there seem to have been two distinct companies active at about the same time and both styling themselves as the Elector's men. One was that of George Webster, Richard Machin and Ralph Reeve,[4] whereas the other was led by John Spencer. Since we know for certain that the former players were in fact protected by Christian, one of the Dukes of Brandenburg and the Elector's brother,[5] and since this company is mentioned in Gdańsk, we may conjecture that the same troupe travelled further east and, having performed on the way at Elbing, reached Königsberg sometime late in September. From a different source we learn that in spring 1605 Machin and Reeve performed at Frankfurt and their company numbered eighteen players and seven musicians.[6] On the other hand, John Spencer seems to have been permanently attached to the Elector's court at Berlin at least from 1604, and it would seem more likely that it was his company that performed at Königsberg in 1605. But the record quoted makes no mention of the Elector's presence there, and it was the Duchess of Prussia Maria Eleonora who hired the company for court performances.

At any rate, it was Spencer who was mentioned in a letter of recommendation, dated 11 July 1609, written from Königsberg by the new Elector of Brandenburg, John Sigismund (1608–19) to the Elector of Saxony, Christian

II (1591–1611). 'Königsberg. The Elector of Brandenburg recommends to the Elector of Saxony one John Spencer, an English instrumentalist, recommended by Franz Duke of Stettin; he stayed at some time at court and his music pleased the Elector very well.'[7] Spencer's company may have stayed at Dresden for almost two years, but the players were certainly back in the Elector of Brandenburg's service in February 1611, when certain items were bought, at the cost of 7 marks and 57 groschen, for the staging of a play by the 'Elector's comedians and musicians'.[8] And in mid-July of the same year John Spencer's company emerged in Gdańsk, but owing to the very small audiences the players decided to return to Königsberg, and on 23 July they were paid 30 marks for a play presented before the Duke Albrecht Frederick (the last of the Hohenzollern–Anspach line). '30 Marks paid as an honorarium on 23 July 1611 to the English comedians who presented a comedy and danced before our most gracious Prince and Lord, Albrecht Frederick etc.'[9]

In autumn, the same troupe accompanied the Elector from Königsberg to Ortelsburg (Polish 'Szczytno'), for which on 7 October they were paid 150 marks.[10] While at Ortelsburg, the Elector ordered suits of clothes to be made for his players and musicians. The order, dated 16 October 1611, was addressed to the Estates at Königsberg.

Because of the forthcoming investitute, we have the wish to provide costumes for our instrumentalists and comedians. Therefore, it is our gracious wish and command that you should – according to the design on the two enclosed sheets – provide galloons of black silk thread, braided on plain white English cloth, for the coats, hoses and doublets. We have already summoned here our court tailors and it is demanded that you should immediately send to us plain English white cloth, black silk cord of average quality, and also all the necessary additions as linings and white knitted stockings, and all this not only for the persons mentioned on the list, but also for five or six additional persons.[11]

The official ceremony of receiving the investiture of the Duchy took place on 16 November 1611 in Warsaw. The order of clothes seems to have been part of the preparations for the event. Several days after the order had been sent, a reply came from Königsberg stating that a wagon had already been sent, loaded with 'all the necessary things for the costumes, as cloth, linen, stockings, silk buttons and galloons in the amounts given in the enclosed list'.[12] The list mentioned has also been preserved and it includes the following items:

979¾ ells of white Kersey, in 32 pieces and 7 separate pieces
492 ells of lining-cloth in 17 pieces and 16 additional ells
287 ells of linen
 41 pairs of white stockings
  2 pounds of silk thread for tailoring and one pound of thread for quilting
123 dozen of iron buttons
883 ells of silk galloon. The rest, that is 2,397 ells we shall send at the earliest opportunity.[13]

The list provides us with a unique opportunity for establishing the necessary materials for the making of costumes for Spencer's company and for six additional persons. From a different source we learn that the company numbered nineteen players and sixteen musicians, bringing the total to forty-one. If we divide the above figures by forty-one, we shall obtain approximate amounts of materials for the making of one costume: around 23.9 ells of white cloth, 12 ells of lining-cloth, 7 ells of linen, 1 pair of stockings, 3 dozen iron buttons and 80 ells of silk galloon. (An 'ell' was a measure of length varying in different countries. The English ell was 45 ins, the Flemish ell 27 ins.) It seems, however, that these were not theatrical costumes, for they were intended to look the same (as is apparent from the order itself), and were also provided for persons outside the company proper. It is therefore possible that the Elector wanted to have a train of liveried servants for the official ceremony in Warsaw.

The players may have gone with their lord to Warsaw and back, for we find them back at Königsberg together with the Elector at the end of November. On the Elector's arrival he was welcomed by the burghers with great splendour and extravagant celebrations.[14] A couple of days later the players received a large sum of money: '720 marks to the English players to the account of their salary of 400 thalers at 36 groschens, paid 30 November 1611.'[15] Most Königsberg records, uncovered and published by E.A. Hagen, are connected with payments either to the players or to various craftsmen and artisans for the making of sundry items necessary for the staging of plays. These form a long list which deepens our knowledge and understanding of the 'technical' side of English theatrical activity on the Continent, and especially of those companies that were attached permanently to noblemen's courts. For example, the entry of 30 November 1611 quoted above, suggests that whenever the players were employed on a permanent basis, they were paid an annual salary, presumably agreed upon in a special contract. This is confirmed by another entry in the Electoral book of expenses:

1,080 marks, being 600 thalers at 36 groschen, to John Spencer comedian, the balance which was still due to him on the contract made with his Electoral Grace, which he received on 4 February 1612.[16]

And in 1613 another payment was made:

1,229 marks 24 sh. to John Spencer, comedian, for silk goods received from Henry Klehe, part of 683 thalers at 36 groschen which is to be deducted from his salary at Berlin.[17]

And in 1620 the same John Spencer wrote an application to Count Schwartzenberg at Berlin, in which he asked for the payment of his annual salary and, in addition, 1,000 thalers, which he claimed to have spent procuring foreign actors for his company.[18]

Apart from the annual salary, the players were often given additional fees for particular performances, and it seems that their other expenses were often reimbursed. For instance, when in August 1617 a company of English players performed at Dresden, they were paid 300 thalers in addition to 'what they had consumed at their landlord's, before they had been supplied with their meals at court, and whatever else they had required and used in the way of rooms, closets and beds'.[19] We find similar entries among the Königsberg records:

26 marks 9 sh. in redemption of his Electoral Grace's comedian, John Spencer, who had lodged with Christopher Hertlein from 28 October to 8 November 1612. One week.

47 marks 48 sh. in redemption of the Electoral comedians, who had lodged with Hans Jacob in the year 1612, of which in the fourth and fifth week 47 marks 16 groschens were paid and now is the rest. 13 March.[20]

Some of the Königsberg records have been published by Hagen and translated into English by A. Cohn in his *Shakespeare in Germany* (1865), but Cohn omitted a number of entries and to my knowledge these have not hitherto been reproduced in English. Besides, neither Hagen nor Cohn arranged the entries in chronological order, and chronology seems to be very important if we are to examine how the court performances were prepared by the English players. For these reasons, it seems worthwhile to present here a full list of extant records arranged chronologically. It should be added that early in 1612 Spencer and his men were preparing a particularly grand performance at the Königsberg court.

9 January 1612 – 30 ells of coarse linen cloth for comedians for the erecting of the city of Constantinople
      – 300 ells of light linen ordered for the comedians in four pieces
9(?) January[21] – 25 ells of flax linen for the comedians for the erecting of the city of Constantinople
      – 70 ells of flax linen in three pieces for the comedians
21 January – Lining-cloth graciously given. 297 ells of red lining-cloth in 11 pieces for the English comedians on the order of the Prince
21(?) January – 189 ells of lining-cloth in 7 pieces for the comedians
      – 30 ells for monks' habits, also 81 ells of red lining-cloth for covering the theatre in the old great hall.
24 January – 351 marks 7 sh. 3 pf. for 2,809 ells of ribbon at $2\frac{1}{2}$ gr. for 16 musicians and 19 comedians and Mr Grabau, the coachman, for the hemming of their coats, hoses and doublets; and 4 marks 57 sh. for 11 measures of silk thread for the comedians to sew the ribbon at 9 gr. from Adrian the ribbon-maker.
1 February – 7 marks 12 sh. paid to Hans Tanapfel, carver, who has carved four death's heads and one shield for the comedy
      – 227 marks 30 sh. for 70 ells of red linen-cloth at 65 gr.
      – 3 marks 45 sh. for 50 ells of red cord at $1\frac{1}{2}$ gr.
      – 1 mark 12 sh. for 3 measures of Scottish-weight(?) red silk thread at 8 gr. and 1 mark for brass rings. Everything for the English comedians collected from George Grunau.
7 February – Christian Salbert, cutler, has made a sword with a gilt hilt for the comedians.[22]

All of the above entries seem to refer to one particular performance, for which it appeared necessary to erect the 'city of Constantinople' on stage, and to cover the walls in the old great hall with red linen, not to mention items like death's heads, monks' habits, a sword, a shield etc. After the last entry, dated 7 February 1612, in the extant records there is no mention of the English players, or of expenses connected with their productions, until May, and this may well indicate that the première of the play took place early in February. The records quoted above certainly confirm our earlier observation that, whenever possible, the English players tried to add splendour to their productions on the Continent, and it also suggests that in such favourable conditions as at Königsberg, the staging of plays must have been similar to that in London.

The entry of 21 January referring to the 'old great hall' ('alten groszen Saal') has attracted little attention. Interestingly, in the Ducal castle at Königsberg (Illustration 7) there actually was a hall traditionally labelled the 'groszen Saal'.[23] The hall was located in the east wing of the rectangular edifice, adjoining the 'Frauenzimmer', i.e. the Duchess's chambers. No pictorial evidence has been preserved for its interior, and the only thing we know about the hall is that it measured 59 × 68.3 feet (approximately 18 × 20.9 metres), and that it was the largest room in the castle, used frequently for feasts, official ceremonies and entertainments of various kinds. Its outer façade (facing the castle yard) had a sort of gallery, extending from the ground level up to the second storey, which was used for public ceremonies as shown in illustration 10. There had been a long tradition of converting similar halls into temporary theatres in England, and the players were obviously acquainted with all the technical difficulties involved.[24]

Before an attempt is made to identify the Constantinople play, the remaining entries in the court book of expenses are worth closer consideration, for they seem to refer to items that appeared necessary for recurring performances of the same drama.

26 May 1612 – 124 marks 47 sh. for firewood bought by the comedians for their need when they stayed here
17 June – 6 marks for the hire of 18 large and 17 long plumes lent by Andrew Körner for the Turkish Triumph Comedy.
1 July – 23 marks 9 sh. for various articles turned in wood, ordered from the court-turner by the players.
21 August – 235 marks 54 sh. for blue, red and white cloth, soft wool, red coarse golden ribbon and other items for the comedians collected from Master Dietrich Schlemmer who made the clothes
– 81 marks 33 sh. for blue, body-colour and black canvas and fringes, all for the clouds for the Triumph Comedy, paid to Master Dietrich.
– 87 marks 39 sh. for various carvings for the Triumph Comedy, made by Alexander Crause, carver.
– 111 marks 15 sh. for various articles of joiner's work for the Triumph Comedy, made by Christopher Dosin, joiner.

19 September – 117 marks 42 sh. to Daniel Rose, court-painter, for various works executed by him for the players at the Elector's order, paid according to the itemised invoice.

16 October – 1 mark 30 sh. for the blade, fitted on the order of his Grace the Elector etc. for the comedians.

20 December – 7 marks 30 sh. paid to the comedians for vittals.[25]

Owing to the fact that Hagen did not follow chronology when publishing materials he had uncovered, all of the above entries have been considered by scholars as referring to one play only, i.e. *The Turkish Triumph Comedy*, which has been identified as George Peele's *The Turkish Mahomet and Hyrin the Fair Greek*.[26] However, when the pieces of evidence are put in chronological order as above, it becomes apparent that preparations were being made, in fact, for two plays, the first of which, 'A Play of Constantinople', was staged in February, whereas the other, *The Turkish Triumph Comedy*, was staged at the end of August. In the following year, when Spencer's company visited Nuremberg, performances of this troupe were described in a local chronicle in the following terms:

1613. On Sunday the 27th of June and a number of days thereafter, with the gracious permission of the Honourable Council, the Elector of Brandenburg's servants and the English Comedians have put on and acted beautiful comedies and tragedies of Philole and Mariane, also of Celide and Sedea, also of the Destruction of the cities of Troy and of Constantinople; of the Turk, and other such histories, besides graceful dancing, delightful music, and other entertainments, here in the Hailsbrunn Court, in good German language, in rich masquerade and costumes.[27]

From the above description, it appears obvious that the play *The Destruction of Constantinople* cannot be identified with *The Turkish Triumph Comedy*, undoubtedly identical with the play 'of the Turk' mentioned in the source quoted above. The latter play, as has already been noted, may be identified with Peele's play, or, perhaps, with John Mason's *The Turk* (1610).[28] This would support the conclusion that there were in fact two première shows at Königsberg, each of a different play.

The Nuremberg chronicle quoted above provides us with further details connected with Spencer's repertoire shortly after he had left Königsberg. *Philole and Mariana* seems to have been Lewis Machin's *The Dumb Knight* (1608), a German manuscript of which, together with a German version of John Marston's *Parasitaster, or the Fawn* (1606) entitled *Tiberius and Anabella*, has been preserved in the collection of the City Library in Gdańsk.[29] It is plausible that both of these manuscripts, written in the same hand, may have come down to us directly from Spencer's company. This is supported by another piece of evidence. Before the players reached Nuremberg, they had stopped at Leipzig, where their presence was recorded in April 1613,[30] and John Spencer was referred to as 'Hans Leberwurst', which seems to have been his first stage-name, subsequently changed to Hans

Stockfish. Interestingly, it is Hans Leberwurst who appears among the *dramatis personae* in the Gdańsk manuscript of *The Dumb Knight*, which implies that the play was in Spencer's repertoire and the extant manuscript may have been the company's property. *Celide and Sidea* is probably Jacob Ayrer's 'comedy of beautiful Sidea' (1595), the action of which takes place in Lithuania, the major characters being the Duke of Lithuania, his daughter Sidea, and Julia, a Polish Princess. This play, indeed, would have added local colour to performances at Königsberg, for Lithuania and Poland were Prussia's largest neighbours.

Returning to the performances of 1612 at the Königsberg court, we see that apart from the efforts of particular members of Spencer's company, a number of craftsmen and artisans were engaged in the preparations for a première show. There was 'Adrian the ribbon-maker'; Hans Tanapfel, the carver; Christian Salbert, cutler; Andrew Körner, who lent his plumes; the court-turner; Master Dietrich Schlemmer who made the clothes; another Master Dietrich who made the clouds; Alexander Crause, another carver; Christopher Dosin, the joiner; and Daniel Rose, the court-painter. The expenditure on staging suggests that the designs must have been elaborate. And certainly some of the stage properties and costumes could be used by the players for performances elsewhere.

Early in 1613 we see John Spencer's company still at Königsberg, where the players received a surprisingly high sum of money, over 1,200 marks, as the reimbursement for 'silk goods' the players had purchased from a certain Henry Klehe.[31] These 'silk goods' may have been ordered for the making of new costumes, prepared for the forthcoming tour of other towns and countries. On 16 April 1613, Spencer received a letter of recommendation from the Elector of Brandenburg to the then Elector of Saxony John George I (1611–56):

The bearer of this letter, the English comedian John Spencer, has spent a considerable time in our service, and in his humble waiting on us has so borne himself, that we have derived a gracious pleasure therefrom. But since he has now proposed to visit other places, and among the rest also to exhibit his art and comedies in Dresden, it has pleased us to give him this recommendation. We would request Your Highness to condescend not only to grant him this for four weeks or more, but also show him all favour in other respects.[32]

This indicates that by April 1613 Spencer had been dismissed from the Electoral court at Königsberg, at least temporarily, for he would return there three years later. One of the reasons for this may have been the Elector's surprising and sudden conversion to Calvinism in 1613, which caused tremendous tension between John Sigismund and the Prussian Estates, which were Lutheran, and which forced the Elector to return to Berlin in order to avoid the political storm. And while in Berlin, John Sigismund employed another English company for court performances.[33]

The players, having left Königsberg, went to Dresden via Leipzig, where they were recorded at the end of April 1613. However, for some reason the company did not stay in Dresden for long, for in June John Spencer emerged in Nuremberg. Thereafter, the fortunes of the troupe may be traced in numerous Continental towns, and John Spencer became widely known and popular under the stage-name Hans Stockfish. He may have returned briefly to Königsberg in autumn 1616, when the presence of an unspecified company of 'English comedians' was recorded there:

> 7 November 1616 – 112 marks 30 sh. as gratuity for English comedians.
> 8 November 1616 – 112 marks 30 sh. for the English comedians in addition to the previously paid 50 Reichsthalers as a gratuity from His Electoral Grace which will be paid on 8 November.[34]

On the other hand, this may equally have been Robert Archer's company which was recorded in Gdańsk in 1615 as the Brandenburg troupe, and also in Berlin in May 1616.[35]

In 1618 it was certainly John Spencer who appeared once again at Königsberg, when in March he was ordered to bring his company over from Elbing. The players stayed at the Elector's court until June 1619, when they were paid 200 guilder, but when in July the same company appeared in Gdańsk, the players indicated in their application to the City Council that they had been ordered to leave Königsberg for Berlin. Having been refused leave to play in Gdańsk, Spencer's men headed straight for Berlin, where they stayed until 1620. However, after the death of John Sigismund in 1619, the new Elector of Brandenburg, George William (1619–40) was not, it seems, such an admirer of theatre and 'protector of the arts' as his predecessor. In addition, there was a dispute between the players and the Elector's treasury in 1620, about some overdue payments, as a result of which the company was dismissed outright. The cause of this may have been Spencer's petition to Count Schwartzenberg, in which he asked for the payment of his annual salary, in addition to 1,000 thalers, which he had spent in procuring some foreign actors to the company. The Elector George William's answer, dated Königsberg 4–14 March 1620, included a promise that arrears would be paid, provided the petitioner proved that he really had disbursed the mentioned sum of money for the company's affairs. However, the Elector also indicated that he had been credibly informed that this was not the case, and that 'the certificate submitted to his favour by the comedians, which he had presented, had been surreptitiously obtained'.[36] And thus ended the long career of John Spencer alias Stockfish at the Brandenburg court. His company was presumably dissolved shortly after the above incident. An isolated entry in the records of Nuremberg informs us that Spencer was still active on the Continent in 1623,[37] but after that date he is not heard of. It may be added that soon after the Berlin incident, in July 1620, a company of English players styling themselves the Elector of Brandenburg's servants was given permission to play at Utrecht. Surprisingly, the manager of the company mentioned by name in the records was not John Spencer, but John Green.[38]

No English company appeared at Königsberg until a peace treaty was signed between Poland and Sweden in 1635. In the following year, Robert Archer and his men appeared in Gdańsk and, in their application of 28 July, the players indicated that after the death of the King of Poland Sigismund III in 1632, at whose court they had stayed for many years, they visited Holland, Denmark, Holstein and Königsberg. We can be certain only that Archer's men performed at Königsberg some time between 1632 and 1636, the years 1635–6 being the more likely. The latter date coincides with the King of Poland's visit to Königsberg in July 1635.[39] If the English players were actually there, Vladislaus IV would have had an opportunity to meet the company that had for many years been attached to his father's court in Warsaw. That this happened seems to be confirmed by Archer's own application of 28 July 1636 to the councillors in Gdańsk, in which he indicated that he had been waiting in Gdańsk for the King's decision as to whether the players should go on to Warsaw or to Vilnius in Lithuania. This means that the company must have been in touch with the King before summer 1636. The grand celebrations connected with the King's visit to Königsberg in 1635 provided the actors with an excellent opportunity to present all their talents before His Majesty and to vie for employment at his court. Their efforts seem to have been fully successful, for from 1636 we find the English players back in Warsaw, where they stayed, again, for many years. Thus it seems highly probable that Archer's company came to Königsberg in July 1635 on the occasion of the Royal visit there.

Yet another company was attached to the Electoral court by the late thirties. Two entries in the Königsberg book of expenses, both dated 1639, refer to English players' presence there, and are of particular importance as they include one of the few extant records informing us about the means of transportation used by the English on the Continent.

> 18 October 1639 – 69 marks for transporting diverse luggage and also the players, strollers, trumpeters, and other things and persons of this kind, from here to Brandenburg by sea in two boats to the Electoral place [depot?]. Paid by Reinholt Klein.
> 5 December – 675 marks to the Secretary Dieter or 150 Reichsthalers as payment for the English players, which Reinholdt Klein advanced and which was repaid to him out of the wood fund.[40]

Königsberg was an important sea-port, and sailing was certainly the quickest and cheapest way to reach Brandenburg, presumably via Stettin in Pomerania. The players, apparently employed for a longer period of time on a salary basis, may have stayed in Berlin over the winter but in July 1640 we see them back at Königsberg, when they received a letter of recommendation from the Elector. The two companies joined forces around May or June 1640, and it is this new company that is mentioned in the letter of recommendation:

We George William, by the Grace of God Margrave and Duke of Brandenburg, inform each and every one, and particularly whoever might be interested and ought to know, of the following: last year, after the English players bearing this letter had come to us, namely: Robertt Rennols, Aaron Asken, Willhelm Roe, Joannes Weyd, Eduard Pudey and Willhelm Wedwer [sic], asking us humbly whether they might present some comedies for our Ducal House, we bestowed on them our gracious favour, for which they were most grateful, and they have shown great skill in their art and have thus proved themselves . . . Because it is now their wish to move on from here, and to prove their skilful art in other lands as well, and because they have humbly implored and begged us for our gracious permission, we have not opposed their most humble request.[41]

The letter is dated 11 July 1640, and the names of actors have already been identified. Having left Königsberg, the company went via Gdańsk to Warsaw, where the players found, again, permanent employment at Vladislaus IV's court, undertaking occasional travels in the summer 'theatrical season'.

The same company (although without Robert Reynolds who died in or shortly before 1642) visited Königsberg again in 1644, as we learn from the players' Gdańsk application of 29 July. Similarly, the company that emerged in 1648 at Riga in Livonia indicated in an application to the councillors there that the players had come from Gdańsk and Königsberg after performances in those towns. The application in question is undated, but it is undoubtedly linked with another, dated 21 January 1648.[42] This indicates that the players must have performed in Gdańsk during the St Dominic's Fair of 1647, and thereafter gone to Königsberg where they may have stayed for a couple of months. The extant Gdańsk application of this company is signed by John Wayde and William Roe, and this leaves no doubt that these two were the leading actors who performed at Königsberg later during that year. Apart from these, among the company's members there are unidentified players from England, the Netherlands and Germany,[43] which, in turn, is a characteristic feature of the changes that the originally purely English companies had undergone by the middle of the century. Owing to the lack of fresh supplies of players from England, the companies had become international, with the English veteran players still being the managers of these congregations. After their Königsberg visit of 1647, which in fact remains the last known presence of the English players there, Wayde and Roe travelled via Riga to Stockholm, and thereafter their names still appear in various Continental records for a number of years.[44] Incidentally, Wayde was last mentioned in 1671 in Dresden, and if our previous conjecture is correct, he was sixty-four years old by that time.

4 Pomerania

POMERANIA had been subjugated and made tributary to Poland, and remained so until, towards the end of the twelfth century, it became dependent on Frederick Barbarossa and thus a principality of the Empire. Pomerania remained a part of the Empire until its dissolution as a result of the Thirty Years War in 1648. For centuries the Duchy was ruled by a native dynasty of the Greifens, Slavic in origin, but Germanised through close political and personal links with Germany, especially with Brandenburg. The constant attempts of the Pomeranian dukes to gain independence culminated in 1529, when Margrave Joachim I Hohenzollern concluded a treaty with the Greifens by which he renounced his claims to the feudal overlordship of Pomerania and received in exchange the right of succession of his line, if the ducal line of the Greifens were to die out. This meant, in practical terms, that Pomerania ceased to be Brandenburg's fief and became one of the numerous independent units of the Empire. However, the Brandenburgs kept the right to use the title of Dukes of Pomerania, and the Greifens used the titles of Dukes of Stettin and Dukes of Wolgast. The latter distinction was due to the fact that in the sixteenth and seventeenth centuries Pomerania was basically divided into two duchies, the Duchy of Stettin (Polish, 'Szczecin') and the Duchy of Wolgast (Polish, 'Wołogoszcz'). Pomerania experienced its period of greatest cultural and economic growth during the reign of Bogislav XIII (1544–1606) and his eldest son, Philip II (1573–1618). This was followed by a calamitous war, and after the death of the last Duke of Stettin, Bogislav XIV (1580–1637), the Duchy remained under Swedish occupation until 1648, when it was divided between Sweden and Brandenburg. The partition lasted until 1720, when Frederick Wilhelm I of Prussia bought the Swedish domains for two million thalers.[1]

Pomerania lay on the way from Northern Germany to Poland, Prussia and further east to Livonia (see Illustration 1). It is likely that English acting companies would have attempted to win the favour of local dukes and to perform at their courts on the way, say, from Cologne to Gdańsk, or Königsberg. Unfortunately, the scanty evidence which has been preserved for the English players' activity in Pomerania probably bears little relation to the frequency of visits. The first recorded visit took place in 1606 in Western Pomerania, i.e. in the Duchy of Wolgast.[2] The Wolgast branch of the Greifens was then represented by Duke Philip Julius (1584–1626), the son of Ernest Ludwig and Sophia Hedwig of Brunswick. To English theatre historians Philip Julius is well known, because in 1602 he went to London and attended performances there in the Blackfriars. The Duke's secretary has left us an invaluable description of actual productions.[3] Perhaps it was this London visit and the great impression that English players made on the Duke that tempted him to hire a company of his own. As is apparent from the pieces of evidence provided below, the company in question was invited several times to Wolgast by the Duke himself, the players were called his servants, and these visits cannot be treated as incidental.

The first known reference to English theatrical activity in Pomerania comes from a diatribe against the players who had allegedly desecrated a castle church at Loitz. This is dated 26 August 1606, and is addressed to the Duke personally. The writer complained

that the comedians, invited by Your Ducal Grace, have allowed themselves to be tempted and yesterday sneaked off into the Ducal castle church, where they set up for themselves a market or a palace for their playing, leaping, acting and other activities . . . that the same foreign servants of Your Ducal Grace arranged and presented in the House of God, which is the house of prayer, their jugglery, leaps, dances, songs and fantasies, and in this way turn the House of God into a theatre, a dancing-place, a jumble-stall of farces, and a fools' market.[4]

The above was accompanied by another complaint, written by the same pious citizens and carrying the same date, but addressed to the Duke's mother, as if the authors were convinced that nothing would be more effective than a mother's scolding.

Because the Calvinist and Baptist foreigners offer for sale and sell the pigeons of their fancy and their comedies; and combine and interlard with holy histories of Isaac and others all the useless forbidden coin of their foolery, tricks, songs, dances, and jugglery (which are really the main point of their entertainment); and thus disgracefully invert and abuse the Name and Word of God as a cover to their licentiousness and folly (which they pursued *ex professio*) . . . It would be a great wrong if we were to allow the Word of God and the histories of the Holy Bible to be preached in our churches in the same new style by these foreign and Calvinist players of comedies and dancers.[5]

The complaints apparently did not appeal either to the Duke or to his mother, for two days later Gregorius Hogius, the leader of the outraged citizens, wrote a third complaint, this time addressed to the councillors of Loitz. This is dated 28 August 1606.

Because their comedies are written and presented in an unknown language, it is not known who their master and author is, and what they include and deal with besides the histories themselves, and whether it is in accord with the Word of God, with the Christian faith, with our own pure Evangelical religion, with God-fearingness, decency and chastity.[6]

It is interesting to note that the first two complaints were written on the day immediately following the first performance of the English in the castle church. Its authors, however, admitted openly in their application of 28 August that one of the things that worried them was the fact that they did not understand the language in which the plays were given. Thus, most of the

accusations were simply fabricated by the fanatical burghers who were infuriated by the very thought that the players may have been Calvinists; and of course they were appalled by the fact that the performances were given in church. It may be added that the above is the last known instance of performances given in English on the Continent.

Having performed at Loitz, the players accompanied their new patron to Wolgast (Illustration 8). We learn about the company's presence there from yet another complaint, this time signed by the Duke's own councillors and court officials. The document is dated Wolgast, 6 October 1606,[7] and includes numerous accusations against the English, who are, it appears, not only the 'trouble-makers' at court, but whose maintenance also costs a lot of money. The players may have stayed at Wolgast over the winter of 1606–7, but they certainly left the town during the early months of 1607, for in June of that year they were given a passport ('Passbrieff') by Duke Philip Julius to return safely from Hamburg to Wolgast.[8] We learn from this document that the company numbered '5 Musicanten', and that they were ordered to reach Wolgast in 'great haste'. On their way to the Duke's court, the players stopped over at Loitz again, at the court of Philip Julius' mother, the Duchess Sophia Hedwig. Two documents connected with their stay there have been preserved, both signed by the Duchess and dated 10 August 1607.[9] The first of these informs us that the players were heading towards Wolgast, where they were to wait for their Lord. The second document is worth quoting, for it includes an order – one of the few of its kind – for the provision of the means of transportation for the players.

Our Gracious Lady and Duchess wishes herewith to command by the power of this writ that in view of this writ the village magistrate of Negendheim should without delay convey Her Ducal Grace's Son's servants to Wolgast in a carriage and three wagons, and should permit nothing to hinder this.[10]

Yet another extant document informs us that the players reached Wolgast on 11 August, i.e., after one day's journey. This is a letter of 12 August 1607,[11] which confirms the company's arrival from Hamburg, and includes, as usual, a number of complaints. When the players appeared at court, they presented the Duke's passport and immediately demanded board and lodging. This was, of course, provided, but the problem was that the company turned out to be much larger than the one mentioned in the passport. Consequently, the court cook had to arrange an additional table for 'those strangers' and serve them the same food as the English (which indicates that the additional persons were not English). The letter is addressed to the Duke, and its author is curious to know how he should treat the intruders. This was accompanied by another letter, bearing the same date and sent to the Duke by his councillors.[12] The latter also show the signs of worry about the unexpected visit of the English company and about the costs involved.

There are no more records referring to this particular company, no names

9. The ducal castle at Stettin

of actors are given, no titles of plays, and so on. This makes the identification of the troupe under discussion difficult indeed. It may have been, however, the same company that in 1609 was recommended by the Duke of Stettin to the Elector of Brandenburg. In the source referring to this event, which is quoted in the previous chapter, it is stated expressly that this was John Spencer and his men, and that the players had stayed at the Duke of Stettin's court 'for some time' (Illustration 9). It is therefore very likely that after the performances at Loitz and Wolgast, the company was recommended by Philip Julius to his cousin the Duke of Stettin, Philip II. Before entering the service of Philip Julius, Spencer's company was recorded in June 1606 at The Hague,[13] and having stayed at the Duke's court over winter, the players reappeared in Germany early in 1607,[14] and thereafter found employment again at Wolgast in 1607 and in 1608–9 at Stettin. This identification of the company and a reconstruction of the players' fortunes in this period remains, of course, to a certain degree conjectural. However, of the remaining companies active about this time, all have to be excluded from consideration. At the time of the players' first visit to Pomerania, Robert Browne's company was recorded in August 1606 at Ulm.[15] John Green was recorded at the same time at Frankfurt,[16] and Thomas Sackville's company was then permanently attached to the court of Henry Julius, the Duke of Brunswick-Wolfenbüttel.[17] That this was in fact John Spencer's company that visited the Duchy of Wolgast in 1606 and 1607 is indirectly confirmed by another source. As mentioned above, the Greifens were related to the Hohenzollerns and Philip Julius was no exception: in 1604 he married the daughter of John George, the Elector of Brandenburg. Since it is known that Spencer was in the Elector's service in 1604 (when he emerged at Cologne he was carrying the Electoral recommendation), it is possible that he performed for the first time before Philip Julius during the wedding celebrations in 1604, and was invited to pay a visit to the Duke's court in 1606 and later in 1607.

At any rate, John Spencer's company was recommended early in 1609 by Duke Francis I (1577–1620), one of Philip's brothers, to the Elector of Brandenburg at Königsberg in Prussia. We learn about this from another letter of recommendation referred to above, dated 11 July 1609, written by the Elector of Brandenburg to the Elector of Saxony. It is not very clear whether Spencer performed at Stettin, which was the capital city of Pomerania, or in Bytów, where Francis had his court after 1606. It may also have been Köslin (Polish, 'Koszalin'), where Francis, as the Bishop of Cammin (Polish, 'Kamień Pomorski') had his residence.[18] Spencer must have made a good impression on the Duke, and it seems probable that the winter of 1608–9 was not the only occasion when this particular company performed before Francis. As is apparent from the letter of recommendation, Spencer went to Saxony in the summer of 1609, and a year later he may have met Duke Francis again, this time at Dresden, during the wedding celebrations of Francis and Sophia of Saxony (the daughter of Christian I).[19]

The presence of English players at Wolgast was recorded again in 1611. From an anonymous letter to Duke Philip Julius, dated 26 June 1611,[20] we learn that the English had submitted an application, seeking permanent employment at the Duke's court. This, however, was rejected by the marshal of the court and other officials, and the players were only provided with board and lodging for a 'certain period of time'. The authors of the letter express their hopes that the players would change their mind and leave for some other place, which would be more profitable to them than the meagre maintenance at the Wolgast court. Again, no names of players are given, and the identification of the company is just as difficult. This may have been John Spencer again, who appeared in Gdańsk a month later.

When Robert Archer's company arrived in Gdańsk in 1615, the players informed the councillors there that they were the Elector of Brandenburg's servants and that they had brought 'testimonials' from Duke Philip of Stettin and Duke Francis of Köslin.

After which we were soon decided to visit this Royal port and city [of Gdańsk] before all others . . . and to present new historical [comedies] . . . before your Noble Graces and other praiseworthy citizens of the town . . . but were graciously put up in the meantime for a good while by his Ducal Grace Duke Philip of Stettin and Duke Francis of Köslin, by the power of the testimonials herewith enclosed.[21]

Thus the players indicated that they had performed in Pomerania for a considerable period of time. Not much is known about this particular company, and the scraps of evidence are discussed elsewhere in this book.[22] Although this remains the last piece of evidence for the English presence in both Stettin and Köslin, a look at the map suffices to show that both of these towns, lying on the way from northern Germany to Gdańsk and to Prussia, were in fact the threshold of the Baltic route that the English players established early in the seventeenth century. It is probable that visits by English players were much more frequent than appears from the extant records, especially in the period before 1627, when the Thirty Years War still had not affected Pomerania.

At any rate, English players' activity in Pomerania is considered by several scholars to have been connected with the somewhat puzzling publication of *Englische Comoedien und Tragedien* in 1620. It was Johan Nordström who first discovered that one Frederick Menius, a practising lawyer in Wolgast in the period between 1617 and 1621, claimed to be the author of the volume in question.[23] The problem of authorship has been scrutinised by G. Fredén,[24] and some of his conclusions are worth mentioning here. According to Fredén, Menius attended the performances of English players at the court of Philip Julius at Wolgast, and he noted and memorised, as best he could, the text and the particulars of staging and on the basis of his notes he reconstructed the plays. The arguments in support of Fredén's theory are the following: firstly, there are many anglicisms in the text; secondly, even more striking, is the abundance of Latin words and names, nearly all of which have correct suffixes; thirdly, the language of all the texts in *Englische Comoedien und Tragedien* is regularly tinged with Low German, which leads us to the conclusion that it had to be the work of one man (either the author, or the editor); fourthly, the alleged author made use of his education and knowledge, for in the plays we find scenes based upon German folk literature and *commedia dell'arte*, we encounter reminiscences of Plautus and Terence.[25] If accepted, this theory would provide us with an additional proof for the English presence in Pomerania in the period between 1617 and 1620 and, what is equally important, the volume of *Englische Comoedien und Tragedien* would serve as a direct reflection of the repertoire of a company that performed at Wolgast some time before 1620.

It was in Wolgast that English players were last seen in this part of the Continent. On 30 August 1623 an application was submitted to Duke Philip Julius, signed by Richard Jones, Johan Kostressen and Robert Dulandt. This has already been published in the original by C.F. Meyer,[26] and an excerpt will suffice here.

As Your Ducal Grace may kindly recall, we are the same persons whom You had previously installed for one year, when we humbly waited upon you with our music, so that we hope Your Grace is graciously satisfied with us. Because a year has now passed, and we have, for urgent reasons, decided to go to England again.[27]

Richard Jones is of course the well-known veteran actor, and his name recurs frequently in other chapters of this book. It may be noted here, however, that before his employment at Wolgast, Jones had for many years been in the service of the Prince of Poland, Vladislaus, beginning in 1617. Whether Johan Kostressen and Robert Dulandt had been associated with Jones before their Wolgast appointment of 1622 is not known. Since Jones' name appears as the first one on the document, this indicates that he was the manager, or the principal actor of the company. 'Kostressen' hardly sounds English, but 'Dulandt' may with all certainty be identified with Robert Dowland, the son of the composer John Dowland.[28] From their application it appears that the three have been employed since 1622, and decided, for some urgent reasons, to leave the ducal service and return to England. This could imply that both Kostressen and Dulandt were in fact English, although this may just as well have been a pretext given to the Duke to obtain dismissal. These 'urgent reasons' for their departure are referred to in Jones' next application to Philip Julius, dated 10 July 1624.

Your Ducal Grace will know that I left Your Ducal Grace for the duration of one year for the following reason: that Jürgen [George Vincent ?] my countryman, had at that time written to me from England that I should take my leave of Your Grace and come to England, where the Prince had promised to pay me so much then that it would suffice till the end of my life; but now I have learned that all this was a pack of lies, and therefore I have come here again with reverence, and desire to offer my service for the second time to Your Ducal Grace, and because I am an old man and I am tired of travelling, I am submitting to Your Ducal Grace my request to enter Your service again and to show all faithfulness and diligence in this.[29]

This time the application is signed by Richard Jones alone, who labelled himself 'an Englishman and musician' ('Engelender undt Musikant'). It is clear Jones departed in 1623 in hope of financial gain. He was promised a lucrative position by a Prince, presumably Prince Charles, who is the only one that seems likely.[30] It is not known whether Jones found employment at Wolgast again,[31] but he was certainly back in London in 1626,[32] a date that coincides with the death of his Pomeranian patron. Thus ended Jones' Continental career, which began as early as 1592. The last record of him in England comes from Worcester, where in 1630 Jones and two others were indicted for forging a licence from the Master of the Revels.[33]

5 Livonia

THE meagre evidence for English theatrical activity in Livonia[1] is limited to Riga and to the short period between 1644 and 1648, i.e., towards the end of the Thirty Years War. One may suspect, however, that the players' visits were much more frequent than the extant records suggest. As shown elsewhere in this book, early in the seventeenth century, English companies established the Baltic route, leading from Wolgast and Stettin in Pomerania to Königsberg in Prussia. Further east, Riga was the largest and wealthiest town, and it was the capital of the province (Illustration 1). Although Livonia had been Poland's fief since 1561, in the first quarter of the seventeenth century it fell into Swedish hands, and Riga was governed by Swedish authorities from 1617. It would seem natural that the players would have attempted to incorporate Riga, and perhaps some other towns in Livonia, into their strolling route. By doing so, a company attached permanently, say, to the court at Warsaw, could visit Gdańsk, Elbing, Königsberg and Riga one after another, for all these towns were relatively close to each other. If scheduled beforehand, and with permission to act guaranteed, a tour of this sort would certainly be profitable, and in addition it would not be too tiring and would not force the actors to seek fortune in distant countries.

However, the available evidence leads us to the conclusion that no regular English theatrical activity ever took place in Riga. The silence of the records may be accounted for by the complex political situation in the region. Poland never gave up hopes of regaining Livonia, and the hostility between the two countries was deepened both by succession claims for the Swedish throne by the Polish branch of the Vasas and by the general international situation. In 1626, a war broke out between Poland and Sweden and this made any travel impossible until 1635, when a peace treaty was signed. In spite of this the situation in the region remained complex and dangerous. This was partly due to the policies of the Elector of Brandenburg, John George, who in May 1635 signed the Peace of Prague, by which he found himself at war with Sweden.[2] However, the Swedish forces stationed in Livonia did not attack Ducal Prussia, because the Duchy was Poland's fief, and from the formal point of view Sweden was only at war with Brandenburg, of which the Duchy was no part (as it was not a part of the Empire). The hostilities between Brandenburg and Sweden eventually ended in June 1644 with the signing of a separate peace treaty between the two countries.[3] Interestingly, the latter coincides with the first recorded visit by English players to Riga.

Johannes Bolte in his *Das Danziger Theater* referred to an entry in the Council records at Riga, from which we learn that an unspecified English company of players stayed in that city from 11 April to 24 May 1644.[4] Unfortunately, Bolte does not reproduce the entry, which is now, as far as I know, lost. However, this visit is confirmed by a hitherto unknown document from Gdańsk: an application from a company that came to Gdańsk in July 1644, where we read the following: 'we the English comedians, having performed this year at Riga and Königsberg, and having now reached Elbing, have further decided to visit the glorious city of Gdańsk'.[5] According to E. Herz,[6] this was the same company that in March 1644 performed at Osnabrück in Northern Germany during the peace talks that were held there. This seems highly probable. The company's presence at Osnabrück and performances given before the highest officials from many countries, provided the players with an excellent opportunity to win the favour of some of the nobles and to secure appropriate letters of recommendation and testimonials which could be useful in other parts of the Continent. And we know for certain that the company that acted at Osnabrück was given a certificate of this sort by the town councillors.[7] One may suspect that the players were also given a letter of recommendation from one of the Swedish nobles present there, like Johan Oxenstierna or Johan Adler Salvius, and this enabled them to obtain permission to play in Swedish Riga. One is even tempted to suspect that this particular visit of English players to Riga may have been connected with the separate peace talks between the Elector of Brandenburg and Sweden. This is partly confirmed by the fact that the company in question stayed for a surprisingly long period of time in Riga, whence the players went straight to Königsberg, after the peace treaty had been signed. This is proved beyond doubt by the Gdańsk application of July 1644 quoted above.

The company is not difficult to identify due to the fact that the players themselves admitted that they had performed in Gdańsk previously.

we submit our most humble petition and request to the High [etc.] Lordships to show us grace and to allow us to perform again during the St Dominic's Fair in the traditional place in the Fencing-School, where we have performed before.[8]

This company must therefore be the former Reynolds–Archer troupe, now led by another pair of veteran players, William Roe and John Wayde.[9] From the Gdańsk application we learn that the company numbered eighteen players, but no other names are given and nothing can be said about the players' repertoire. Details concerning the company's further fortunes may be found in other chapters of this book.

The last pieces of evidence for English players' presence in Riga, are the two applications of the same company, both dated 1648.[10] These have already been published by Bolte, and excerpts will suffice for our purposes here.

we, the English comedians who performed here four years ago following the gracious permission of Your Highly Learned and Gracious Lordships, would like to inform you that we have come here desiring to present publicly our comedies, tragedies and histories, etc. once again. When this our whole request reaches Your Noble and Gracious and Praiseworthy Lordships, we would humbly beg you to take into account the great expenses of our journey by land (namely from Gdańsk and Königsberg, where we have lately performed) and to grant us the space for our scheme, just as was done at Königsberg and Gdańsk.[11]

The above application is not dated, but we may follow Bolte's assumption that it must have been submitted shortly before the other one which carries the date 21 January 1648:

we have been told by the Steward in the name of the Royal Burgrave that we should cease to perform . . . It was our intention to go from here to Stockholm . . . At the present time it is impossible to undertake a journey of this sort; Your Noble and Gracious and Praiseworthy Lordships may kindly consider that although we have received a good deal of money, we have at the present time, as we have mentioned before, not yet recovered our expenses, and even less have we earned a penny to subsist on for a further journey . . . The state of things at the present time is such that we cannot properly go anywhere else. It is impossible to go by water, and to travel by land to the nearby towns is arduous, expensive, and not worth either the trouble, or the expense. Nor is it the custom in any town to welcome us at this time of year . . . and as Your Noble Lordships have previously done us the honour of attending a performance of a lowly comedy, we herewith submit to you our request, that you allow us to perform a tragedy (of Dorothea the Martyr) in your most desired presence.[12]

From the above we may draw the conclusion that this was the same company that visited Gdańsk in August 1647, the one led by John Wayde and William Roe. As is apparent from the players' Gdańsk application, the company was composed of English, Dutch and German players. And from their Riga application we learn that this was the same troupe that visited that town in 1644. Having performed in Gdańsk and Königsberg, the actors reached Riga on their way to Stockholm, which was their ultimate destination.

Not much can be said about the actual performances at Riga. In accordance with the tradition developed elsewhere, the players invited town councillors for a première show, presented in their honour. The magistrates seem to have been impressed by the show and, consequently, the company was allowed to perform in public. As we learn from the players' second application, the permission to act was for some reason cancelled by the order of the Royal Burgrave. The hopelessness of the situation in which the players found themselves is moving indeed, but we do not know whether this had any influence on the councillors' final decision. At any rate, the company eventually made its way to Stockholm, and in July 1648 performed at the Royal Castle there before Queen Christine.[13] And this remains the last piece of evidence for the English players' presence at Riga.

PART II

The noble patrons: the Habsburgs and the Vasas

6 Warsaw

English theatrical activity in Warsaw exemplifies clearly that the notion of the so-called 'strolling companies' is slightly misleading, for the ultimate goal of the 'wandering comedians' was to find a patron at whose court the players could find permanent employment, undertaking occasional travels, or none at all. As I said, the theatrical season in sundry Continental towns was limited to the time of local fairs, festivities and celebrations of various kinds, and only experienced companies, well acquainted with local tradition could plan their tours beforehand in such a way that they could coordinate the festival season in different places into one longer tour. This, of course, was much easier to achieve in densely populated areas of the Continent, which was not the case of Central and Eastern Europe. In addition, the outbreak of the Thirty Years War in 1618 made travel highly risky, if not impossible in a number of countries, and this led to the dissolution of a number of companies. Some players returned to England, and those who remained active on the Continent continued their activities in relatively more peaceful regions. Poland was one of those countries where the English players found refuge during the War, and – as shown below – it is this calamitous period in European history that marks the apex of their activity in Warsaw. That Poland remained neutral during the War may have been one of the facts which attracted the English players there; the other reason was the favourable conditions offered to the actors by the King of Poland Sigismund III (1566–1632), and his son Vladislaus IV (1596–1648), for the English players enjoyed the Royal patronage for many years.

Unfortunately, almost nothing concerning the English theatrical companies in this period has been found in the Warsaw records. Most of the archive materials were destroyed or looted during the various wars that devastated the country, and the last irretrievable loss was caused by the Second World War when the collection of old records in the National Library was burned during an air raid. Therefore, the picture of the English players' activity drawn below on the basis of pieces of evidence scattered in Continental and English archives has to be treated as incomplete and imperfect. Moreover, some extant pieces of evidence are only circumstantial. For instance, an isolated entry in the Cologne archives tells us that a company of English (?) players that visited that city in August 1606, styled itself as 'Polinischen Comedianten' (i.e., 'Polish Comedians'). Since nothing is known about Polish strolling companies in that period, we could perhaps vaguely assume (tenuous though the evidence may be) that this may have been in fact an

English company that found permanent employment and patronage at the Polish court. But even if we concentrate on direct pieces of evidence only, the meagre records at our disposal today leave no doubt that Warsaw was one of the important centres of English theatre in Central Europe, a fact generally neglected in scholarship on the subject.[1]

It is not unlikely that the first visit paid by the English players to Warsaw took place in November 1611, when the Elector of Brandenburg John Sigismund went there to participate in the official ceremony of receiving the investiture of the Duchy of Prussia. On the way from Königsberg, the Elector stopped at Ortelsburg (Polish, 'Szczytno'), and on 16 October ordered suits of clothes to be made for his 'instrumentalists and comedians'. This company, composed of nineteen players and sixteen musicians, has been identified as John Spencer's. The order had been accomplished at great speed by 24 October. Zbigniew Raszewski was the first to suggest that the above order was made as part of preparations for the celebrations in Warsaw and that the players accompanied the Elector to Poland's capital.[2] However, no direct evidence can yet be provided to support this conjecture. The only indirect piece of evidence that I have come across is a letter written by an Englishman, one James Hill, apparently the Elector's courtier or servant, who on 25 October 1611 wrote to Robert Cecil from Ortelsburg where he had accompanied his lord. In this letter we find the following passage:

Newes is kom this daye, that the parliament att Wersaw have agreed my Lorde shall reseyve the Leave and that we doo expecte with in 5 dayes Imbassanders from the Kinge to conclude apon the day of my Lordes kominge thether so that her is greate preparation made agaynste the Solemnytie.[3]

This 'greate preparation' could, of course, include the provision of new clothes for the players, and if we bear in mind the King's well-known admiration of theatre and music,[4] the idea of bringing a company of players to Warsaw may have been a part of the Elector's policy to win Sigismund's favour. Thus we have some justification for assuming that the performances by the English did actually take place and that they added splendour to the pomp of the official ceremony that took place on 16 November 1611 in Warsaw.

The same event was referred to in a letter by another Englishman, Patric Gordon, again written to Robert Cecil, who apparently had a number of informers in Poland.

The king of Polland, at the parliament latelie holden at Varsavia, enterteaned the Duke Elector of Bradenburg most kyndlie and brotherlie, and with consent of the whole estates did give unto him feudum Ducalis Prussiae, and he as beneficiarus Regis did swear the oath of fidelitie, with divers conditions.[5]

The letter is dated 6 January 1612, 'Kunigsberg in Prussia'. There seemed to have developed a tradition of giving theatrical performances on the occasion of the Electors' visits to Poland. For example, when in October 1641, Frederick William who succeded George William (†1640), came to Warsaw he saw an opera piece, *Enea*, staged in the newly built Royal theatre (within the castle walls), and the production was even dedicated to his honour by the author of the libretto, Virgilio Puccitelli.[6]

The first direct evidence for a planned visit to Warsaw by the English players may be found in John Green's application to the City Council, written in Gdańsk and dated 25 August 1616.

We have been advised as regards His Royal Highness the King of Poland and Sweden,[7] to wait for his gracious decision on whether His Royal Highness will express his desire of our services. But since a number of days will pass, before we receive His Royal Highness's decision and our position will not suffer us to remain in this difficult situation without earnings from which to live; and since in other respects we have also had great expenses, which we have not made up by takings; and since we are not acting; we therefore submit to Your Lordships our great request, that in the mean time, and in especial honour of His Royal Highness, you indulge our wishes and permit us to prevent our present losses and to earn our subsistence by performing comedies and tragedies. This will serve to please His Royal Highness most graciously, and we shall most humbly praise it to the same, humbly and readily announcing and commending Your Noble Lordships' great favour and most friendly affection, and we will do so elsewhere besides, to other potentates and in other lands.[8]

Perhaps it should be recalled here that John Green was one of the leading English strollers on the Continent in the period between about 1603 and 1626. In 1616 he came to Gdańsk from Denmark, and he signed his application of 25 August together with Robert Reynolds, who was to gain unparalleled fame under the stage-name 'Pickleherring'. Sigismund III's decision was favourable to the players and, as we learn from a different source, the whole company stayed in Warsaw during the winter 1616–17. The only information about this visit comes from a letter, dated 17 March 1617, written by the Archduke Charles, who was then the Bishop of Breslau (Polish, 'Wrocław'), to Cardinal von Dietrichstein at Olmütz (Czech, 'Olomounc') in Moravia.

When we remember that, during the life-time of our late most beloved lady mother of highly honoured and praiseworthy memory, just these same persons have performed their comedies at Graz, quite honourably and decently, always with our most gracious pleasure and satisfaction, but that now they have come to us with royal recommendations and good testimonials from Poland, where they have for some months exhibited such comedies before their Royal Highnesses, and have respectfully presented themselves.[9]

Although no names are given in the letter, there is no doubt that the company in question was John Green's. Firstly, reference is made to the performances at Graz during the lifetime of Charles' mother, the Archduchess Maria. Since the Archduchess died in 1608, the letter quoted must refer to Green's recorded appearance at Graz in winter 1607/8. This, in turn was described in detail by the Archduchess Maria Magdalena in a letter she wrote to her brother Ferdinand. The details of the Graz visit are discussed elsewhere in this book, and for our purposes here it will suffice to say that it was undoubtedly John Green's company that stayed in Warsaw during the winter of 1616–17.

The fact that the English players stayed at Sigismund III's court for a couple of months and received a favourable letter of recommendation from their Royal Highnesses indicates that they were warmly received there. It should also be added that the personal and cultural links of the Royal Court in Warsaw with the Archduke Charles' court at Neisse (Polish, 'Nysa'), in Silesia, and with the Habsburgs in general were by no means accidental or sporadic. To begin with both the families, i.e. the Vasas and the Habsburgs, were related through the Jagiellons – a dynasty ruling in Poland since the late fourteenth century until the death of the last male heir, Sigismund Augustus, in 1572. When in 1592 Sigismund III married the Archduchess of Austria Anne Habsburg (the Archduke Charles' sister), he was actually marrying his distant cousin. In addition, the Emperor Ferdinand II was their son's godfather. Therefore, it is not surprising that both families kept in close touch and frequently visited one another. Visits of this sort were often an occasion for grand celebrations, which of course included theatrical performances and musical concerts. For example, when in 1624 the Prince of Poland Vladislaus (the future King Vladislaus IV) went on a long tour of Europe, he stopped on the way at several friendly courts of the Habsburgs and at every one of them he was entertained with either music or theatre or both.[10] Green's stay in Warsaw in 1616–17 and the letter of recommendation he received from their Royal Highnesses may also serve as an example of how noble patronage extended far beyond the court of a given aristocrat.

The Royal family at Warsaw must have been greatly impressed with the art and skills of the English players in 1616–17, for it was decided that an English company should be employed at court on a more or less permanent basis. From the documents among the Acts of the Privy Council[11] we learn that it was the young Prince of Poland Vladislaus who felt a capricious and extravagant desire to bring a whole company of players and musicians directly from London to Warsaw.

[22 June 1617]

A letter to the Erle of Suffolke, Lord Highe Treasurer of England

Whereas George Vincent, servant to the Prince of Poland, hath made provision here of certeyne necessaries for the use of the Prince his master and for the King and Queene of Poland, vizt: 36 paire of silke stockinges, black and coloured, and 15 paire of gloves, and thereupon hath made humble suite unto us that hee might have leave to transport them custome free. Theese are therefore to pray your Lordship to give order to the searchers and other officers of the porte of London to licence the sayd Geo[rge] Vincent to transporte those thinges above mentioned without paying any custome or impost for them. And this shall be unto your Lordship a sufficient warrant.

Ut ante.

A passe for the sayd Geo [rge] Vincent to goe over to the Prince of Poland, and to carry over with him to the sayd Prince his master these musicions, Richard Jones, Wm. Corkin, Donatus O'Chaine, Thomas Wite, Wm. Jackson, Tho. Sutton, Valentine Flood and John Wayd.

Ut supra.[12]

Another pass was granted to George Vincent by the Council on 24 August of the following year:

A passe for George Vincent to retourne into Poland to the Prince, his master, and to take over with him such thinges as he hath bought for the Kinge, Queene and Prince of Poland vizt. a perfumed sweete bagge and two bever hattes, one wastcot and four paire of ritch gloves six wastcottes and six night capps, a dozen of ryding gloves and such instruments of musicke as he shall have use of for his maister's service, together with his wife and childrenn and also five musitians for the service of the Prince of Poland, and the wife of one Joanes residing in Poland.

This passe was graunted upon significacion of his Majesty's pleasure by letter from Sir Robert Cary, knight.[13]

Of the names given above, only three may at present be identified as actors. George Vincent, who seems to have been responsible for the organization of the company for the service of the Prince of Poland, was first recorded on the Continent in 1615, when in May he was paid 100 thalers for performances at Wolfenbüttel.[14] Richard Jones was a well known player, first in the Earl of Worcester's company, where he was associated with Robert Browne, with whom he went on the Continent in 1592, and later, until 1602, as one of the Lord Admiral's men.[15] The last mention of Jones in Henslowe's *Diary* reads as follows: 'Lent vnto the company to geve vnto m^r Jonnes m^r show at thire goinge a waye fyftye powndes wch is not in this Recknynge I say'.[16] And John Wayde seems to have begun his long and successful Continental career in Warsaw, for no earlier records of him are known. He may have in fact been a boy-actor in Jones' company, for one 'John: Wade of Yarmouth of Norff' was mentioned as thirty years of age in 1637.[17] Thus, Wayde would have been only ten in 1617, and if this conjecture is correct he may have played women's parts. Incidentally, a fourth name on the list has been identified: Valentine Flood was a well known musician, and his presence on the Continent was recorded until 1637.[18]

The importance of the Privy Council documents quoted above lies not only in the fact that they help us to track down the individual names of actors and musicians active on the Continent, but – even more so – in their broader implications. They inform us that the vogue of keeping an English acting company at one's court had reached Warsaw by 1617, and, secondly, they prove beyond doubt that the frequent visits of the players to Warsaw were not accidental and that the Vasas' patronage was not adventitious.[19] They remain, in fact, the only known documents of their kind, and serve as an invaluable piece of evidence for unprecedented 'theatrical import' directly from London to Warsaw.[20] It is worth noting that it was not Sigismund III, but the young Prince, Vladislaus, who initiated this enterprise. The easiest and quickest way to reach Poland from England was to sail to Gdańsk or to Elbing, and undoubtedly, this was exactly what the players did in the summer of 1617. It was only George Vincent who was sent back to England in the summer of the following year, whence he returned to Poland again accompanied by his own and Jones' wives, his children, and also by five additional 'musitians'. All this implies that the players' employment was on a permanent basis.

The available evidence seems to indicate that the players stayed in Warsaw for approximately two years without undertaking any travels. It is only in June 1619 that we learn of the company temporarily leaving Warsaw for Gdańsk. The players' application, dated 7 June, to the town councillors is reproduced and discussed in Chapter 1, but at this point only a short passage is relevant, because it includes a reference to the players' employment in Warsaw. 'Since our company has for some time stayed at the court of His Royal Majesty in Poland and intends to return there again towards winter.'[21] This indicates that Jones' company not only stayed in Warsaw during the period between July(?) 1617 and May(?) 1619, but was back there in winter 1619–20. The latter is additionally confirmed by a letter that Jones' wife wrote in April 1620 to Edward Alleyn. We know that Mrs Jones followed her husband on his Continental tours and her presence overseas was recorded in 1615–16 and again in 1620.

Ladvo [?] from dansicke The ffirste of Apriel 1620
my Aproved Good ffrinde m^r Allin your helleth wished in the lord witith your Good wife trvsting in God you Ar both in Good hellth As I was at the wryting her of thes few lines is to tre[a]te your worshyp to stand owr Good frind As you hath been before I sent, you A leeter of Atorny by m^r bapties Abowte the lebickes hed I Cnowe not whither you hath Reseafed it or no I wowlld intreate your worship to send me word m^r Rowly hath delte with me for my Rente by his baerher of my Husband Is with the prince And as yt I am hire in dansicke locking Evry daye to Gooe to him thvs desierin God to bles you with your Good wife I Commyt you to the all myty God

> Your pore frinde to
> Command haris
> Joones + H J

To the Rite wofo m^r Edward Allin deliver this at dvlige nere Londo.[22]

It has been claimed that the 'prince' mentioned in the above letter was George William, the Elector of Brandenburg from 1619, but this is very unlikely. The Elector was no prince, and had the title of a duke. The only 'Prince' that may be taken into consideration here is Vladislaus, the Prince of Poland.[23] The fact that Mrs Jones did not specify exactly which prince she actually had in mind indicates that she expected Edward Alleyn to know at whose court his old companion had been employed since 1617. Thus, Mrs Jones' desire 'to Gooe to him' would indicate Warsaw rather than Berlin or Königsberg.

The above pieces of evidence show that touring the country in summer was customary for almost all English companies that found protection and patronage at a nobleman's court. It is, however, impossible to determine precisely how long Vincent–Jones' troupe stayed in Warsaw after the players had returned from Gdańsk. There is a slight possibility that John Green joined this company sometime during the 1619–20 season, for when he emerged in Cologne at the end of April 1620, he presented his company as 'Polish comedians' ('Polnische Comedianten').[24] Since Richard Jones in his application to the Duke of Wolgast, dated 30 August 1623, indicated that he had been in the Duke's service for one year, and since he was not accompanied there by any of the actors mentioned above, it may be assumed that the company had split up by summer 1622.

Warsaw remained one of the safer places during the Thirty Years War, and companies could find refuge there. The first indication of an English presence at the Warsaw court in this 'dark period' is provided by Robert Archer's application to the City Council in Gdańsk, dated 28 July 1636, and beginning 'Following the death of King Sigismund the Third of blessed memory, whom we, the English comedians, have served for many years.'[25] Sigismund III died in 1632 and the fact that the players had stayed in his service 'for many years' implies that Archer's company was hired sometime in the 1620s. In 1627 Archer was still a member of Robert Reynolds' company, and a Torgau list provides us with the names of players. Apart from Reynolds and Archer, the list included: 'Jacob der Hesse', 'Johann Eydtwartt', 'Thomas die Jungfraw', 'Johann Wilhelm der Kleiderverwahrer', 'der Engländer', 'der Rothkopf' and 'vier Jungen'.[26] Several of these have been identified: 'Jacob der Hesse' was presumably Jacob Teodor (a German player), 'Johann Eydtwartt' may have been John Edwards,[27] and 'Johann Wilhelm der Kleiderverwahrer' may have referred to John Wayde and William Wedware.[28] Soon after performances at Torgau, the company split up. When Reynolds emerged in May 1628 at Cologne,[29] he was accompanied by only three players from the above list, Edwards, Teodor and Robinson. It seems that Archer formed a new company together with Wayde and Wedware, and with these players may have reached Warsaw by the time Reynolds' presence was recorded at Cologne. This would indicate that Archer's troupe stayed at the court of Sigismund III from about 1628 to 1632, which would accord with the reference to 'many years' spent there.[30] If we assume that Wayde was among Archer's men, then this hypothetical reconstruction of the company's fortunes will appear even more plausible, for Wayde, it should be remembered, had stayed in Warsaw earlier with Richard Jones' company, and may have had a good reputation there.

In his Gdańsk application of 1636, Archer also indicated that his company was waiting for the King's, i.e. Vladislaus IV's, 'resolution' whether the players should go to Vilnius or to Warsaw to attend on him. There is no direct evidence for English theatrical activity in Vilnius (Polish, 'Wilno'), although kings of Poland, as Grand Dukes of Lithuania, often visited that city and even resided there for longer periods of time, and the players may have accompanied their lords. An indirect piece of evidence for such an event was discussed by W. Tomkiewicz in his 'Court Performances During the Renaissance':[31] he conjectured that the players were brought to Vilnius on the King's order in 1639, to add splendour to the celebrations on the occasion of the Duke of Curland's oath of allegiance to the King of Poland. A contemporary account tells us that a theatrical performance was to take place on a special stage arranged *ad hoc*, but owing to some clash of a political nature between the Duke and the King, the show was cancelled; the King, offended by the Duke, ordered the 'theatre' erected in the castle courtyard to be demolished.[32] If this conjecture is accurate, although this account does not tell us whether the company was English, it is reasonable to suppose that this was Archer's company, and that Archer was again permanently attached to the Royal court in Warsaw, at least from 1636 to 1640, undertaking – as we shall see – occasional travels to Gdańsk and other towns in the region.

The company that visited Gdańsk in 1640 indicated in an application to the City Council, dated 18 May, that the players had been refused leave to play in that city a year before, during the St Dominic's Fair, i.e., in August 1639. This is followed by a reference to the players' stay in Warsaw:

Later we stayed with His Royal Majesty in Warsaw, where we served him according to his convenience and his desire; we received leave of absence from thence for some time, on the condition, however, that we should return again after a time.[33]

These certainly were Robert Archer's men, and the players, having been refused permission to act in Gdańsk in May 1640, soon joined forces with Robert Reynolds at Königsberg. Apart from these two leading actors, the Elector's patent of 1640 gives us the following names: William Roe, John Wayde, Edward Pudsey and William Wedware.[34] Wayde and Wedware, it seems, were faithful companions of Archer's; they went with him to Warsaw around 1628 and may still have been members of his company in 1636 and in May 1640. Edward Pudsey was mentioned as Reynolds' companion in 1636 in Amsterdam.[35]

Thus, on the basis of the above application we may ascertain that Robert Archer's company spent the winter of 1639–40 in Warsaw, once again enjoying the Royal patronage, and that in spring 1640 the players left Warsaw and went via Gdańsk to Königsberg, to return to Warsaw later in that year. That this particular company did in fact return to Warsaw some time after July 1640 is confirmed by a reference to English players' activities in the Warsaw–Gdańsk–Königsberg triangle made by an English traveller, Peter Mundy who stopped in Gdańsk in 1642:

Some Summers come here [i.e. to Gdańsk] our English commediens or players which representte in Netherlandishe Dutche, having bin att Coninxberg beffore the prince Elector of Brandenburge; Allsoe att Warsowe beffore the king of Poland. Among those Actors was one here Nicknamed pickled herring, much talked off and admired For his dexterity in the Jesters partt, Amo. Itt is said off him thatt hee could soe Frame his Face and countenance thatt to one halffe off the people on the one side hee would seeme heartily to laugh and to those on the other side bitterly to weepe and shedd teares – straunge. Hee died att Warsaw. His wife now liveth here in towne [and] hath allowance From the king For her Maynetenance.[36]

This leaves no doubt that the company in question was still attached to the court in Warsaw in the period between July 1640, when the players left Königsberg, and early 1642, when the news of Reynolds' death had reached Mundy in Gdańsk. This piece of information is of particular relevance, for Reynolds was one of the most important English players active on the Continent. That the King of Poland gave an 'allowance' to Mrs Reynolds indicates how popular the English players were at the Polish court.[37] This, however, remains the last direct reference to an English company's stay in Warsaw. Only an isolated entry in an application dated 1643 by the English players to the councillors in Gdańsk tells us that the players had been refused leave to play three and five years before and consequently they had to seek the patronage 'of someone else'.[38] This indicates 1638 and 1640, and this 'someone else' stands here, of course, for the King of Poland. This is additionally confirmed by a letter written in support of the players by one Roszawen, a citizen of Gdańsk, to the councillors there. The letter, dated 1 August 1650, includes a passage telling us that the English company of players expected to arrive soon in Gdańsk was the same one that had been attached to the court of the late King [i.e. Vladislaus IV], who died in 1648.[39]

To conclude, we may claim with confidence that from 1616, if not earlier, for approximately thirty years, the court of Sigismund III and Vladislaus IV was an important centre of English theatrical activity on the Continent. During the calamitous years of the Thirty Years War, Royal patronage provided the players with a refuge and enabled them to survive. The players stayed there, indeed, for many years, undertaking occasional expeditions in summer. The evidence provided contradicts the frequently stated opinion that Vladislaus IV favoured Italian opera above all else.[40] The theatre built in 1637 within the castle walls equipped with the newest refinements of contemporary theatre architecture served both English and Italian companies. The architectural details of this theatre are discussed in a separate chapter of this book, and it will suffice here to make a final remark that Vladislaus' permanent court theatre provided the English players with an excellent opportunity of getting acquainted with new trends in staging from Italy.

*

At the end of the sixteenth century and beginning of the seventeenth century the Habsburg dynasty was undoubtedly the greatest power in Europe. Members of this family were Kings of Bohemia and of Hungary, Archdukes of Austria, Kings in Spain and Portugal and Naples. They owned Burgundy, the Low Countries and parts of Alsace, the fiefs of Silesia and of Finale and Piombino in Italy; they also reigned in the New World over Chile, Peru, Brazil and Mexico. The list could be made much longer if we added smaller countries and tiny duchies scattered across Europe, some of these being only twenty square miles in size. Bearing this in mind, it is clear that the influence of the Habsburgs and of their policies went beyond the bounds of Germany. Nevertheless, or, perhaps, precisely for this reason, the Holy Roman Empire of the German nation, when ruled by the Habsburg emperors, did not unite the numerous independent states of Germany. Just the opposite: we observe in the period under discussion Germany's total disintegration. As late as the turn of the sixteenth century primogeniture was not an established principle in the Empire, and princes divided their lands between their sons, forming in this way smaller and smaller units of almost equal independence. At times, the number of these fragments exceeded two thousand.

In this book only two countries that were both a part of the Empire and a part of the Habsburg dominion will be discussed: the Kingdom of Bohemia and the Archduchy of Austria; which were to be ruled by the members of the Habsburg family for over six centuries until the end of the First World War.

*

7 Bohemia

THE first indication of the English players' presence in Bohemia comes to us in a letter written on 18 March 1596 by the Landgrave Maurice of Hesse to his agent in Prague, Johan Lucanus, in which he announces

that our comedians have arrived and have humbly begged our gracious permission to visit other places, too, and perform various comedies, since we now meet these their wishes, as it is also our gracious desire: should our said comedians happen in the course of their travels to come near Prague, and perform several comedies there, would you provide them with all possible good assistance.[1]

Although no names of players are given in the letter, we know for certain that the company attached at that time to the Landgrave's court at Kassel was led by Robert Browne.[2] In August 1595 he was mentioned at Wolfenbüttel as the Landgrave's comedian, together with Thomas Sackville and John Bradstreet (both of whom had been members of the Lord Admiral's company in London until 1592) and Anthony Jeffes, a boy-actor of whom mention may also be found in Elizabethan records.[3] The players may have visited Prague some time between March and July 1596, for in July they re-appeared in Germany and performed at Nuremberg and Augsburg,[4] and they were back at Kassel in October.[5] If the company had made its way to Prague, the players' repertoire would have included plays that were staged by them in the period between 1592 and 1596: *Gammer Gurton's Needle*, some plays by Christopher Marlowe, *Abraham and Lot* and *The Destruction of Sodom and Gomorrah*.[6] A claim has been made for Thomas Sackville's visit to Prague in 1598 when, in August, Sackville, 'the Duke of Brunswick's servant', was paid a gratuity of 116 florins and 40 kroner.[7] Nothing more is known about this visit.

Another English company of players may have come to Prague in April 1610 but, again, this visit remains conjectural.[8] That was the year when the Emperor Rudolf II (1576–1612) summoned the Austrian Archdukes and some German dukes to Prague to settle his continuing conflict with his brother Mathias who was then the King of Hungary. In keeping with long tradition, Rudolf as the King of Bohemia was also Emperor at the same time. However, strong opposition by Protestants in Bohemia to the radical actions undertaken against them by Rudolf led to his deposition in 1611, and to the election of Mathias as the King of Bohemia. But in 1610 Rudolf was still the man in power. Among the guests arriving at Prague, there were the Archdukes Ferdinand of Graz, Leopold of Passau, Maximillian of Tirol, accompanied by the Duke Julius of Brunswick and the Landgrave Maurice of

10. The Hradschin Castle in Prague

Hesse-Kassel. The latter name is, of course, of particular importance to our purposes here because the Landgrave, being a great admirer of theatre, had kept a company of English players at his court since 1594.[9] On the Landgrave's arrival, he was accompanied by forty-eight men, all of whom stayed in Prague from April to September.[10] Johannes Meissner conjectures in his book on the English players' activities in Austria that among the accompanying servants there were the Landgrave's comedians,[11] although no direct evidence has been preserved.

Presumably the players went on from Prague to Jägerndorf in southern Silesia (Czech, 'Krnov') on the occasion of the wedding celebrations of the Duchess Eva Christine of Saxony and the Margrave John George of Brandenburg, and their performances were recorded there in June 1610. The political division of Silesia in the sixteenth and seventeenth centuries was particularly complex, owing to the fact that the region in the course of the centuries had been frequently fragmented into small duchies, and although Silesia as a whole had been Bohemia's fief since the fourteenth century (in other words, it was a part of the Empire) we may distinguish at least three families contesting the region. Traditionally a territory governed by the Silesian branch of the Polish Piast dynasty, in the early sixteenth century (after the death of most members of this large family) Silesia became the object of rival claims, first between the Czechs and the Hungarians, then between the Polish-Lithuanian Jagiellons and the Austrian Habsburgs and the Brandenburg Hohenzollerns.[12] Thus as early as 1523 the tiny duchy of Jägerndorf was bestowed as a fief upon the Margrave George Hohenzollern (of the Anspach line) by King Lodovick of Bohemia.[13] After the Margrave's death in 1543, all his possessions in Silesia, of which the Duchy of Jägerndorf was only a part, were inherited by his son, George Frederick and his successors. Therefore, it is no surprise that we find German nobles in Silesia and that they invited the English players to Jägerndorf in 1610, since both the courts in Dresden and Berlin were well acquainted with their art.

However, on the basis of documents uncovered by Hans Hartleb,[14] it appears that the players went to Jägerndorf not from Prague, but from Berlin, where they had been entertaining the court for some time before June 1610. From a letter, dated November 1609, written by the Duke of Brandenburg John George (who was the Elector's brother) to the Landgrave Maurice of Hesse, we learn that the English company under the latter's patronage had been 'lent' for some time for court performances in Berlin, and the Duke was asking the Landgrave to permit the players to stay a while longer until the ducal, i.e. his own, wedding.[15] The celebrations took place at Jägerndorf in June 1610, and a contemporary record of the performances has been preserved:

> 6 June – And after supper, a comedy from the Amadis was played by the Englishmen (who had also played before at Stuttgart).

> 9 June – In the afternoon another comedy was played by the above mentioned Englishmen.
> Sunday the 10th – After dinner a fencing-match in the palace-court, immediately after which another comedy was acted.[16]

These, indeed, may have been the 'Hessian musicians and comedians' who were recorded, eleven in number, in May 1609 at Stuttgart.[17] E. Herz in his influential study identified this company as that of Webster, Machin and Reeve who had been active together since about 1600.[18] This company numbered eighteen players when they were recorded at Frankfurt.[19] Before their Prague (?) and Jägerndorf visits the players, styling themselves 'fürstlich hessischen Komödianten und Musicanten' performed at Stuttgart (May, 1609), Ulm (May), Nördlingen (June), Nuremberg (July), and again at Ulm (August), and in Berlin (winter 1609–10).[20] In spring 1610 they emerged at Frankfurt still as 'hessischen Komödianten und Musikanten', and from Frankfurt they may have gone either to Prague, or straight to Jägerndorf.[21]

In his second letter to the Landgrave Maurice of Hesse-Kassel, dated 25 June 1610, the Elector John George expressed his gratitude for the kind 'loan' of the comedians.

> After our ducal wedding, we have ordered the English comedians Your Grace had sent to us to be dismissed, and we consider it a great honour that Your Grace has shown such kindness and sent them to us, for which we remain most thankful.[22]

The only play mentioned in the sources quoted as actually performed at Jägerndorf, the *Comedy of Amadis*, may have been a German piece: in 1587 at Dresden a play was recorded under the title *Historia von des . . . Ritters Amadiseus auss Franckreich*.[23] At any rate, the English must have made a good impression on the Hohenzollerns, for three years later the same company performed at another wedding at Anspach, that of the Margrave Joachim Ernest, the Elector of Brandenburg's uncle.[24]

More evidence has been preserved for the visit of English players to Bohemia in 1617. This company, identified as John Green's, was first recorded in March at the court of the Archduke Charles at Neisse (Polish, 'Nysa') in Silesia, after they had been recommended by the Royal court in Warsaw. Charles, who was a Habsburg and the Bishop of Breslau (Polish, 'Wrocław'), received the players kindly and although no direct evidence is available, we may assume that the players stayed at his court for some time and gave performances there. We learn about their visit from a letter of recommendation, dated 18 March 1617, written by the Archduke to Cardinal von Dietrichstein.

> The English comedians bearing this document, have respectfully requested us to give them a written recommendation to Your Eminence, and to assist them in their humble end, that it might be permitted them by Your Eminence to practise their skill and comic acting in Your Eminence's residence . . . Accordingly, we could not well refuse them the desired recommendation to Your Eminence for the salutary favour and hereby kindly request

Your Eminence to allow the same often-mentioned persons to be recommended on our part to all favour and good will, to the end that they may humbly learn, how our friendly intervention with Your Reverence may prove both agreeable and effective.[25]

The fact that Charles welcomed the players at his court at Neisse and gave them the recommendation quoted, suggests that John Green and perhaps some of his companions were Catholic. Ever since the Archduke became the Bishop of Breslau, he had been undertaking energetic actions against the Protestants in his bishopric. In 1610, for example, he prohibited public and open confessions of faith by the dissenters,[26] and fought fanatically against them throughout his life. Following the outbreak of the Thirty Years War, Charles had to flee from Neisse, and in 1619 he emigrated to Poland to return in 1622, after the Margrave John George Hohenzollern, the leader of the Protestant army in Silesia, had withdrawn his troops from the Duchy of Neisse. Charles did not learn much from the war, and until his death in 1624 continued his ruthless Counter-Reformation actions, imposing hard fines on Protestants, prohibiting Protestant services in towns, and so on. To strengthen the Catholic party in Silesia, Charles brought Jesuits to Neisse and founded their famous college there, the *Gymnasium*, in later years called the *Carolinum*.[27]

The Bishop's Palace, originally a medieval edifice, was located in the east corner of the old town (today's Grodzka Street), but owing to numerous reconstructions, remodellings, and so on, the oldest part of the palace (as it stands today) may be dated to 1615. This part, however, is of some interest to us because it was built on the order of the Archduke Charles, and accommodated a 'reception-hall'.[28] The hall was large, rectangular, and it was vaulted and richly decorated. Fragments of the ornamentation have even survived to our times. And, it seems, this 'reception-hall' was used both for official ceremonies and for entertainment, so that if the English performed at Neisse in 1617, this was probably their temporary theatre.

The company's further travels in Bohemia in 1617 were again connected with political affairs. The monarchy in Bohemia was not hereditary, but, as in Poland, elective. For two centuries the Kings of Bohemia had been, with some exceptions, Habsburgs, and in spite of constant disputes between the Catholic rulers and predominantly Protestant Estates, not to mention national differences, the Czechs followed the tradition in 1617, when on 17 June, in Prague, they elected Archduke Ferdinand King of Bohemia,[29] with Mathias (1612–19) remaining the Emperor. Thus the players, having stayed for some time at Olmütz (Czech, 'Olomounc') where the Cardinal von Dietrichstein had his residence, and having paid a short visit to Vienna, went to Prague on the occasion of the coronation of the new King, who was also the brother of their sponsor from Neisse and of the Queen of Poland. Interestingly, all the expenses involved were covered not by the newly elected King, but by Emperor Mathias. The aging Emperor like most of the

Habsburgs, was a great admirer of theatre. When, for instance, he went to Regensburg in 1613, he paid for the entertainment of two English companies there. One was that of Robert Archer, who played with his men before the Emperor on 19 September and received 20 florins for his trouble.[30] It is unusual to hear of players from countries other than England but on the following day a French comedian was paid 14 florins for his show. Then, on 24 October John Spencer was given 200 florins for performances which must have lasted for a number of days.[31] The latter fact is confirmed by another source in which it is mentioned that Spencer had played 'many wonderful plays before the Emperor Mathias'.[32] The Emperor must have been very pleased with Spencer's art, for he rewarded him with a patent which naturally helped the players in their wanderings, especially in the Catholic countries of the Empire.[33]

Thus it was no surprise that the company hired in 1617 for court performances at Prague was English. However, in the Emperor's register of expenses, there are two entries connected with performances of two distinct English companies about the same time in 1617.[34] One of these has already been identified as John Green's. And the first entry in the register of expenses tells us that on 28 July 1617 John Green of London, an English comedian, was paid 200 florins for performances given before His Imperial Majesty. The second entry, however, is not connected with Green, but with John Spencer, who on 12 August received 100 florins as a fee for his efforts at court.[35] Interestingly, there was yet another troupe performing in Prague at the same time: a company of German players under the management of one Heinrich Schmidt.[36]

That Green appeared during the celebrations following the coronation of Ferdinand as the King of Bohemia is by no means surprising, for Ferdinand had known this particular player since 1607–8 when Green performed at Ferdinand's court at Graz. Green also had letters of recommendation from the Royal court in Warsaw, and from the Archduke Charles at Neisse, and, presumably, from Cardinal von Dietrichstein who may have actually brought the company with him. But why a second company was hired remains an open question. Of course, the Emperor Mathias had known Spencer since his performances at Regensburg in 1613, and it is not unlikely that this company may have been invited to Prague by Mathias himself as a rival troupe to the one hired by the Graz branch of the Habsburgs. A sort of theatre festival may have taken place. In addition, the managers of both the companies were, it seems, Catholic, which was essential to winning the favours of the Habsburgs. The Emperor must have been particularly pleased with Spencer and his recent conversion to Catholicism. We learn about this event from an English chronicle of the Franciscan order:

Twentie fowre Stage players arrive out of Ingland at Collen, all Inglisch except one Germanian and one Dutchman. All Protestants. Betwixt those and father Francis Nuget disputation was begunne and protracted for the space of 7 or eight days consecutively: all of them meeting at one place together. The chiefs ammong them was one N. Spencer, a proper sufficient man. In fine, all and each of them being clearly convinced, they yielded to the truth, but felt themselves so drie and rough hearted, that they know not how to pass from the bewitching Babylonian harlot to their true mother the Catholic church, that always pure and virginal spouse of the lamb.[37]

The event aroused much interest and was even recorded in local chronicles at Cologne,[38] but it remains an open question whether the conversion was serious, or whether it was a cunning policy of the players to win the favours of Catholic magistrates of that city and elsewhere on the Continent.

Perhaps another reason for employing Spencer for performances in Prague was that his company offered a different sort of entertainment from that of Green's troupe. Spencer specialised in music and dances and in spectacular shows, requiring elaborate scenery, rich costumes and numerous stage properties.

However, it is not certain that Spencer was paid for performances actually given at Prague. Pieces of evidence uncovered by Johannes Meissner show beyond doubt that the Emperor left Prague at the end of July 1617 and went, accompanied by King Ferdinand, to Dresden where he stayed until about the middle of August.[39] This could suggest that the payment made on 12 August was connected with Spencer's performances given before the Emperor at Dresden. But, as is apparent from other extant records, a separate payment was made to Spencer in Dresden, where on 19 August he received 300 thalers from the Electress for the performances he had given at her court.[40] Thus, two explanations are equally plausible: one that Spencer came to Prague in July, performed there together with Green's company and accompanied the Emperor to Dresden, where he was paid by Mathias for the entertainment in Prague, and separately by the Electress for the performances at the Dresden court; or alternatively, that Spencer never came to Prague, but presented plays before the Emperor at Dresden for which he was rewarded by both Mathias and the Electress.

After his Prague visit, all trace of Green is lost for some time,[41] and it seems likely that he soon joined forces with his old companion, Robert Browne, who went on his last Continental tour in 1618.[42] About that time, Spencer was back at his former patron's court at Königsberg. In the meantime, the political situation in Bohemia was growing tense, as events led with ever-increasing speed towards the outbreak of the Thirty Years War. Generally speaking, there were two political parties in Bohemia, one supporting the Habsburgs, Spain and the Catholic League, and the other being a dissident opposition against the Habsburgs and remaining in loose alliance with the Netherlands, England, Sweden, France and the German Protestant Union. In spite of the fact that King Ferdinand, soon after his election, guaranteed the so-called Letter of Majesty, by which Protestant worship was tolerated, the Protestant party remained full of suspicion, remembering well Ferdinand's ruthless actions against dissenters in Styria. This suspicion was strengthened when in autumn following the election two edicts were issued, one of which gave the King's judges the right to be present at all local and national meetings, and the other introducing royal censorship. In this atmosphere, a trifling incident, a conflict over the erection of two Protestant churches, led to an angry outburst and consequently to an open mutiny against both the King and the Emperor. In March 1618 two meetings of Protestant officials and deputies from all over Bohemia were called in Prague. The second of these ended with the well-known siege of the royal castle of the Hradschin and the attempted murder of the two Imperial governors, Count William Slavata and Jaroslav Martinitz, who were thrown out of the castle window, but were, in fact, miraculously saved.[43] Soon afterwards, a provisional government of thirteen Directors was appointed by the Protestant assembly, and when neither political nor military solution was found, the confederate states of Bohemia, Lusatia, Silesia and Moravia declared that the election of Ferdinand was invalid and that he was no longer their king. This stern decision was made on 19 August 1619, following the death of the Emperor Mathias in March, and on 26 August the Bohemians elected their new king, the Elector Frederick of the Rhenish Palatinate who, strangely enough, was a Calvinist. Ironically, two days later at Frankfurt Ferdinand was elected Emperor, still taking the traditional place among the Electors as the King of Bohemia. It may be recalled here that the Palatine's wife, Elizabeth, was the daughter of James I and naturally the King-elect could expect both military and financial help from England, and this may have been one of the reasons why Frederick eventually accepted the Bohemian offer to become what has been known in history as the 'Winter King'. The additional irony was that a Calvinist German prince was taking the leadership of a Lutheran Slavonic rebellion against the Holy Roman Empire of the German nation represented by a Catholic Austrian.

In autumn 1619 Frederick and his beautiful wife were enthusiastically welcomed in Prague. Among the festivities following the coronation of the two, there were of course theatrical performances given by the English players who, it seems, were brave enough to cross the Bohemian border from Germany or from Poland. It is indeed difficult to understand what induced these men to take the risk. At any rate, they were determined to reach Prague for the festivities and made their way there in spite of all the dangers involved. The leader of this company was the indefatigable Robert Browne who went on his last Continental tour in 1618. He was first recorded at Nuremberg on 28 May;[44] and emerged at Strasburg in June accompanied by a company of seventeen actors, among whom we find Robert Reynolds and Robert Kingsman.[45]

We learn about Browne's visit to Prague from a later source, when the company, having left Bohemia, emerged first in February 1620 at Nuremberg,[46] and in March, at Frankfurt-on-Main.[47] In an application to the councillors at Frankfurt, signed by Robert Browne, the players offered 'beautiful new national dances and music' in addition to 'beautiful new comedies'.[48] In the application no indication is made of the players' stay in Prague, but a passage from another application submitted by a local woman, Anna Catherina Hausen, and dated 30 March 1620, tells us that the English players had recently arrived in town from Prague in Bohemia.[49] And this remains the last Continental record of Robert Browne, one of the most remarkable English players active on the Continent.

The Thirty Years War had, of course, made theatrical activities in Bohemia impossible, and only after the signing of a peace treaty at Münster in October 1648 could the players venture their fortune there. And just as in Gdańsk, when the first English company appeared in that city just one year after the end of the Polish–Swedish war in 1635, the presence of the English players was first recorded in Prague in 1649.[50] This was the same company that in 1640 received a patent from the Elector of Brandenburg, in which Reynolds, Archer, Wayde, Roe, Pudsey and Wedware were mentioned by name. Reynolds died in Warsaw about 1642, and Archer, who started his Continental career in 1608, must have been very old by that time and may have returned to England, for his name is not mentioned in any Continental records after 1640. Similarly, Pudsey and Wedware disappear from the records, and it is only John Wayde and William Roe who continued their activities overseas. Their company had become international: when Wayde and Roe visited Gdańsk in 1647, they indicated in their application to the councillors there that the troupe was composed of English, German and Dutch players. Before the Prague visit of 1649, they were mentioned together with Gideon Gellius, presumably a German actor, at the Frankfurt fair.[51] It is probable that this was the same company that visited Pressburg (Slovak, 'Bratislava') in February 1649. A record of this visit has been preserved in the municipal archives there.[52]

Wayde–Roe's company emerged in Prague again in December 1651,[53] and, fortunately, a list of plays performed by the English has been preserved. This included the following tragedies: *Tragedy of Dorothea*; *Tragedy of a Cruel and Unheard of Murder in Spain* (*The Spanish Tragedy?*); *Julius Caesar*; *The King of Rhodes*; *Doctor Faustus*; *The Jew of Malta*; and comedies: *The Prodigal Son*; *The King of Cyprus and the Duke of Venice*; *Orlando Furioso*; and several others.[54] We learn about their presence in Prague from a memorial the players wrote to the Royal Stadtholder in that city, carrying the date 15 December 1651, in which the English complained that:

at the lately issued gracious prohibition of your Most Noble Excellency and Grace we have ceased to play, and in as much as the maintenance of the company costs a great deal we have incurred no small expense, thus besides this, a great part of our clothes and property had been previously stolen and lost.[55]

In their plea, the players further asked for leave to play for four additional days, and declared in conclusion that, formerly in Vienna, they had performed even during Lent, before Cardinal von Dietrichstein and the

Archduke Leopold of Austria (i.e. the future Emperor Leopold I, 1657–1705). It may be recalled here that in November 1650 the same company received the Emperor's patent, which indicates that the players enjoyed the Habsburg patronage again during that period. This may in fact have been the Archduke Leopold's company, active since about 1649.[56] The complaint of the players met with a favourable reply, granting them leave to play, and a few days later the English asked the authorities for permission to play for three more weeks after the forthcoming Christmas holidays, giving their approaching departure for Vienna as the reason for their request. Interestingly, in this application, the players remarked by the way that: 'two masters among our company are devoted to the Roman Catholic religion, and that we in other respects also use all decency both in words and actions'.[57]

An isolated reference to the English players' presence in Prague in 1658 is the last of the known sources for their activities there. This may have been Wayde–Roe–Gellius' company again, or rather what was left of it, and we learn of it from a decree of the magistrates, dated 10 May 1658, in which it was ordered that the authorities had to be notified of all the strangers passing through or stopping over in Prague. In the decree, examples were provided to prove that this rule had not been observed by owners of inns and other persons of this kind. One was that the envoy of the King of Poland had passed through the town without the authorities being notified; the other was that 'some comedians, called the English, undoubtedly heretics, have for a long time been staying here': about which, again, the authorities were not informed.[58] According to another source, referred to in a recent history of Czech theatre, these comedians, 'called the English', were indeed English, and they presented to the citizens of Prague *Romeo and Juliet* among other plays. A contemporary account tells us that 'Pickleherring was excellent and very funny'.[59] Of course, this 'Pickleherring' should not be identified with Robert Reynolds, who was dead by 1642, but with a stage-type originally created by George Vincent and Reynolds.

It must have been the same company that visited Breslau (Polish, 'Wrocław') in Silesia in August 1658. A record of the players' performance there, neglected in major scholarship on the subject, is to be found in a diary of Elias Maior (1588–1669), who was the Rector of the *Elizabeth Gymnasium* in Breslau.[60] The diary, written in Latin and preserved in manuscript in the former city library, now the University of Wrocław Library, begins on 1 January 1640, and under 1658 includes the following entries:

> 22 August – some English players have come here, and presented tragedies, not known to me, in the roofed house under the golden eagle.
> 23 August – The English players acted for the second time.
> 24 August – The English players acted for the third time.[61]

This remains the last record of English companies active in Bohemia.

8 Austria

THE first recorded visit by the English players to Austria took place in 1607 and was, of course, sponsored by the Habsburgs: strictly speaking by the Styrian branch of the family with their residence at Graz (Illustration 11). The earliest reference to the presence of the English at the Graz court is a payment order signed by the Archduke Ferdinand, later Emperor Ferdinand II (1578–1637). Ferdinand was the eldest son of the late Archduke Charles (1540–90), and in accordance with the Habsburg internal settlement was the head of this branch of the family.

We have graciously ordered 300 Reichsthalers to be graciously given as payment to those particular English comedians who came here following our gracious wish and who have several times presented their comedies for our gracious pleasure.[1]

The above entry is dated 11 November 1607; on the 19th, a performance by the English players was mentioned in a letter from the Archduchess Maria Anna, Ferdinand's first wife, to her husband who had left Graz for Regensburg eight days earlier. In the letter, the Archduchess indicated that the English had presented on that day a comedy about 'the King of England who was in love with a goldsmith's wife'.[2] Again, no names are given which would help us to identify the company, but since the Archduchess used the plural form 'die engellender' we can at least be certain that it was a whole company of players performing at Graz, and not a single actor (as suggested by the payment order).

Ferdinand, having left Graz on 12 November, was in no hurry, and stopped in several towns on the way to Regensburg. One of these was Passau, where Ferdinand's younger brother, Leopold, Bishop of Passau, had his residence. It seems that the players, having given their last performance at Graz on 19 November, followed Ferdinand. Their presence was recorded at Passau sometime between 19 and 28 November, and we know that they presented two comedies there. One of these was *The Prodigal Son*, the other, *A Play of a Jew*,[3] which could either be Shakespeare's *The Merchant of Venice*, or Marlowe's *The Jew of Malta*. At present, no evidence is available to determine whether the players followed the Archduke to Regensburg, or whether the company returned to Graz.

At any rate, a contemporary account tells us that the English players were certainly back at Graz in February 1608, and performed a number of plays at the court there. Detailed information about these performances is included in one of the most interesting first-hand accounts of English theatrical activities on the Continent, a letter written by the Archduchess Maria Magdalena

11. A view of Graz showing the archducal Castle

(1589–1631) to her brother the Archduke Ferdinand, who apparently was at that time still at Regensburg. The letter is dated 20/22 February 1608 and in 1974 was published in a new English translation by Irene Morris.

[20 Feb.] . . . But I must tell you, too, about the English players and the plays they gave. Well, after they arrived on the Wednesday after Candlemas, they recovered from the journey on the Thursday, and began on the Friday with *The Prodigal Son*, the same play as they had performed at Passau; this was followed on the Saturday by *The Godly Woman of Antwerp*, truly a very good and proper play. On the Sunday they performed *Doctor Faustus*, and on Monday a play about a Duke of Florence who fell in love with a nobleman's daughter, on Tuesday they gave *Nobody and Somebody* – that was vastly agreeable. *Fortunatus and his Purse and Wishing-cap* was also very enjoyable on the Wednesday; on Thursday they gave another of the plays they had performed at Passau, the one about the Jew, and on the Friday they and ourselves all had a good rest . . . On Shrove Sunday the cooks had their holiday, so we had dinner at five o'clock and in the evening the English players gave another performance: this was about two brothers, King Louis and King Frederick of Hungary – terrifying play with King Frederick stabbing and murdering everybody non-stop; on Shrove Monday they acted another play about a King of Cyprus and a Duke of Venice and that was very enjoyable . . . After the performance [given by the Jesuits] we again had dinner at five o'clock and the English players gave another play about the Rich Man and Lazarus. I cannot tell you, my dear, how pleasurable that was, not the least little bit of love-making in it, and we were all deeply moved they had acted it so well. There is no doubt about it, they really are good actors.[4]

Even though no names of players are given in the Archduchess' letter, the titles of plays she referred to make the identification of this otherwise unspecified company possible. Of the eleven plays mentioned, seven are included in an extant list of plays performed in 1626 by John Green's company at Dresden:[5] *The Duke of Florence, Nobody and Somebody, Doctor Faustus, Fortunatus, The Jew of Malta, The Duke of Venice* and *The Prodigal Son*. Before his Graz visit, Green had already been recorded on the Continent as one of the leading players of the Landgrave Maurice of Hesse-Kassel.[6] In August 1606 he emerged at Frankfurt-on-Main, accompanied by Robert Browne and Robert Ledbetter;[7] in March 1607 he was still with Browne at Kassel (this time Ledbetter's name does not appear in the records), where the 'Hessian comedians' offered a comedy about 'the King of England and the King of Scotland'.[8] In July the company was recorded at Elbing, and a month later in Gdańsk.

The extant repertoire of the troupe that performed in February 1608 at Graz, has made its identification possible as John Green's company, as other pieces of evidence confirm. For instance, in the well-known letter that the Archduke Charles wrote in March 1617 to Cardinal von Dietrichstein, recommending a company of English players who had arrived from Warsaw with good testimonials from the Royal court, we find the following passage:

When we remember that, during the life-time of our late most beloved lady mother of high honoured and praiseworthy memory, just these same persons have performed their comedies at Graz, quite honourably and decently, always to our most gracious pleasure and satisfaction.[9]

The mother of the Styrian branch of the Habsburgs, the Archduchess Maria, died in 1608, which leaves no doubt that this was a reference to the performances in 1607–8 at Graz.

There is yet one more piece of evidence that this was in fact John Green's company. In a postscript to the quoted letter of Maria Magdalena, dated 22 February, the Archduchess meticulously described a local incident, in which one of the English players, 'the one with long red hair who always played the little fiddle',[10] killed a Frenchman in a duel, and was himself badly wounded.[11] And in the lodging-list of Green's men in Saxony in 1626 one of the players, perhaps Green himself, was entered as 'der Roth-kopff', i.e. 'the red-head'.[12] This may have been coincidental, but fortunately the remaining pieces of evidence leave no doubt as to the company's identity. A manuscript copy of the German version of *Nobody and Somebody* has been preserved, in which we find a Latin dedication of the play to the Archduke Maximillian who was present at Graz at the time of Green's visit there.[13]

The performances of the English are also referred to by the Graz court doctor, one Hippolyt Guarinomi, in his book on man's pleasures and ribaldry, among which the doctor distinguished 'comedies and tragedies and plays'.[14]

This kind of play for the eyes and for the ear can be found today in Germany, and I have myself seen these comedians coming from the Dutch and English towns, wandering from one place to another, presenting their amusing farces and jugglery, without, however, paying any taxes on the money collected from those who wish to see and hear them – insofar, that is, as they can make themselves understood in German and by using gestures.[15]

This was published in 1610, and the author's last comment suggests that the English players' knowledge of German was still not impeccable by that time.

Having performed at Graz in February 1608, Green's company left Austria and, presumably equipped with a letter of recommendation, headed for another Habsburg country, the Spanish Netherlands. We learn about this from various pieces of evidence uncovered by H. R. Hoppe[16] and, more recently, by W. Schrickx.[17] That Green was no longer the manager of the 'Hessian comedians' early in 1608 is proven by an application of the Landgrave Maurice's men, dated 3 March 1608, and signed by Ralph Reeve who, apparently, had taken over the leadership of the company by that time.[18] It is, therefore, possible that after the Graz visit, the company split into two separate troupes, one of which returned to Kassel to enjoy the patronage of their lord, the Landgrave Maurice of Hesse, whereas the other was inclined to accept the new patronage of the Habsburgs and went to the Spanish Netherlands. Green continued his activities and provided entertainment for the Spanish branch of the Habsburgs until about 1615, when he reappeared in Wolfenbüttel (May) and in Gdańsk (August). He emerged in Gdańsk again in the following year and, as mentioned above, came to Bohemia via Warsaw and Neisse, and took part in the celebrations connected with the coronation of the Archduke Ferdinand as the King of Bohemia.

During the players' travels in this region of Central Europe in 1617, the company paid a short visit to Vienna, the first record of English theatrical activity in that town (Illustration 12). In 1886, Karl Trautmann suggested that the first visit to Vienna may have taken place in 1610, when the presence of some English players was recorded in Bohemia, but no evidence can be provided to support this conjecture.[19] This may seem surprising today, when Vienna has for the last two or three centuries been considered the unrivalled cultural centre of this part of the Continent, or even at times of the whole Continent, but in the first half of the seventeenth century Vienna was still a relatively small provincial town, overshadowed by the splendour and size of Prague, which until the outbreak of the Thirty Years War was the capital of the Holy Empire of the German Nation. We learn about the English players' first visit to Vienna from a later piece of evidence, namely, an application of one of Green's companions who in 1620 was recorded as the manager of a company in Frankfurt-on-Main. This 'Komedianten Meyster' stated that he had in 1617 'played for the gracious and noble lords at Vienna', and while still together with Green had played also on some later occasion at Frankfurt.[20] This enables us to reconstruct the players' route in 1617: in March they reached Neisse from Warsaw; left Neisse during the same month and, carrying the Archduke's recommendation, went to Olmütz (Czech, 'Olomounc'), where they stayed at Cardinal von Dietrichstein's court. Later, they accompanied the Cardinal to Vienna, performed there, and reached Prague in June, just in time for the coronation.

During the Thirty Years War even the protection of noble patronage often appeared insufficient. The English players disappeared entirely from Austria for several decades, or at least no evidence has been preserved for their activities there. An isolated entry in the book of expenses of the Royal court in Warsaw, dated 13 December 1639, tells us that some players or leapers were paid for going away to Vienna.[21] It cannot be proven that the players in question were English at all, although we do know that there was an English company of players at Warsaw in 1639. There is also some indication that English players may have paid a brief visit to Vienna even earlier, in 1628. This was the company attached from about 1626 to 1631 to the court of the Elector of Saxony John George I (1585–1656), under the management of Robert Reynolds. When the company visited Strasburg in June 1628, the players, sixteen in number, in support of their application to the town councillors submitted an Imperial patent ('Passbrieff'), or passport, which indicates that the players must have performed before the Emperor earlier, though not necessarily at Vienna.[22] Incidentally, Reynolds had apparently

Univerſ:

Wien.

left the company by 1628, for the Strasburg application was signed by his former companion Edward Pudsey.

Thus the English players re-emerged in Austria only after the Peace of Westphalia had been signed in 1648, their first brief visit being recorded in 1649. We learn about this particular visit from the players' application to the councillors of Cologne, dated 2 November 1649:

> Because we have now stayed for some time at Vienna in Austria, and we recently presented at Nuremberg our comedies and actions on the subject of the beloved conclusion of peace, before many highly esteemed envoys and generals, and from thence we have come to Cologne.[23]

And in the court book of expenses for 1649 we read that this company was paid 100 guilder for performances given before the Emperor.[24] Presumably the same company paid a longer visit to the Emperor's court at Vienna in 1650. The then Emperor Ferdinand III was the son of Ferdinand II, i.e. the Archduke responsible for bringing the English players to Graz in 1607–8. In connection with the players' visit to Vienna in 1650, one most interesting document has been preserved, a patent given to the players by the Emperor himself on 10 November of that year. Since the names of players are mentioned there, the identification of this company offers no difficulty: it was the same troupe that had been active from 1640 in the Gdańsk region and also in Warsaw. The text of the patent and its English translation have already been published, but it is so relevant to the matters now under discussion that it must, however familiar, be recalled at some length.

> We, Ferdinand the third, by the Grace of God etc., publicly declare and make known to all men by means of this letter: After the bearers of these, William Roe, John Wayde, Gideon Gellius, Robert Casse and their companions, being English comedians, had most kindly given us to understand how they for a considerable time past had publicly exhibited and acted all sorts of amusing plays and entertaining comedies at the courts of various high potentates, as also at other places from time to time, humbly beseeching that we would likewise grant them our gracious permission to act such things publicly for a certain time in our Imperial residence, and we graciously granted them the said permission yet only on condition that they should entirely refrain thereby from all improprieties as well in their words as in their actions . . .
>
> Graciously regarding this their most humble and respectful petition, but more especially taking into consideration, that all the time in which we have graciously permitted them to act their comedies here in our city of Vienna, and yet more, in our Imperial court itself, they have comported themselves in such manner that no complaints have been made against them: We, with due consideration, good counsel, and right knowledge, have shown them this Imperial grace, and given them licence, that they may without hindrance publicly exercise, carry on, and use this their intended profession in all places, as well in the Holy Roman Empire as also in other of our hereditary Kingdoms, Principalities, and lands, and that they suffer no damage, impediment or confoundment from anyone, whoever he may be; however, they themselves must display all honour, and certainly refrain from all unseemly speech and actions.

This is followed by an order to nobles and magistrates of all ranks:

that they allow the said company of English comedians, together with their people, horses, and effects to pass and repass freely at all places, by water and land.[25]

It is worth noting that in 1650 it was still the behaviour of the English players that attracted most attention, and the Imperial patent was given 'regarding this their most humble and respectful petition, but more especially taking into consideration that . . . they have comported themselves in such manner that no complaints have been made against them.' Moreover, the patent is valid on condition that the players 'abstain from all unseemly speech and actions', which indicates that this also was a frequent accusation against English actors in that period. From the Imperial patent we learn that the company had also given public performances at Vienna: the first indication of such performances there.

From Vienna the players went to other places and eventually reached Prague, where they were recorded in December 1651 and from their application to the councillors there we learn that the company intended to return to Vienna after their Prague visit, early in 1652. In April 1653 an English company performed before the Emperor again, and the players' manager was the veteran actor John Wayde.[26] This means that Wayde had split up with Roe by the spring of 1653, and each of these players became managers of independent companies. It may be recalled here that Roe appeared in Gdańsk in 1654 as the leader of a company. Wayde's company, presumably enjoying the patronage of the Archduke Leopold, continued its activity for many years,[27] but it seems that in the period after 1650 relatively few of the players were actually English,[28] and the last two members of the former 'Imperial' company, Gellius and Wayde, are mentioned together in 1671.[29] Thereafter, both of these veteran players disappear from Continental records.

Although it goes beyond the scope of the present enquiry, yet another English player was active in Central Europe from about 1650; this was George Jolly who is generally considered to be the last of the great English strollers.[30] Among other places, Jolly performed in Gdańsk, and also in Vienna, where his presence was recorded in May 1653 and in 1659.[31] The first of these visits is conjectural, for on the basis of available evidence a claim has been made that the actual performances took place in Regensburg.[32] However, one of the sources connected with Jolly's activity in Central Europe provides us with a unique piece of evidence, namely, a list of players in his troupe. The preserved names are the following: 'moy' (i.e. Jolly himself), 'Samel' (Sambelain Harvey ?), 'Tom' (Thomas Knowles ?), 'Jackob' (Johann Jakob Müller), 'Burckhadt' (Burckhardt Belzer), 'Ursel' (Maria Ursula Cärer), 'HM' (Hans Martin ?), 'Wolgeha.' (Johann Wohlgehaben), 'HGE' (Hans Georg Encke) and 'Castrin' (Catharina

Faszhauer).³³ This, to my knowledge, is the first piece of valid evidence for the use of actresses in an English company active on the Continent. The same company may have visited Vienna once again in 1654, for in this year the death of Burckhardt Belzer was recorded there. And in spite of the fact that his name does not sound English, he was referred to as 'ein Engeländischer Commediant'.³⁴

In 1659 Jolly with his two principal actors, Peter Schwarz and Ernst Hoffmann, gave performances which shocked the Viennese, because they were 'spiced with the most scandalous obscenities'.³⁵ This may have been the reason why thereafter the English players are not heard of in Vienna. In 1659 Jolly styled himself an 'English and Heidelberg comedian', and offered with his companions 'such notable comedies and tragedies that the like had never been seen in Germany before, or ever acted by others'. The councillors, however, were far from enthusiastic about Jolly's appearance at Vienna, being of the opinion that

although one cannot derive any good from such comedies, and, as is well known, idleness and scandal of all sorts are only increased by them, moreover money, which any how is very scarce at present, is taken out of the country, we leave it to Your Grace's pleasure to decide whether Your Grace will advise His Imperial Majesty, that the petitioner may perhaps be allowed to practise his performances next year during the Carnival, or whether the same shall be dismissed altogether.³⁶

In 1653 Jolly acted before the Emperor at Vienna (or at Regensburg), for which he was paid 75 florins on 15 May, but on the basis of the above record, we may assume that by 1659 the ear of the Emperor had become harder to reach, the way more set about with obstacles. It may be added that again one of Jolly's actors died in Vienna: this time it was Andreas Hart.³⁷

The pieces of evidence quoted above suggest clearly that before the Thirty Years War the visits of English players to Austria were sporadic and limited to court performances only. During the War, the theatrical activity of the English ceased almost entirely, with the possible exception of one or two brief visits to the Emperor's court at Vienna. It is during the relatively short period after the peace treaty had been signed in 1648 that the English presence in Austria becomes somewhat more conspicuous, their visits more frequent, and performances were also given in public.

PART III

The theatres

An exhaustive discussion of all the theatres, both temporary and permanent, that were in use in Central Europe in the first half of the seventeenth century would demand writing a separate book. Precisely for this reason only two theatres have been selected for a brief analysis here: a public theatre in Gdańsk, called the Fencing-School, and a court theatre in the Royal Castle in Warsaw. The choice was additionally justified by two other factors: firstly, both of these theatres were the first of their kind in Central Europe, and, secondly, they were closely linked with English players' activity in the region.

The Gdańsk playhouse, erected in c. 1610, was the first permanent public theatre in Central Europe, whereas the Royal Theatre in Warsaw, built in 1637, was the first permanent court theatre in the region designed in the Italian manner and adapted for complex opera productions. Both of them illustrate clearly the major tendencies in theatre architecture of the period, one coming from England, the other from Italy, and are therefore worth closer examination. Moreover, it was in the Royal Theatre in Warsaw that English players had a first opportunity to get acquainted with the new trends in staging which were becoming the fashion.

*

9 The Gdańsk Fencing-School

IN what follows I present pictorial and written evidence for an early seventeenth-century playhouse built in the city of Gdańsk, a playhouse which is reminiscent of and perhaps modelled on London's Fortune theatre.[1] The engraving showing the Gdańsk theatre (Illustration 3) is attributed to a Dutch artist, Peter Willer, who included it in his cycle of illustrations made for the first written history of Gdańsk by Reinhold Curicke.[2] This was written in 1645, but, due to a conflict with censors, was not published until 1687. Since Willer was active in Gdańsk from 1664, the engraving must have been made sometime between 1664 and 1687. However, the evidence available shows us that the playhouse was built much earlier.

The Gdańsk theatre is first mentioned in documents on 30 May 1600, i.e. several months after the Fortune contract had been signed in London, when one Conrad Heidemann[3] made application to the City Council for permission to build a 'Fencing-School' ('Fechtschule') in which, apart from fencing exercises, other performances ('allerley Schawspill') would also take place.[4] However, this astonishing coincidence of dates cannot lead us to suspect that it is Conrad Heidemann who was responsible for the actual erection of the theatre, for we have no proof that his project of 1600 was the same as was realised later on, since he was not given a permit in that year and, to my knowledge, is not mentioned in any theatrical documents again. The first evidence of theatrical performances in the Fencing-School comes from 1612, which means that the theatre must have been erected sometime between 1600 and 1612.[5]

Although the resemblance of the Gdańsk theatre to the Fortune – as described in the builder's contract – is striking, it remained unnoticed until recent years.[6] Thus, our second task will be to establish how this typically English theatrical form made its way as far as Gdańsk, and to establish the cultural background of such an unprecedented and peculiar 'import' of an architectural concept.

Let us begin with the engraving proper (Illustration 3), which shows the south-western corner of the Main City, which was the centre of old Gdańsk, with the object of our interest in the foreground. Behind the theatre some municipal buildings are shown (thus the engraving is entitled 'der Stadthoff'); these were erected by Jerzy Strakowski in the 1620s and are described in Curicke's book. The towers (which were built in the second half of the fourteenth century) are the remains of a medieval defence system. All of these, with the exception of the theatre, have survived to our times.

Unfortunately, Willer's engraving remains the only known pictorial evidence for the Gdańsk theatre; this is readily accounted for by the fact that the building adjoined a huge military defence system that encircled the city, and on numerous views and panoramas it is simply concealed by one of the bastions.[7]

The theatre itself is a wooden structure erected on what seems to be more solid foundations, presumably made of stone, which, as in the Fortune contract, are 'wroughte one foot of assize att the leiste aboue the grounde'. The frame consisting of four wings encloses an inner open yard and is covered with a single-slope roof, which leads to the suspicion that the galleries were not very deep (they were $12\frac{1}{2}$ feet deep in the Fortune). It seems probable that, as in the Fortune, the frame roof in the Gdańsk theatre was tiled, especially in view of the fact that tiles are clearly marked on the right wing.

The roof above the front façade bears a diagonal Latin inscription, which is somewhat puzzling. The first five letters are clearly visible: 'AVDII', but what follows is not easy to decipher. At first glance the first letter seems to be a 'w' – non-existent in Latin, and therefore it is more likely that it stands for double 'v', followed by an 'E'. Thus, we obtain 'AVDII VVE', which undoubtedly is an abbreviation of a sentence. My suggestion is that the inscription stands for 'AVDII VERBUM VERITATIS', meaning 'I listened to the word of truth', which denotes the theatrical function of the building. Another possible explanation of 'AVDII VVE' is that it stands for 'AVDI IBI VERBA ET VOCES EXEMPLARIA' meaning 'Listen there to the words and voices as an example [of life]', which is an echo of Seneca's *Epistulae morales* 108.6: 'Quidam veniunt ut audiant, non ut discant, sicut in theatrum voluptatis causa ad delectandas aures verbo et voce vel fabulis ducimur.'[8] Probably this inscription was not on the roof of the actual theatre, and it is more likely that this is a 'comment' made by the artist himself.

The strange-looking projecting element on the righthand side of the roof is a chimney constructed in 1646 when heating was installed in a special compartment of the gallery for the Queen, Maria Ludvica Gonzaga, wife of Vladislaus IV, when in February an Italian opera was staged there in her honour as a part of celebrations to welcome her to Gdańsk.[9]

A large wooden double gate, reinforced with iron hinges and opening outwards forms the main entrance to the Gdańsk theatre. The same arrangement is quite possible in the Fortune for no evidence can be provided for the actual location and form of its main entrance. The front façade of the Gdańsk theatre, made of vertical wooden boards, is supported by a system of seven buttresses, but it is not certain whether these were erected according to the builder's plan or, what seems more likely, whether they were added afterwards when there was a danger that the building might collapse. The number of buttresses on both sides of the main entrance is not equal, for we have four on the left-hand side and three on the right, where the corner buttress is for some reason missing. This could have been caused either by the artist's omission or by the fact that this part of the façade was sufficiently supported by the adjoining building.

The staircases are not visible on Willer's engraving, which leads us to suspect that they were incorporated into the frame. The Fortune contract states that the 'steares' are to be constructed in the same way as those at the Globe, and in view of the available evidence most reconstructors have insisted that the latter must have been attached to the frame, not incorporated into it. The lack of windows in the Gdańsk theatre is not surprising, and we have no evidence about whether there were any in the Fortune, apart from 'windows and lightes glazed to the saide Tyreinge howse'. There is also no hut, but again we do not have evidence for one in the Fortune.

Although the whole frame has a somewhat trapezoid shape it is not unlikely that it may in fact have been rectangular, or even square, if we take into consideration some inaccuracies in perspective and the presumed attempt of the artist to show as much of the interior as possible. Thus, he managed to show the top gallery for spectators in the two wings of the frame, one opposite the main entrance (which is backed by a pitched roof of a building behind the theatre) and the other adjoining it on the left-hand side. The shape of these galleries recalls both the pictorial evidence we possess of London theatres and their reconstructions. It is worth noting that the lower part of the galleries is equipped with solid barriers instead of railings and are surmounted by lambrequin ornamentation, i.e. with their lower edge scalloped.

In order to explain other features of Willer's engraving, we have to look for some other sources of information. Not much, for instance, can be said about the actual size of the playhouse and we can only deduce its measurements from the height of the people standing nearby: a calculation which, of course, cannot be accurate. Besides, the number of galleries is not certain. One of the courtiers accompanying the Queen to the performance in February 1646, Jean Le Laboureur, wrote a brief but nevertheless interesting description of the theatre,[10] in which he noted that it was a wooden structure, with several galleries for spectators ('avec plusieurs galleries'), some of whom stood in the yard, around the stage, which was also a common custom in London theatres. He also provides us with a striking piece of information, estimating the number of spectators as 3,000, which is exactly the same as that recorded by De Witt when he visited the Swan in 1595, and confirmed by the Spanish ambassador who visited the Second Globe in 1624. Given the number of spectators, we can come to the general conclusion that, even if the capacity of the theatre is exaggerated (as it could well be in the case of the Swan and the Second Globe), the Gdańsk theatre was similar in size to a 'typical' London playhouse. Although the number of galleries is not mentioned, the quoted 'plusieurs' means more than two. However, as is noted by C. Walter Hodges,[11] the word could have been used in reference to galleries on several sides of the building, irrespective of how many tiers of galleries there were in the vertical dimension. In spite of this ambiguity, Mr Hodges is inclined to guess, and I agree, that there were indeed three galleries, as shown on the conjectural reconstruction of the theatre (Illustration 4). This is also confirmed by some further evidence, namely late seventeenth- and eighteenth-century theatrical posters, which are now in the collection of the Polish Academy of Arts and Sciences in Gdańsk. From them we learn that the auditorium of the theatre was divided into sections and that different prices were charged accordingly. Thus, a seat in a 'loge' costs 1 'Tympff'; in the 'parterre', 1 guilder; for 'other seats' ('andern Platz') one had to pay 18 groschen; for a gallery, 12 groschen; and for the 'last seats' ('letzten Platz') 6 groschen:[12] these last three seem to indicate the existence of three tiers of galleries.

The number of rows of benches in each gallery is also not certain. The only evidence I have come across is a note that in 1695 three rows were dismantled in order to accommodate a special compartment for an orchestra. To sum up, in the highly conjectural reconstruction of the frame of the Gdańsk theatre (Illustration 4) I suggest three storeys of galleries, approximately of the same height, of which the two lower galleries are equipped with three rows of benches each, and the top gallery with only two.

Having analysed the frame in great detail, let us now turn to some other elements of the Gdańsk theatre. Simply by looking at Willer's engraving, nothing can be said about the actual location and form of the stage and the tiring-house. As far as the location of the stage is concerned, at least two possibilities may be taken into consideration. First, that it was situated opposite the main entrance; second, that it adjoined the inner façade of the right-hand wing of the frame. It seems likely that in the period before 1646 the stage in the Gdańsk playhouse was temporary, erected *ad hoc* for performances, and therefore could have been attached to either of the two wings. In the conjectural reconstruction presented in illustration 4 it faces the main entrance. However, in 1646 elaborate machinery was installed for complex opera productions, and it seems possible that the stage of 1646 was used for later performances too. And the available evidence suggests that this stage was attached to the right-hand wing of the frame. This may be additionally supported by two factors. First, that the buildings outside the theatre, adjacent to this wing, could have been a part of the tiring-house, which was also (as shown on Willer's engraving) equipped with a separate entrance for the players. This arrangement was not unknown in the contemporary playhouses of London, which is confirmed by both written and pictorial sources. Secondly, it seems likely that the heated compartment arranged for the Queen in 1646 would have been directly below the chimney, as close to the stage as possible.

Concerning the physical conditions of the stage in the period of English players' activity in Gdańsk, we have to keep in mind that no direct pictorial evidence is available. The only indirect source known to me is an early seventeenth-century painting by an anonymous Gdańsk artist.[13] It shows an allegorical scene, which takes place on what seems to be a theatrical stage, which is equipped with a trap at the front of the stage, and curtains at the back. However, it is impossible to determine whether the Gdańsk artist had any particular stage in mind when painting his 'theatrum mundi', or whether it was simply a product of his imagination.[14] Thus, we have to rely exclusively on written sources, among which the most important are stage directions included in plays performed in Gdańsk, especially in those written by native authors for that particular stage.[15]

It should be remembered that in the first half of the seventeenth century, Gdańsk was not only the largest and wealthiest city in this part of the Continent, but also that it was an important cultural centre, with literary and theatrical circles founded by scholars and students of the Academic Gymnasium, poets and playwrights. Owing to the fact that Gdańsk was a multi-national city, literature was written there in a number of languages, above all in Latin, German and Polish. Unfortunately, most of the plays staged at the Gdańsk theatre are known only by their titles or by the names of their authors; only a few seventeenth-century dramas written to be staged in that theatre have been preserved, either in print or manuscript.

But in spite of this scarcity of material, some useful information may be gathered from an analysis of stage directions in the extant plays. For instance, in an anonymous Polish play *Tragedia o bogaczu y Łazaru* (*A Tragedy of a Rich Man and Lazarus*) written in 1643,[16] we find a number of interesting facts provided by the text. Actors made their entrances and exits through the door, or doors, which are mentioned several times. Simple stage properties were used, such as a bed, a table, chairs; music was played and a trumpet blown. Some sort of machinery must have been used, since we encounter entries like: 'Angels take Lazarus's soul to the bosom of Abraham', and there must have been at least one trap, in this case leading to the 'abyss'. The stage may have also been equipped with a place for concealment since in one of the entries the actors are directed to 'hide and whistle'.

Summing up, we may conclude that the stage of the Gdańsk theatre was presumably (at least, before 1646) a removable raised platform, erected *ad hoc* before the performance just as, for instance, in the Hope theatre. It was probably arranged in similar way as in London theatres, i.e., projecting into the yard and at the back adjoining the tiring-house façade. It must have been reasonably large and equipped with at least one trap, a place for concealment, and some sort of machinery.

In spite of the fact that the stage of the Gdańsk theatre may have differed in detail from that of the Fortune, the general resemblance the theatre bears to the Fortune is remarkable. This seems to have been recognised by contemporaries. When in June 1619 a company of English players came to Gdańsk, in their application to the City Council, the players referred to the building as 'publicum theatrum', which is a Latinised version of the characteristically English form, 'a public theatre'. There is little doubt that the players had in mind not only the fact that the theatre was 'public', but also that its architectural form was reminiscent of the theatres they had known back in London. And it may be recalled here that the leader of this particular company was Richard Jones, a former Lord Admiral's man, who had performed in the Fortune until 1602. However, owing to the fact that in the seventeenth century the building also functioned as a fencing-school, in most documents quoted elsewhere in this book it is referred to as a 'Fechtschule'. In a relatively puritan city like Gdańsk, there had to be not only a moral pretext for erecting a permanent theatre, but also an economic one: officially theatrical performances could only take place during the St Dominic's Fair in August. This rule, of course, was not always observed and plays and operas were staged occasionally throughout the whole year. For instance performances of various plays were recorded in February 1629, June 1631, September 1636, February 1646, January 1648, and so on.[17] Besides fencing exercises and tournaments, animal baiting took place there, another feature shared by some London playhouses, with the Hope being an obvious example. It may be added, that the 'Fencing-School' was occasionally referred to as 'Theatrum', whereas in later periods it was usually labelled a 'Comedienbude'.

The fact that two theatres, obviously belonging to the same architectural type and similar in a number of details, were built almost simultaneously in two cities so far apart cannot be a matter of mere coincidence. The question remains, how did this indisputably English theatrical form make its way to Gdańsk? No doubt a number of Gdańsk citizens, merchants, travellers, and students, visited London, and obviously the London theatres were known at least to some of the members of the large English colony in Gdańsk, which in the first half of the seventeenth century was one of the largest English colonies on the Continent (totalling almost one thousand poeple). Some written evidence can be provided. For instance, the anonymous author of *Descriptio Urbis Londini in Anglia*, written in Gdańsk before 1615, mentions 'comediarum theatra' as places of interest he recommends seeing in London.[18] The idea that the missing Fortune plan was brought to Gdańsk seems too implausible to be taken seriously. The most convincing explanation in this case is that the notion of erecting an English type of theatre in Gdańsk had been suggested to its founders by the actors of the English companies, especially by those who had either performed in the Fortune itself or had close relations with the theatrical life of London and who may be traced in Gdańsk between 1600 and 1612. The erection of a theatre like this was not a complex architectural project, and an experienced carpenter would have had no difficulties with the construction, provided he was given the concept. An amateur sketch would have sufficed in this case. Any actor acquainted with the architecture of London's public playhouses would have been capable of providing such a sketch.

Among the actors dealt with in the chapter on Gdańsk, several are recorded as active in London after the Fortune had been built and a few of these visited Gdańsk in and before 1612. These were Robert Browne in 1601; John Green with Richard Jones and Robert Ledbetter in 1607, and again in 1612. Of course, it may be argued that almost all the players of the English companies active on the Continent had seen at least some of the London theatres, including the Fortune, but since there is direct evidence for the three mentioned, it could have been one of them who was responsible for providing someone in Gdańsk with detailed information about the architecture of the Fortune.

These actors were members of the Lord Admiral's company and the Fortune was their home theatre. That Poland and Gdańsk were not completely unknown to this company may be evidenced by three plays that I know of from their repertoire thematically connected with that country. The first one, *Voyvode*, for which Henslowe paid one pound to Henry Chettle on 29 August 1598, was probably, as Greg suggested, 'an old play belonging to Alleyn revised by Chettle on the occasion of its revival'.[19] 'Voivode' is a title equivalent to governor of a province in Poland, hence the country is divided into 'voivodeships'. It seems likely that the play was written after Olbracht Łaski's visit to England in 1583. Łaski was a voivode at Sieradz and was known in England as 'Alasco', and his visit aroused a good deal of interest all over England (it was described, for instance, by Holinshed and Camden).[20] The second play, *Strange News out of Poland*, was bought by Henslowe on behalf of the Admiral's men from Haughton and one 'mr Pett' on 17 May 1600. Unfortunately, nothing is known of this piece. And last but by no means least is Henry Chettle's *Tragedy of Hoffman, or a Reuenge for a Father*, which is of particular importance to us, for its action takes place in Gdańsk and is based on events from local history. On 29 December 1602, Henslowe lent 5 shillings to an actor, Thomas Downton, 'to geue vnto harey chettle in pte of payment for a tragedie called Hawghman'.[21] The plot of this piece is centred around a son's cruel revenge for the death of his father, one Hoffman, who was once an admiral, but having fallen into disgrace with the Duke, became a pirate and eventually was captured and executed. It is revealed by the Gdańsk archives that a pirate named 'Hans Hofeman' was beheaded in 1590. This must have been Chettle's source and it is possible that he learned about the tragical events in Gdańsk from the players who visited this city in or before 1602.

The 'Fencing-School' in Gdańsk functioned as the city's only permanent theatre for approximately two hundred years. Being a wooden structure it underwent numerous repairs, renovations and reconstructions. It was, for instance, repaired in 1635 and a sort of 'Lords' room' for the rich citizens was installed within the frame. In 1646 heating was installed in one of the compartments of the gallery, as mentioned above, and an Italian architect was employed to adapt the theatre to sophisticated opera productions. In 1695 three rows of benches were dismantled to accommodate a 'choir' for an orchestra. The building was repaired again in 1714, and in 1730 a roof was constructed over the whole, after which the entire theatre was heated. Around this time the theatre was described as a 'Bear Garden' by an English merchant, who, in his description of Gdańsk, wrote that it was 'a large Are[n]a for the Baiting of Bulls, Bears and wild Beasts, Amphitheatre-like, capable of containing a vast Number of Spectators, strongly inclosed with Wood, and having convenient Galleries for that Purpose, one above another'.[22] The theatre's condition was appalling by the end of the eighteenth century and Joanna Schopenhauer, the philosopher's mother, complained in her memoirs that it looked like a shed rather than a theatre. It was repaired again in 1795, but this did not help much. It was last mentioned in 1809 and the playhouse was presumably dismantled afterwards since a new theatre had been built by Carl Samuel Held and on its site a synagogue was soon erected which did not survive the Nazi era.[23]

The Gdańsk public theatre, erected within the first twelve years of the seventeenth century, seems to be a unique example of an English theatrical model implanted in a foreign country. It bears a number of features in common with the London playhouses, and we may say that the origin of its architecture is probably to be sought in London's Fortune. Both of these theatres were wooden structures, similar in shape, containing three storeys of galleries, which were built round an open inner yard which accommodated both the stage and some of the spectators, and their capacity (i.e. the actual size) was, if not the same, not very different. They were built almost simultaneously, shared some of the actors (who seem to have been responsible for bringing the idea and architectural details to Gdańsk) and a number of the same plays were staged in both of these theatres. The congruity of the Gdańsk theatre as shown on Willer's engraving with some of the features of the Fortune as described in the contract enables us, with some restrictions, to incorporate this engraving into the meagre file of the pictorial evidence for the Elizabethan and Jacobean theatre architecture.

10 The Royal Theatre in Warsaw

PREPARATIONS for the erection of a permanent theatre within the Royal Castle in Warsaw were first recorded in July 1637 by the nuncio M. Filonardi in his message to Cardinal F. Barberini.[1] From about that time the theatre was sometimes referred to as 'sala del teatro'. Vladislaus IV, a great admirer and connoisseur of opera and theatre, had long entertained the notion of having a real court theatre of his own, designed according to the newest developments in theatre architecture and equipped with modern and elaborate stage machinery, changing scenery, etc. Vladislaus was well acquainted with the newest trends in theatre design, and had seen a number of theatres in Italy – at that time the leading country in this field. From 1628 operas were staged in the Royal Castle in Warsaw,[2] but all the necessary arrangements were temporary and were prepared *ad hoc* for a particular performance. It was not until 1637 that the King found a pretext which would justify the considerable expense of his project: his marriage with Cecilia Renata provided an excellent opportunity for carrying out his extravagant plans.

The actual location of the theatre within the Royal Castle has been a highly controversial issue among scholars. The variety of often contradictory opinions, always supported by seemingly valid evidence, makes a decisive conclusion difficult to reach. One of the major causes of such a conflict of opinion is the fact that the castle interiors were often reconstructed and re-modelled, and nothing survives of Vladislaus' original theatre. Besides, most of the early accounts and descriptions of the theatre are far from precise. Of the latter, the most authoritative appears to be an inventory of the castle's interior made in 1696. In this document we read that in the south wing of the castle

above the stairs, there is an oblong hall with solid doors with a good lock and with undamaged windows, as it had been before. In this hall there is a divided comedy-hall, preserved even with benches, choirs, perspectives, heavens, columns and a ceiling above the theatrum, as it used to be.[3]

That the theatre was actually located on the upper storey of the castle is confirmed by the brief account of a German spectator who saw the production of *St Cecilia* in 1637.[4] For this reason, most writers today are inclined to consider a large hall on the second storey of the south wing as the actual site of the theatre. This hall was about 48 metres long and about 12 metres wide, and the stage had a depth of 24 metres.[5] The auditorium could accommodate about one thousand spectators.[6]

The theatre was designed by an Italian architect, Agostino Locci, who may have been influenced or perhaps even ordered to base his project on the work of Lorenzo Sirigatti, *La Practica di Prospettiva* (1625), the first edition of which was dedicated by the author to 'Ladislao Sigismondo, Principe di Polonia e di Svezia'. Locci, who bore the title of 'His Royal Majesty's Engineer', may have been assisted in the whole enterprise by another Italian 'engineer', Bartolomeo Bolzoni, who was also in the service of the King, and, perhaps, by Giovanni Battista Gisleni who was the court stage-designer. It may be noted that Gisleni was the author of a project for the theatre's plafond, presumably the one mentioned in the inventory quoted above.[7] This is a rectangular design, covered with rich ornamentation and congruous with the extant description of the actual ceiling: 'And under the top the theatre has its own heavens / With clouds, seemingly bright, / The sun, the Moon and with the stars, / The heavenly planets.'[8]

The auditorium in the Royal Theatre was divided, according to court tradition into two sections, one of which was reserved for the royal couple and their guests of honour, all of whom were seated in comfortable armchairs. A contemporary account tells us that the King's chair stood on a carpet and on a white bear's skin, and that it was one of the three armchairs covered with red damask-cloth and decorated with golden fringes. And

At the back and on the sides there sat the senators and voivodes who are attached to the court, together with selected ladies, on benches covered with red cloth, whereas the remaining ladies and gentlemen watched the ballet standing.[9]

Some of the extant records, however, suggest that there were separate seats, or even compartments for the ladies, and one of the accounts tells us that the ladies watched the performance through 'the windows'.[10] This, of course, would not be in accordance with the tradition in Italian theatres where there was no separation of the sexes.

A contemporary Polish poem describing, among other things, the Royal Theatre, mentions the following architectural details: the beautiful 'theatrum' (i.e. the stage) was built with 'perspectives' (perspective vistas?, or, perhaps, periaktoi?) and with 'columns'; the interior was lit with 'candles', and there were also 'porches' (boxes?) and double 'windows' wide enough to accommodate two persons. The poet, Adam Jarzębski who was also a professional court musician, was impressed above all by the various wonders of the changeable scenery.

The stage was designed after the Italian fashion, and was equipped with changeable scenery and periaktoi, a fact confirmed by numerous contemporary sources.[11] During Vladislaus' travels to Italy, which preceded by more than ten years his theatrical enterprise in Warsaw, periaktoi were still considered the highest achievement of theatre machinery; already in use in England, they were to be found in Italy well into the middle of the seventeenth century. Whether wings were used in the Warsaw theatre is not certain. Periaktoi were, of course, located on both sides of the stage proper and through their rotation they changed the painted perspective. That periaktoi had been known in Poland even before the Royal Theatre was built, may be demonstrated by a treatise on the subject, *De Perfecta Poesi*, written by a notable Polish poet, Casimir Sarbiewski (1595–1640). Sarbiewski studied in 1623–5 in the Jesuit *Collegium Germanicum* in Rome, and apart from the theatre in that particular college, he must have seen a number of other theatres in Italy. One of the chapters of his treatise (written c. 1626) is devoted entirely to theatre, and among other scenic devices and machines, periaktoi are mentioned. They should be constructed in the form of a prism, Sarbiewski explained, and each side of the prism should be covered with canvas

stretching from the very upper part of the stage to the floor, with a picture of a forest, painted precisely after the rules of perspective, and similarly, on the second side they all will have a perspective representation of clouds, on the third, fire; and on the fourth, palaces and buildings, and they all may be turned at the same time to one and the same side.[12]

Thus, the periaktoi in the Warsaw theatre flanked the stage, and the back of the stage was concealed by a removable illusionistic painting, i.e. the prospect. This was changed either by rolling, simply pulling it up, or drawing it aside, and thus uncovering another painted prospect or the stage space.

It seems that all these techniques were used in Vladislaus' theatre, judging by contemporary descriptions of actual performances in the extant opera librettos. For instance, the poet Adam Jarzębski indicated in his description of the theatre that 'one painting goes down, the other goes up lifted by weights'.[13] In the libretto of *Armida*, staged in Warsaw in 1641, we read that the stage prospect 'opened', and a sea was uncovered.[14] In Virgilio Puccitelli's *La Maga Sdegnata* (1640) a rock 'changes into a palace, exposing a view of a rich vaulted hall'.[15] The use of periaktoi in the Royal Theatre is further indicated by stage directions. For instance, in *Giuditta* (first staged in 1635) we find the following entry: 'Suddenly, the stage turns on which one can see buildings, towers, churches and streets of a town'; in *Andromeda* (staged in 1644) we read that 'thus the theatrum turns from a sea into a royal palace'; and a contemporary biographer of Vladislaus IV, Everhart Wassenberg, had periaktoi in mind when he mentioned a 'versatile theatrum' in the Royal Castle.[16] In addition, some sort of a 'flying' apparatus must have been used, for in the extant librettos we encounter entries like 'Here June is seen descending in golden cart from heaven.'[17]

A detailed analysis of all the available evidence and of the architectural features of the Royal Theatre in Warsaw lies beyond the scope of the present inquiry. The Royal Theatre in Warsaw was the first of its kind in Central Europe with which English players had an opportunity to get acquainted. It may be recalled here that English companies were permanently attached to the Warsaw court in the periods ?1628–32, and 1636–42; or even longer than that. And for our purpose the most important fact is that in the latter period the players had a unique opportunity of watching Italian opera productions, performed by Italian artists. They could uncover all the mysteries of the changing scenery, illusionistic painting, complex machinery and the new techniques in staging. Employment at the court in Warsaw, apart from providing the players with a refuge during the calamitous period of the Thirty Years War, turned out to be an important theatrical experience, not without relevance to their future fortunes.

The documents

The original texts of English players' applications to the City Council in Gdańsk have been preserved in the State Archives in that city and are catalogued under two entries: 300, 36/67 and 300, 36/68. The texts reproduced below have never hitherto been published and their language form follows the originals in every detail, i.e. no attempts have been made to modernise or alter the syntax, spelling and punctuation. Every application is followed by the Council's decision, which in the original manuscripts is always recorded on the reverse side of the last page of a given application. Most of the abbreviations are explained in square brackets.

1. **English players' application of 7 June 1619; State Archives in Gdańsk: 300, 36/67, fos. 103–6**

Edle, Ehrnveste, Groszachtbare Vndt Hochweise Herrn Bürgermeister Vndt Rath, groszgünstige patronen Vndt Fürderer,
Ale Ehrnv[este] Vndt Weiszheiten geben wir endszbenante underdienstlich Zuerkennen, dasz, demenach Vnsere Compagnia Welche sich vf eine Zeit bey kön: Maijtt: in polen Verhalten, auch gegen den Winter wiederumb dachinn begeben wirdt, so Viel erlaubnusz gebeten, diese Vndt andere angräntzendt Städte in etwasz zu frequentiren damenhero wir bedacht Zukünftige Dominici Mess auch allhier Vnter, E[dle] Ehrnv[este] Vndt Weiszh. löblichen Jurisdiction Vnsere wenige qualiteten zu exerciren, teilen aber nicht allein bräuchlich, sondern an ihne selbsten recht Vndt billich, dasz E[dle] Ehrnv[este] alsz dieser hochberümbten Policey löblicher Magistrat, hierunter, Zu forderst Vmb consens begrüsset Vndt erstichet werde,
Alsz gelanget an denselben Vnsere dienstfleissige pitt, in groszgünstiger betrachtung, dasz Comoediae Vndt Tragoediae andersten nichts dann theatra morum Vndt Specula ingeniorum seindt, welche den cursum menshlicher müheseligkeiten, auch wie endtlichen Engstendt belohnet, laster aber vndt Untugendt gestraffet werden ad vivum repraesentiren, Ein Ehrnvester Hochweyser Rath wolle Vnsere Exercitia Vndt Actiones vf obbestimbte Zeit in publico theatro zu tractiren, Vnsz groszgünstig erlauben Vndt gestatten, Vnsz belangendt wollen wir unsz bester müglichkeit dachin accomodiren, damit Scandala Vermidten, Vnsere Spectatoren contentirt auch ein hochlöbliecher Magistrat inn nichtem offendiret werde, E. Ehrnvh. Vndt sl: [= seligen?] göttlichen obhalt hiemit zu Friedlichem Regiment Vndt aller glückseligen wohlfart treulich empfehlendt Vndt gewüriger Resolution erwartende.

Englische Comedianten.

[The Council's decision:]
Lect. 7 Junij An. 1619.
E.E. Radt weisz Supplicanten nicht einzuwilligen.
Act. 6 Junij Anº 1619.

2. **English players' application of 18 May 1640; State Archives in Gdańsk: 300, 36/68, fos. 45–8**

Herr Bürgermeister, Edle Ehrnveste, Namhaffte vnd Hochweise Groszgünstigste Herren,
E.E.E. Her[r]l[ich]k[eiten] werden sich danno groszgünstigst erinnern, dasz am

negsthingewichenen Dominicksmarckt bei denenselben wir bitlich angehalten haben, dasz uns, wie vor diesem zum öftern geschehen, vergönnet werden möchte, unsere Comedien der Bürgerschafft in der Stadt zu exhibiren, weil es aber damahlen E.E.E. Herlkn. wegen hin vnd her sich euszerender posto bedencklich gewesen, vnd wir dennoch die reise unkosten nicht vergeblich möchten gethan haben, hat uns die notwendigkeit gezwungen auf dem Bischoffsberge etwas auffzubauen, wiewol kaum die unkosten daselbst verdienet sein: Nach der Zeit haben wir uns bei I[hr] K[önigliche] M[ajestä]tt zu Warschau aufgehalten, vnd deroselben nach behagen vnd begeren auffgewartet, auch auf eine Zeit dimiszion erhalten, doch mit dem verschprechen, das in gewiszer Zeit wir uns wieder daselbst einstellen sollen: Sowie nun dafür dem Allerhöchsten Danck gesaget sey, Die gefahr der seuchen von dieser Stadt abgewendet worden, vnd inmittels, das unser Termin zu Hofe wieder zu erscheinen einfelt, nicht gerne müssig vnd gar notürfftigen unterhalt sein wolten, Alsz gelanget an E.E.E. Hrlkn. vnser dienstgefliszener bitten, dieselbe unsz die hohe gunst und gewogenheit erzeigen vnd nachgeben wolten, dasz wir ungefehr umb Johannis allhie unser exercitium haben, Vnd mit demselbigen die Bürgerschafft erlustigen mögen, welches das so modest und höfflich angestellet werden soll, dasz niemandt einig ergernisz darausz zunehmen sondern viellmehr allerhand Instructionis gemeinene leben zu schepfen haben wiedermaszen wir das auch erbötig saindt der bitteren hiebe nicht zu vergessen, sondern was die billigkeit immer lindern wird in acht haben. Sie wie nun aus beigefügter Recommendation ihrer K.Mtt: E.E.E. Hrlk. abnehmen können, dasz deroselben dieses unser exercitium auch in diesen Orten nicht zuwieder ist, also seint wir der Zuverlasziger Zuversicht, E.E.E. Hrlk. unserem demütigen bitten groszgünstig raum und statgeben werden, welches wir jederzeit zurühmen und mit gefliszenen Diensten zuverschulden uns wollen angelegen sein laszen.

E.E.E. Hrlk.

Dienstgeflieszene
Englische Comedianten

[The Council's decision:]
Englische Comoedianten
Lect[um] in Sen[ioribus] 18 May Anno 1640
Vnd siehet E.E. Rahtt nicht, dasz supplicanten in ihrem petitio könne gefüget werden.

3. English players' application of 16 July 1643; State Archives in Gdańsk: 300, 36/68, fos. 49–52

Herr Bürgermeister, Edele Ehrenueste Nahmhaffte, Vndt hochweise Groszgönstige Herren. E[dle] E[hrenveste] G[estrenge] Herren, E[dler] E[hrenvester] Rath dieser Löblichen weitberümbten Stadt Dantzig, haben wir die ganze Compagnia der Englischen Čommedianten, selbe bitlichen anzulangen Keinen vmbgang nehmen wollen, Sondern E.E.G. Herren ihrer vertröstung so sei vnsz vor 3 Jahren gethan erinnern wollen, Nemlichen da wir auch bittlichen E.E.G. Herl[ichkeiten] angelanget, den Plaz der Fechtschul begehret aber uns abgeschlagen worden. Nur dabey vertröstung gethan wen wir anderer Zeit wieder kommen würden, allszdas von E.E.G. Herl. diese Gunst haben, vndt vnserer bitte vielleicht gewehret werden möchten, da wir vnsz den zu der Zeit vor 3 iahren, wie auch vor 5 iaren, vnter anderer Herschafft vnsz behelffen müszen. Gelanget derowegen vnser Vnterdienstliches bitten E.E.G. Hrl. wollen günstig der unsz gethanen vertröstung eingedenck sein, Vndt in erwegung des weitten fernen weges den wir zu dieser Löblichen Stadt gethan, keine fehlbitte thuen lassen, sondern vnsz hierin ihre Gunst erzeigen, dafür wir auch wegen der armen 200 R[eichs] thal[e]r zu entrichten schuldig sein werden, welche grosze Gunst E.E.G. Hrl. E.E. Rath dieser Stadt wir mit dem klahrenn

Hertzen erkennen vndt solches hoch zu rühmen, Uhrsach haben werden, Erwarten hierauf erfrewlicher Antwortt.

E.E.G. Hrl.

Dinstgefliszene
Die gantze Compagnia der
Englischen Commedianten

[The Council's decision:]
Comaedianten
Lect[um] in Sen[ioribus] 16 July Ao 1643
Vnd will E.E. Raht supplicanten zwar in ihrem petzto gefüget haben, dasz sie ihre comodien allhier in der Stadt vier wochen land, (auszgenommen des sontages) agiren mögen iedoch dasz sie sich erbaulich verhalten v keine leichtfertigkeit vorbringen, das wen solches vermercket würde, solen sie der freyheit vnfehlbar verlustigk sein. Über dieses werden sie schuldigk sein Zum besten des Zuchthauses, so ferne nicht ein mehrs bey ihnen zu erhalten sein möchte, 200 Rthl. zu aufs geringste zu geben, vnd nicht mehr von den Zuleuten zu nehmen so wol wegen des obern als vntern sizes als zu stemen 9 fl.

4. English players' application of 15 January 1644; State Archives in Gdańsk: 300, 36/68, fos. 57–60

HochEdle, Gestrenge, Ehrenveste, Groszachtbahre, Hoch vnd Wollweise Herren Bürgermeister vnd Raht, vnser allezeit Hochgeehrte vnd Groszgustige Herren, vnd Mächtige Befonderer.
Nach dem wir vergangönen Dominick alhier in Dantzig aus L.H.E.G.L.G.G. gnädigster Zulassung eine Zeitlang agiret haben, sind wir zwar willens gewesen, vnser Reyse weiter an andere Öhrter forzustellen, solches aber ist durch einen vnvcr hofften Zufall verhindert worden, alsz das wir vns haben Zimlich geraume Zeit mit auffgehenden wielen Vnkosten alhier auffhalten müssen, (insonderheit ich, als ein Einwohner dieser löblichen Stadt, mit Weibe, Kindern vnd gesinde), auch nun, mehro vnser Reyse in dieser Winterszeit, weder Zu wasser noch zu lande anders wohin wenden oder richten Können, alder wir bey solchen grossen Auszgeben, wiederumb ein wenig erwerben möchten; So wehren wir gesonnen itziger Zeit Wegen fasznacht noch eine Zeitlang alhier offendlich Zu agiren. Dieweil aber solches ohne erlaubnüs vnd nachgeben L.I I.E.G.L.G.G. nicht gechehen mag, Als gelanget an E.H.E.G.E.G.G. vnser gantz Vntähnigstes bitten vnd ersüchen, E.H.E.G.E.G.G. wollen vns mit der hocherwünshten Freyheit begaben, dieses vnser vorhaben ins Werck Zu stellen Vorgönnen, vnd Vns die Woche E.H.E.G.E.G.G. beliebung nach 3 oder 4 mahl noch Zu agiren Gnädigst erlauben. Hiermite Verobligiren wir vns, E.H.E.G.E.G.G. vor diese hohe Gnade vnd Gunst, nebenst einem aleZeit danckbahr bereiteten gemühte, den 4 [ten] vnserer einnahme willig vnd dienstlich darzureichen, vnd Zu vberlieffern, wollen vns auch befleissen solche grosse an vns erwiesene Woltaht der pflichtschuldigckeit nach allezeit wiederumb, vermöge vnser Wenigkeit Zu Verschulden vnd Zu werdienen.

[The Council's decision:]
Comediant. EE Rhat Hielt bedenklich den supplicanten zufugen.
Act in Sen: 15 January Ao 44.

5. English players' application of 29 July 1644; State Archives in Gdańsk: 300, 36/68, fos. 61–4

Woledle Gestrenge Ehrenveste Hoch: vndt wolweise Groszgünstige Herren, demnach wir

Englische Comaedianten disz Jahr aber mit agirung unserer Comaedien in Rüege vndt Königsberg zugebracht, vndt nunmehr zu Elbing angelanget, Auch ferner entschlossen, vnsere Reise nach dieser löblichen Stadt Danzigk zu nehmen. Vnd weil wir 18 personen starck, vndt etwas neues zu Ehrenn E[uer] wole[dlen] G[estrengen] E[hrenvesten] He[rren] vnd der löblichen Bürgerschafft sonderlicher recreation zu agiren gesonnen, Alls haben wir zu forderst E. wole. H. G. He. hiermit vnderdienstlich ersuchen vndt bitten wollen, Sie geruehen groszgünstig, vns zu vergönnen, das wir den Domnic aber auf dem gewöhnlichen Plaz der Fecht Schule, wie vor diesem geschehenn, vmb ein leidlichen accord wiederumb agiren mögen, Solches wie es E[uer] wole[dlen] Ge[strengen] E[hrenvesten] He[rren] zu sonderlichem Ruhm vnndt Ehre gereichet, seindt wir es mit vnseren willigsten Diensten nach vestem Vermögen hinwiederumb zu verschulden stets geflissen. Dieselbe hiermit Göttlichem Schuz empfehlend vnd guter resolution dienstlich erwartend.

E[urer] wole[dlen] Ge[strengen] E[hrenvesten] He[rren]

Vnderdienstwillige
Sembtliche Englische Comaedianten
izo in Elbing sich aufhaltend.

[The Council's decision:]
Comaediantenn.
Lect[um] in sen[ioribus] 29 July Ao 44.
Vnd siht EE Raht nicht wie den supplicanten in ihrem ansuchen ullo modo zufügen sey. Sollen demanch ernstlich ermahnet werden sich nicht zu erdreusten am königlichen Artusshofe vnd an den Thören irkeine scarteken oder Intimationes zu affigiren, bey harter preng.

6. English players' application of 5 August 1647; State Archives in Gdańsk: 300, 36/68, fos. 67–70

Herr Praesidfrender Bürgermeister, Wolledle, Gestrenge, Hoch- Vnd Wollweise Herren, E.E. H[err]l[ichkeiten] seind Vnsere Vnterthenigste Dienste bevor; Verhalten daneben Einem Ehrenvesten Hochweisen Raht hiemit Supplicando nicht, wasmaszen wir mit Vnsern Collegis aus Engelland, Niederland Vnd deutschen Hanse Städten an diesen weitberümbten Ort der Königl[ichen] Stad Dantzigk (:nach ausgestandener Meeresgefahr:) angelanget, In der Hoffnung Einen Hochweisen Raht, Vnd die Liebe Bürgerschafft in dieser Dominicks zeit, Vnserer Profession nach, mit newen Vnd Vorhero niemals gehabtenen Comöedijs zu erlustigen.

Wann dann nun aus allen historiend bekand, das etzlichen Comicis (:welche mit nützlichen Lehren Vnd historien dahin trachten Vnd richten, das man daraus sehe, wie man allerhand Laster meiden, Vnd sich dargegen der Jugend Vnd erbarkeit im Leben Vnd wandel befleissigen soll:) so woll wegen ihrer Kunst, als ihrer Jugend halben, grosze ehre, auch offentlich erzeiget worden, wie Vnter andern zu sehen ist beim Macrobio lib. 3 Satunal. Der andern, als Terentij, Plauti, Senecae, Naevij, Coelij, Menanari, Euripidis, Aeschijli u. a. zugeschweigen.

Als gelanget hiemit an E.E.H[err]l[ichkeite]n Vnser Vntertheniges bitten, dieselbe wollen groszgönstig geruhen, Vns in dieser Dominicks Zeitt, da iederman gerne Lust Vnd ergetzlichkeit suchet, zu vergönnen, das wir alhie gutte, nützliche, Vnd dabey angenehme Comödien agiren Vnd halten mögen. Vnd dieselbes an Ort vnd stelle, da E.E.Htn. Vns anzuweisen belieben werden. Es sey auff der Fechtschule, auff der Wage, auffm Schieszgarten, oder sonsten.

Dagegen wir nicht allein erbötig sein, E.E.Htn. zu Vntertenigsten Diensten zu leben, sondern auch deswegen einen billigen recompens zu geben. Dieselbe gesampt Vnd besonders des Allerhöchsten gnedigem Schutz, zu friedsamer Vnd glücklicher Regierung Vnterthenigst empfehlend.

E[inem] Woll Edl[en]
Gestr[en]g[en]
Vnterthenigste
Johan Waide
Vnd
Wilhelm Roh
für sich vnd in nahmen ihrer Consorten

[The Council's decision:]
Supplicatio
Englische Comaedianten
Lect[um] in Sen[ioribus] die 5 August 1647
Vndt hatt ein Hochweiser Rath geschlossen, dasz die Comoediantes auf drey wochen auf der Fechtschulen zu agiren soll vergönnet sein, ein gewisses aber dem Zuchthause deswegen abtragen. Dabei dan wirdt ihnen diese commination angehenz sein, dasz sie sich von allen vnhöflichen dictis et factis gentzlich werden enthalten müssen, vndt in allem die erbar Seitt observiren. Im gegentheil soll ihnen das Agiren bald verbothen sein vnderdessen so Sie erleget, auch verlustig[des] Landt[es] werden; der Sontag soll aber damitt eingestellet sein.

7. English players' application of 29 October 1649; State Archives in Gdańsk: 300, 36/68, fos. 71–4

Hoch Edle, Veste, Groszachtbare, Hochgelährte, und Hochweise Herren, Herren Bürgermeister und Raht,
Insbesonders Hochgeehrte, Groszgünstige und gebietende Herren, nachdem die Compagnie Comoedianten, So Ihr Hochfürstl[iche] Durchl[aucht] Ertzhertzog Leopoldo, zu Brüssel in Niederland eine geraume Zeit auffgewartet, unter welchen entliche Ihr Königl[iche] Maj[est]ät von Engelland Höchstlöbl[iches] gedächtnüs seltsteygene Diener gewesen: angelanget, Zuvors aber noch niemals allhier in Dantzig gewesen, ihnen auch die Zeit und Gelegenheit nicht hat vergönnet, dasz sie vergangenen Dominicks Markt anhero hätten kommen können, haben sie doch nicht unterlassen wollen, hiesige berühmte und löbl[iche] Stadt anitzo auff des Märtins Markt zu ersuchen, und also ihre Action L°. H. E.Hrl. belieben nach, sehen zu lassen. Ist demnach an L°. H. L°. Hl. ihr gantz demütigst bitten, und fleissigst ersuche, Dieselben wollen ihnen die grosse Ehr erzeygen, und, dasz sie ihre Action allhier in Dantzig eine Zeitlang anstellen mögen, hochgünstig vergönnen: Sintemahl sie geübte und meist von Jugend aufgebrachte Actores sind, bey ihnen auch keine Laster oder tadelhaffte Possen eingeführet werden, sonders alles, wasz der Erbarkeit gemäsz presentiret wird, welches annoch eine liebliche und angenehme Englische Musik, so sie selbst bey sich haben, benebenst trefflichen Ballettes, um die Schauer und Zuhörer desto besser zu vergnügen vermehret. Leben demnach der Hoffnung E.H.E.Hl. werden diesz ihr emsiges und bittliches ersuchen nicht abschlagen, sondern ihnen ihr Theatrum anzustellen hochgünstig zu lassen und erlauben; Sie herkegen verbleiben alle Zeit

L.H.L°.Hl.

Demüthigste Diener
und
Comoedianten

[The Council's decision:]
Lect[um] in Senatu die 29. October A: 1649

undt befunden, das bey itziger Zeit Supplicanten nicht könne gefüget werden, sondern da sie einige stücke haben, nechsten künfftigen Dominicksmarck sollen willigen aufgenommeten u. admittiret werden.

8. English players' application of 30 July 1654; State Archives in Gdańsk: 300, 36/68, fos. 99–102

Herr Burgermeister
Woll Edle, Gestrenge, Ehrenveste, Namhaffte, Hochweise, in sonders hochgeehrte Herren.
Demnach nunmehr die Zeit heran Kombt, da der Dominiks Jahrmarckt abermal soll gehalten werden, Zu welcher Zeit denn allerhand Ergezligkeit ufleget erlaubet Zusein, und Wir in Ziemlich groszer Gesellschafft von 24 personen auch anhero gelanget seyn, in willens, da es vergünstiget werden möchte, Uns mit allerhand Geistlichen und Weltlichen, meistentheils neuen sinnreichen, und nicht wenigen erbaren Spielen, Comaedien und Tragoedien, sehen undt hören Zulaszen: Das haben wir E.E.H.Herrligkeiten gebührlich hierumb anzuflehen für nötig befunden damietigst bittende, sie wollen geruhen, Unsz hochgünstig nicht allein solches Zugesteltenn, sondern auch die Fecht-Schule, alsz einen ganz beguemen orte, hier Zu assigniren. Da wir denn Unsz gerne hiviederumb Zu billiger recognition Zu verstehen, danebenst auch so Zu verhalten wiszen werden, dasz Jederman an Uns ein Vergnügen empfinden soll. Erwarten hierauff eine geneigte gevierige Antwortet, und verblieben

Derer [Eurer ?] Selben Gueten
Unterthänige
Ich Wilhelm Rohe zu namen
der gantze Companej

[The Council's decision:]
Demutige Suplication der Engelschen Commediant
lecta in Senatu d. 30 Jul. 1654.
E. Hochn. Rath hatt Supplicanten vergünstiget in der fechtschule Ihre Comoedien Zu praesentiren iedoch mit der vermahnung das sie nichts unerbares u. was wieder Zuchtlauffen möchte, Zu agiren sich gelüsten laszen. Im übrigen sollen sie dem Zuchthause ein billiges Zukehren weszwegen sie mit Her Adrian Engelke der Herl. sich abfinden sollen, an welchen sie auch hiemit verwiesen werden.

9. English players' application of 14 [?August] 1654; State Archives in Gdańsk: 300, 36/68, fos. 103–6

Herr Bürgermeister,
Edle, Ehrenveste, Namhaffte, Hoch vnd Wollweise, groszgünstige Herren, E.E.E.Herl: wünschen wie furs erst glückliche regirung, smabt allem woll ergehen, von Gott den Allerhöchssen, vndt bedanken vnsz demnach in tieffester demuhth gegenst E.E.E.Herl: dasz sie groszgünstig consentiret haben, eine gewisze Zeit auff der fechtshulen allerley spiele, die melancholischen gemühter auffzufrishen, von Vnsz zu agiren vndt vorzustellen, wudurch zum theil vnser wunsh erfüllet worden, in dem wir vor anderen Städten diese weitberühmte Stadt erwehlet, mit vnseren diensten derselben, nach begeren, auffzuwarten, welcher weiter weg dan, weil wir in Zimlicher anzahl personen bestehen, ein groszes gekostet, alsz hatt vnsz aber, wie bekandt den Dominick über, das wetter gar nicht fügen wollen, weil esz meistentheils von oben nasz gewesen, weszwegen dan die Leute, wie auch wegen des bösen wegesz, sich in die Comedien nichtt haben einstellen können, welches dan vnser groszer schade gewesen, auch vnser gemachte gute hoffnung

gar Zu nichte worden. Wir trösten vnsz aber dieses, weil vnsz wolbekand dasz E.E.E.Herl:, ihrer guten gewohnheit nach, noch niemals jemandes shaden begehret, sondern vielmehr in einem vnd andern mittgeholfen, Sie werden auch diesen vnsern shaden, welchen wir wegen cesz masze wetters erhilten, und das disz vnsz weite weg, wie auch das [auffbaren ?] auff Fechtschulen viel gekostet, nichtt begehren, sondern ferner mit gnädigen augen ansehen. Gelanget demanch an E.E.E.Herl: unser unterdienst demütigstes bitten Sie geruchen groszgünstig uns noch eine gewisze Zeit, nach dero belieben, agiren Zu laszen, damit wir wieder in auffnehmen kommen mögen. Solche grosze gnade und gunst, wollen wir mit danckbaren herzen erkennen, undt in der frembde höchlich Zurühmen wiszen, daneben wollen wir auch fur E.E.E.Herl: uns diese weitberühmte Stadt auffnehmen, in unserm gebet, der Allmächtigen Gott stets anruffen, die wie im übrigen den gnadenschuz Gottes befehlen, nebenst erwartung einer erfrewlichen antwort. E.E.E.Herl:

Unterdienstgeflieszenste
Ganze Compagnie der Comedianten

[The Council's decision:]
Comaedianten. Lect: 14 [August?] A.1654. Undt will Ein Rath den Supplicanten in anmerkung es dem Zuchthause mit Zum nutzen gereichet, vergönnet haben, die Comedien besz Zu ende dieses Monats Zuspielen; mit bedinge das sie dem Zuchthause das seinige auch entrichten möchten.

Entrance fees charged by English players in various towns

Date	Town	Entrance fee		
1596	Nuremberg	1 batzen	=	16 pfennigs
1596	Strasburg	3 kreutzers	=	12 pfennigs
1597	Frankfurt	1 albus	=	8 pfennigs
1599	Münster	1 shilling	=	6 pfennigs
1600	Memmingen	4 kreutzers	=	16 pfennigs
1600	Cologne	4 albus	=	32 pfennigs
1601	Frankfurt	1 albus	=	8 pfennigs
1605	Strasburg	3 kreutzers	=	12 pfennigs
1607	Cologne	2–3 kreutzers	=	8–12 pfennigs
1613	Nuremberg	3 kreutzers	=	12 pfennigs
1614	Ulm	2 kreutzers	=	8 pfennigs
1618	Strasburg	1 batzen	=	16 pfennigs
1619	Gdańsk	2 groschen	=	20 pfennigs
1628	Nuremberg	6 kreutzers	=	24 pfennigs
1636	Gdańsk	9 groschen	=	90 pfennigs
1643	Gdańsk	9 groschen	=	90 pfennigs
1650	Gdańsk	6 groschen	=	60 pfennigs

Recorded visits by English players to Central Europe

Date	Town	Company (leading players)
1587?	Gdańsk	The Earl of Leicester's men
1596	Prague	Robert Browne's
1598	Prague	Thomas Sackville's
1601	Gdańsk	Robert Browne's?
1605	Gdańsk Königsberg Elbing (Elbląg)	Richard Machin–George Webster–Ralph Reeve's
1606	Loitz Wolgast	John Spencer's
1607	Gdańsk Elbing Graz	John Green's
	Loitz Wolgast	John Spencer's
1608	Graz Passau	John Green's
1608–9	Bytów? Stettin (Szczecin) Köslin (Koszalin) Königsberg	John Spencer's
1610	Prague? Jägerndorf (Krnov)	George Webster–Richard Machin–Ralph Reeve's
1611	Wolgast	?
	Königsberg Gdańsk Warsaw?	John Spencer's
1612	Gdańsk	John Green's
	Königsberg	John Spencer's

Date	Town	Company (leading players)
1613	Königsberg	John Spencer's
1615	Stettin Köslin	Robert Archer's
	Gdańsk	1. Robert Archer's 2. John Green's
1616	Gdańsk	John Green–Robert Reynolds'
	Königsberg	John Spencer's or Robert Archer's
	Warsaw	John Green's
1617	Warsaw	1. John Green's 2. Richard Jones'
	Neisse (Nysa) Olmütz (Olomounc) Vienna	John Green's
	Prague	1. John Green's 2. John Spencer's?
1618	Warsaw	Richard Jones'
	Königsberg Balga Elbing	John Spencer's
1619	Warsaw	Richard Jones'
	Gdańsk	1. Richard Jones' 2. John Spencer's 3. Robert Browne–John Green's
	Königsberg Elbing	John Spencer's
1619–20	Prague	Robert Browne's
	Warsaw	Richard Jones'
1620–2?	Warsaw	Richard Jones'
1622–3	Wolgast	Richard Jones'
1624–?	Wolgast	Richard Jones'

Date	Town	Company (leading players)
1628?	Vienna?	Edward Pudsey's
1628?–32	Warsaw	Robert Archer's
1635?	Königsberg	Robert Archer's
1636	Gdańsk	Robert Archer's
1636–8	Warsaw	Robert Archer's
1638	Gdańsk	Robert Archer's
1638–9	Warsaw	Robert Archer's
1639	Vienna? Vilnius? (Wilno)	Robert Archer's?
	Königsberg	Robert Reynolds'
	Gdańsk	Robert Archer's
1639–40	Warsaw	Robert Archer's
1640	Gdańsk	Robert Archer's
	Königsberg Elbing	Robert Reynolds–Robert Archer's
1640–2	Warsaw	Robert Reynolds–Robert Archer's
1643	Gdańsk	Robert Archer's? Wayde–Roe's?
1643–4	Warsaw	John Wayde–William Roe's?
1644	Gdańsk Elbing Königsberg Riga	John Wayde–William Roe's
1647	Gdańsk Königsberg	John Wayde–William Roe's
1648	Riga	John Wayde–William Roe's
1649	Gdańsk	George Jolly's?
	Vienna Prague Pressburg? (Bratislava)	John Wayde–William Roe's

Date	Town	Company (leading players)
1650	Gdańsk	George Jolly's
	Vienna	John Wayde–William Roe's
1651	Prague	John Wayde–William Roe's
1652	Vienna	John Wayde–William Roe's
1653	Vienna?	George Jolly's
	Gdańsk	The Archduke Leopold's
1654	Gdańsk	William Roe's
1658	Vienna	George Jolly's
	Prague	?
	Breslau (Wrocław)	?
1659	Vienna	George Jolly's

Principal players active in Central Europe

Name	Approximate period of activity
Robert Browne	1596?–1620
Richard Machin	1605–10
George Webster	1605–10
Ralph Reeve	1605–10
John Spencer	1606?–1620
John Green	1607–20
Robert Archer	1615–40
Robert Reynolds	1616–c. 1642
Richard Jones	1617–24
John Wayde	1617–c. 1658
William Roe	1639?–1654
Edward Pudsey	1639?–1654?
William Wedware	1639?–1654?
George Jolly	1649–58

Notes

Introduction

1. 'Les Anglois se signalerent entre les autres par un Spectacle nouveau, ou au moins inusité jusqu'alors en Allemagne. Ce fut une Comedie sacrée que les Evêques Anglois firent représenter devant l'Empereur le Dimanche 31 de Janvier, sur "la naissance du Sauveur", sur "l'arriveé des Mages" et sur "le massacre des Innocens". Ills avoient déja fait représenter la même Piece quelques jours auparavant en presence des Magistrats de Constance & de quantité de personnes de distinction, afin que les Acteurs fussent mieux en état de faire bien leur rôle devant l'Empereur' (quoted in Hartleb, *Deutschlands erster Theaterbau*, p. 12).

2. *Shakespeare's Europe: Unpublished Chapters of Fynes Moryson's Itinerary. Being a Survey of the Conditions in Europe at the End of the 16th Century*, Introduction by Charles Hughes, published by Sherratt and Hughes, 6 vols. (London, 1907–36). Here I am quoting from vol IV, (1925) p. 304.

3. Ibid.

4. Quoted in Cohn, *Shakespeare in Germany*, pp. CII–CIII; see also Hotson, *The Commonwealth and Restoration Stage*, p. 171.

5. Chambers, *The Elizabethan Stage*, II, p. 272.

6. Ibid.

7. Hartleb, *Deutschlands erster Theaterbau*, p. 12.

8. See Cohn, *Shakespeare in Germany*, pp. XXIV–XXVI; see also Herz, *Englische Schauspieler*, p. 3, and Ravn, 'English Instrumentalists at the Danish Court', p. 556.

9. Cohn, *Shakespeare in Germany*, pp. XXIV–XXVI.

10. Bolte, *Das Danziger Theater*, pp. 22, 25.

11. Hartleb, *Deutschlands erster Theaterbau*, p. 14.

12. See Wikland, *Elizabethan Players in Sweden*, passim.

13. For a complete and accurate version of the passport see Schrickx, 'English Actors at the Courts of Wolfenbüttel, Brussels and Graz', p. 153.

14. Browne and Jones were first mentioned as actors in 1583, when they were members of the notable Earl of Leicester's company; see Chambers, *The Elizabethan Stage*, II, p. 222; more details may be found in Bentley's *The Jacobean and Caroline Stage*, especially in volume II.

15. Quoted in Chambers, *The Elizabethan Stage*, IV, p. 325.

16. Ibid., pp. 303–4.

17. There is also the Statute of 1604. See Chambers, *The Elizabethan Stage*, IV, pp. 269–71, 324–5, 336–7.

18. Ibid., pp. 334–5.

19. *Henslowe Papers*, ed. Greg, p. 90.

20. Quoted in Cohn, *Shakespeare in Germany*, p. XCVI.

21. Chambers, *The Elizabethan Stage*, I, pp. 350–1; for a detailed analysis of actors' economics see pages 348–88. It may be added that also in later periods frequent inhibitions to act in London led to the pauperisation of the city players. For instance, among the dramatic records from the Privy Council Register we find the following significant documents:

    17 September 1637: His Majestys servants ye players, having by reason of

the Infeccion of the Plague in and neare London been for a long time restrained, and having now spent what they got in many years before, and soe not able any longer to subsist and maintain their families, did by their petition to his majesty most humbly desire leave to be now at liberty to use their quallity.

And a similar petition was submitted by her Majesties players on 24 September 1637, from which we learn that 'by the occasion of the infeccion of the playgue in and neere about London, they have for a long time almost to their utter undoing, having noe other Imployement nor means to maintain themselves and their families been restrained from using their quallity' (quoted in Stopes, 'Dramatic Records', p. 113).

22. To my knowledge, the last Continental record of English players comes from 1683, when H.J. Christ. von Grimmelshausen mentioned an English company in one of his works: 'At that time [i.e. in 1683], a company of English actors arrived in the town, who wanted to return home from thence, and were only waiting for a fair wind to sail. I obtained from them a terrible devil's mask etc' (quoted in Cohn, *Shakespeare in Germany*, p. CIII).

23. For a full account of performances at Nuremberg see Trautmann, 'Englische Komoedianten in Nürnberg', pp. 113–36; see also Hysel, *Das Theater in Nürnberg von 1612 bis 1863*.

24. The theatre at Kassel has attracted some attention from scholars; see, for instance, Hartleb, *Deutschlands erster Theaterbau*, pp. 86–143, and a more recent work by Graham C. Adams, 'The Ottoneum: A Neglected Seventeenth Century Theatre' – a paper presented during the annual Shakespeare Association of America meeting in 1980.

25. 'Profert enim multos et praestantes Anglia musicos comoedos, tragoedos, histrionicae peritissimos, e quibus interdum aliquot consociati sedibut suis ad tempus relictis ad exteras nationes excurrere, artemque suam illis praesertim Principum aulis demonstrare ostentareque consueverunt. Paucis ab hinc annis in Germaniam nostram Anglicani musici ... et in magnorum Principum aulis aliquandiu versati, tantum ex arte musica, histrionicaque sibi favorem conciliarunt ut largiter remunerati domum inde auro et argento onusti sunt reversi' (quoted in Chambers, *The Elizabethan Stage*, I, pp. 343–4, fn. 2).

26. For a meticulous analysis of English players' activity under the Landgrave's patronage see Hartleb, *Deutschlands erster Theaterbau, passim*.

27. Quoted from *Grove's Dictionary of Music and Musicians*, II, p. 755.

28. Ibid. pp. 755–6.

29. Hartleb, *Deutschlands erster Theaterbau, passim*.

30. For a full account of Henry Julius' patronage see Zimmerman, 'Englische Komödianten am Hofe zu Wolfenbüttel', pp. 37–45.

31. See Prölss, *Geschichte des Hoftheaters zu Dresden*.

32. Wedgwood, *The Thirty Years War*, p. 62.

33. Trautmann, 'Englische Komoedianten in Nürnberg', pp. 122–3.

34. Herz, *Englische Schauspieler*, p. 44.

35. Bolte, *Das Danziger Theater*, p. 36.

36. See Rommel, *Neuere Geschichte von Hessen*, p. 402; Hartleb, *Deutschlands erster Theaterbau*, pp. 58–62; see also below, chapter 7.

37. Herz, *Englische Schauspieler*, p. 41.

38. See Bolte, *Das Danziger Theater*, p. 36; Cohn, *Shakespeare in Germany*, p. LXXXVII and also below, chapter 3.

39. Bolte, *Das Danziger Theater*, p. 36.

40. Cohn, *Shakespeare in Germany*, p. XCVII.

41. For further examples see ibid.; Creizenach, *Die Schauspiele der englischen Komödianten*, pp. II–XVI; Herz, *Englische Schauspieler, passim.*
42. Quoted in Chambers, *The Elizabethan Stage*, IV, pp. 250, 253.
43. See Schrickx, 'English Actors at the Courts of Wolfenbüttel, Brussels and Graz', pp. 165–8.
44. See Thaler, 'Travelling Players in Shakspere's England', pp. 501–2.
45. Wikland, *Elizabethan Players in Sweden*, pp. 33–5.
46. Trautmann, 'Englische Komoedianten in Nürnberg', p. 119.
47. Wolter, 'Chronologie des Theaters der Reichstadt Köln', p. 92.
48. Herz, *Englische Schauspieler*, p. 49.
49. Cohn, *Shakespeare in Germany*, p. LXXXVIII.
50. Kindermann, *Theatergeschichte Europas*, III, p. 378.
51. Cohn, *Shakespeare in Germany*, p. XCII.
52. Trautmann, 'Englische Komoedianten in Nürnberg', p. 131.
53. Creizenach, *Die Schauspiele der englischen Komödianten*, p. XII.
54. Riewald, 'New Light on the English Actors in the Netherlands', pp. 85, 87.
55. Prölss, *Geschichte des Hoftheaters zu Dresden*, p. 69.
56. For further details see Cohn, *Shakespeare in Germany, passim*; Herz, *Englische Schauspieler, passim*; see also Harris, 'The English Comedians in Germany', p. 455.
57. The number of players named in the Jacobean patents varied from seven to fourteen. Probably the Elizabethan companies ran rather smaller. See Chambers, *The Elizabethan Stage*, I, p. 354.
58. For instance, an interpreter, one 'Hindrich v. Meklnb.', accompanied English instrumentalists at Nyköping in Sweden in 1591/92. See Wikland, *Elizabethan Players in Sweden*, p. 35.
59. See Bolte, *Die Singspiele der englischen Komödianten.*
60. Cohn, *Shakespeare in Germany*, p. XXXII.
61. Ibid., p. XXIX.
62. Ibid., p. LVIII.
63. Crüger, 'Englische Komoedianten in Strassburg', pp. 116–17.
64. Creizenach, *Die Schauspiele der englischen Komödianten*, p. XXII.
65. *The Elizabethan Stage*, I, p. 345.
66. Quoted from Cohn, *Shakespeare in Germany*, pp. LIX–LX.
67. An anonymous Frankfurt poet wrote a satirical piece on the English players, in which we find the following lines:
    > And yet these actors play such stuff,
    > They must themselves oft laugh enough,
    > To think a man his money brings
    > To them, to see such foolish things.

    The full text of this poem was translated and published by Cohn, *Shakespeare in Germany*, pp. XC–XCI.
68. Ibid.
69. Translated by Brennecke in his *Shakespeare in Germany 1590–1700*, p. 8.
70. A number of examples of Puritan attacks against the London theatres may be found in Chambers, *The Elizabethan Stage*, IV. These inform us about 'such wanton gestures, such bawdie speeches . . . such kissing and bussing, such clipping and culling, Suche winckinge and glancinge of wanton eyes' which the players present on stage (ibid., pp. 222–3).
71. Herz, *Englische Schauspieler*, p. 36.
72. Harris, 'The English Comedians in Germany', p. 456.
73. Herz, *Englische Schauspieler*, pp. 21–2, 31; incidentally, Harris mentions only 'one scrap of positive evidence', '2 Jungen' who accompanied Browne at Strasburg in

1618, but even much earlier, in 1598, an English 'youth' appeared among the players at the Landgrave Maurice's court at Kassel (see Hartleb, *Deutschlands erster Theaterbau*, p. 38).

74. Creizenach, *Die Schauspiele der englischen Komödianten*, p. XXII.
75. Cohn, 'Englische Komödianten in Köln', p. 257.
76. Hotson, *The Commonwealth and Restoration Stage*, p. 175.
77. Creizenach, *Die Schauspiele der englischen Komödianten*, p. XXII.
78. Harris, 'The English Comedians in Germany', p. 462.
79. Ibid., p. 461.
80. Quoted in Chambers, *The Elizabethan Stage*, I, p. 333.
81. 'Demenach aber von vnsern bisshero gehabten Spectatoribus dieser Ehrlöblichen policey vndt Burgerschafft wir keinen Vrlaub genommen, auch wider vnsere gewonheit keine Valediction gesprochen, welches alles unss nich allein zur vnhöfligkeit gerechnet, sondern auch, alss wann wir insalutato hospite davon gezogen, ja von vnsern Osoribus anderer orthen, alss wann etwa vns vbel verhaltens willen wir abgeschaffet worden, auss spargiret werden möchte, also zu schimpf gereichen soltte . . . Alss gelanget an E. Ehrnv. vnd gunsten vor dismahl vnser letzte pitt . . . Ein Ehrenvester hochweyser Rath geruhe noch grossgünstiglich zuge-statten, das zukünfftigen Sontagss dero gehorsamen treuen Bürgerschafft zum Valete, gueter nacht vndt gedächtnuss noch eine ergötzliche Comoedi agiren, also mit ehren, glimpf vndt guetem nahmen von hinnen abreisen mögen' (quoted in Bolte, *Das Danziger Theater*, p. 55). See also chapter 1 below.
82. 'Demnach den aber von vnser gesellschafft in gewöhnlichen brauch bisshero observirt worden, dass fur ertzeigte gutt und wohlthaten, wo nicht, wie siches wohl gepurtt jedoch pro viribus, ein zeichen der danckbarkeitt zueweissen vnd seinen hochweissen Magistrat mit einer sonderlich schönen Action zuurehren' (quoted in Bolte, *Das Danziger Theater*, p. 53).
83. Cohn, *Shakespeare in Germany*, p. CII.
84. Ibid., p. II.
85. Ibid., p. XCIX.
86. Quoted in ibid., pp. CXXXIV–CXXXV.
87. Creizenach, *Die Schauspiele der englischen Komödianten*, pp. II–III.
88. This account is found in a letter, dated 13 September 1592, written by Balthazar Baumgartner the Younger to his wife. Quoted from Riewald, 'New Light on the English Actors in the Netherlands', p. 66.
89. See Chambers, *The Elizabethan Stage*, II, p. 551.
90. Quoted from Cohn, *Shakespeare in Germany*, pp. CXXXV–CXXXVI.
91. *Grove's Dictionary of Music and Musicians*, VI, pp. 712–14.
92. Wolter, 'Chronologie des Theaters der Reichstadt Köln', p. 91.
93. See Duncker, 'Landgraf Moritz von Hessen', p. 267.
94. 'Wälsche täntze mit wunderlichen vertrehen, hupfen, hinter und für sich springen, uberwerffen, und andern seltzamen gebertne getrieben' (quoted in Hartleb, *Deutschlands erster Theaterbau*, p. 68).
95. *Grove's Dictionary of Music and Musicians*, I, p. 1009.
96. Ibid.
97. For other examples see, for instance, Hammerich, 'Musical Relations between England and Denmark', pp. 114–19.
98. Supplications of this company were first published by Bolte in his *Das Danziger Theater*, pp. 44–7; see also chapter 1 below.
99. Riewald, 'New Light on the English Actors in the Netherlands', p. 76.
100. Prölss, *Geschichte des Hoftheaters zu Dresden*, p. 68.
101. Creizenach, *Die Schauspiele der englischen Komödianten*, p. XC.

102. Cohn, *Shakespeare in Germany*, p. XXVI.
103. Quoted from Cohn, *Shakespeare in Germany*, p. XCV.
104. We learn about this from the Elector's letter to the Steward, dated 25 October 1586, first published by Cohn, p. XXV.
105. Ibid., p. XXIV.
106. Ibid., p. LVIII.
107. *Henslowe Papers*, ed. Greg, p. 33.
108. 'Und sie stattlich in Essen und Trinken, Kleidung und anderen Sachen unterhalten . . . dass fast in der Rentkammer nichts mehr in Vorrath geblieben . . .' (quoted in Duncker, 'Landgraf Moritz von Hessen', p. 267).
109. 'Auf Ew. Liebden Gesuch zur Verrichtung der Comödie von den alten Potentaten, die waffen, Harnische und Kleidung, was deren bei uns vorhanden, feundlich zu senden, haben wir Befeht gethan' (quoted in ibid., p. 266).
110. See Brachvogel, *Geschichte des Königlichen Theaters zu Berlin*, I, p. 18.
111. Rommel, *Neuere Geschichte von Hessen*, p. 446.
112. Cohn, *Shakespeare in Germany*, pp. LXXXVII–LXXXVIII.
113. Ibid., p. CXXXVI; see also Hartleb, *Deutschlands erster Theaterbau*, p. 21.
114. See Massner, *Die Kostümaustellung im K.K. Österreichischen Museum 1891*. This neglected source is noticed by Professor Zbigniew Raszewski in his article 'Jeszcze o teatrze zawodowym w dawnej Polsce', where he reproduces the photograph of the costume.
115. See Chambers, *The Elizabethan Stage*, II, pp. 281–2.
116. The first two editions, bearing the same title, *Englische Comoedien und Tragedien*, were followed by a third one, entitled *Liebeskampff oder ander Theil der Englischen Comoedien und Tragoedien*, which came out in 1630. Yet another collection, entitled *Schaubühne Englischer und Französicher Comödianten*, appeared in Frankfurt in 1670.
117. A full list of these plays is given by Chambers, *The Elizabethan Stage*, II, pp. 285–6.
118. See, for instance, Creizenach, *Die Schauspiele der englischen Komödianten*, pp. XXVII–LXVI; Herz, *Englische Schauspieler*, pp. 65–138.
119. Trautmann, 'Englische Komoedianten in Nürnberg', pp. 119–20.
120. Riewald, 'New Light on the English Actors in the Netherlands', p. 75.
121. Grabau, 'Englische Komödianten in Deutschland', p. 311.
122. Cohn, *Shakespeare in Germany*, p. CXVII.
123. Ibid., p. XCVIII. A tennis-court was also adapted for theatrical purposes by George Jolly; see Scanlan, 'Notes on George Jolly's stage', pp. 17–18.
124. 'englischen Komödianten J. Spencer einer grosse Bühne, auf die Bühne ein Theater, darinnen er mit allerley musikalischen Instrumenten auf mehr denn zehnerley Weise gespielt, und über die Theater-bühne noch eine Bühne 30 Schuh hoch, auf 6 grosse Säulen, über welche ein Dach gemacht worden, darunter ein viereckiger Spund, wodurch sie schöne Actione verrichtet haben, erbauen' (quoted in Elze, 'John Spencer in Regensburg', p. 362).
125. 'Commedianten zu tag unnd nacht mitt acht Pferden Vorspan darvon sie dann vier vor eine Gutschen, unnd die Andernn vier I einem wagen, daräff sie Ihre Instrumenta Unnd Anders haben unnd fuhrenn müggenn, damitt sie hierduch nicht gehindertt unnd ufgehalten werden' (quoted in Hartleb, *Deutschlands Erster Theaterbau*, p. 41).
126. Quoted from Cohn, *Shakespeare in Germany*, p. CI.
127. Bolte, *Das Danziger Theater*, pp. 42–3.
128. Quoted from a supplication published by Bolte ibid., pp. 38–40.
129. Ibid., pp. 44–7.
130. See Harris, 'The English comedians in Germany', pp. 446–64, and the discussion below.

131. Ibid., pp. 462–3.
132. Quoted in Cohn, *Shakespeare in Germany*, pp. xxv–xxvi.
133. Meissner, *Die englischen Comoedianten zur Zeit Shakespeares in Oesterreich*, p. 52.
134. For instance, in the period between 1601 and 1620, the relation of gold to silver in Gdańsk amounted to 1 : 11.66, whereas in Germany it was 1 : 12.25; and in the period 1621–40 it amounted to 1 : 12.70 in Gdańsk and 1 : 14.0 in Western Europe. The only stable gold currency in the period was a 'ducat', which weighed 3.5 grams of gold ('thalers' were made of silver – 24.317 grams).
135. See, for instance, Harris, 'The English Comedians in Germany', *passim*.
136. According to Harris (ibid.), £60 was equal to approximately 275 thalers, i.e., one pound sterling was worth about 4.58 thalers.
137. Ibid., p. 457.
138. Trautmann, 'Englische Komoedianten in Nürnberg', p. 134.
139. Ibid.
140. Meissner, *Die englischen Comoedianten zur Zeit Shakespeares in Oesterreich*, p. 53.
141. Wolter, 'Chronologie des Theaters der Reichstadt Köln', pp. 91–2.
142. Bolte, *Das Danziger Theater*, p. 76.
143. Some examples may also be found in Creizenach, *Die Schauspiele der englischen Komödianten*, pp. xvii–xviii.
144. All of the above pieces of information were taken from contemporary sources published in scattered articles, most of which have already been referred to.
145. For example, the company that visited Gdańsk in 1643 was given leave to play, provided the players paid 500 thalers; in addition, the players were warned by the councillors that if they tried to avoid paying the money, they would be imprisoned. This indicates that the players may have tried to do so in the past. See also chapter 1, below.
146. One of these bills was reproduced by Cohn in his *Shakespeare in Germany*, who dated it 1628, and by Könnecke in *Bilderatlas zur Geschichte der deutschen Nationalliteratur*, p. 171, who dated it 1650. Another bill, dated 1656, was reproduced by Hotson in *The Commonwealth and Restoration Stage*, p. 175.
147. Riewald, 'New Light on the English Actors in the Netherlands', p. 91.
148. The first mention of this practice in London comes to us in a letter of the Bishop of London to Sir William Cecil written in 1564, in which the Bishop complained that 'histrions . . . now daylye, butt speciallye on holydayes, sett vp bylles' (Chambers, *The Elizabethan Stage*, IV, p. 267). This was prohibited by the Mayor of London in 1581: 'that they doe not at anye tyme hereafter, suffer anye person or persons whatsoever, to sett vpp or fixe anye papers or breifes vppon anye postes, houses, or other places . . . for the shewe or settynge out of anye playes, enterludes, or pryzes, within this Cyttye' (quoted in ibid., p. 283).
149. Ibid., II, p. 547.
150. Ibid.
151. Cohn, 'Englische Komödianten in Köln', p. 256.
152. Ibid., pp. 257–8.
153. 'Mit zweien trommeln und 4 trompeten' – quoted in Creizenach, *Die Schauspiele der englischen Komödianten*, p. xxv.
154. 'Es wird aber E.E. Hochw. Rath hierauf dienstlich berichtet, dass wir mit keinem trommeln oder trompeten öffentlich durch die strassen laufen, sondern es wird nur blos im Anfang Undt Ende einer Comoeti die trommel gerüret Undt durch angeschlagene Brieff wird dem Volk die Komötia kundt gethan' (quoted in Creizenach, ibid., p. xxv).
155. Quoted from Cohn, *Shakespeare in Germany*, p. xc.
156. For a list of these towns see Flemming, 'Englische Komödianten', p. 272.
157. Such, at least, are the periods in which records are silent about visits by English

players. See bibliography for articles on the English presence in particular towns. See also a table in L.M. Price's *English > German Literary Influences*, between pp. 136 and 137.

158. Quoted in Cohn, *Shakespeare in Germany*, p. xcviii.
159. Riewald, 'New Light on the English Actors in the Netherlands', pp. 85–6.
160. Hotson, *The Commonwealth and Restoration Stage*, pp. 167–8.
161. See Cohn, 'Englische Komödianten in Köln', pp. 268–9.
162. Hotson, *The Commonwealth and Restoration Stage*, p. 171.
163. Quoted in Cohn, *Shakespeare in Germany*, pp. civ–cv.
164. 'ut iam apud nos Angli histriones omnium maxime delectent . . .' (quoted in Chambers, *The Elizabethan Stage*, I, p. 344, fn. See the discussion of the subject in Willem Schrickx's recent article, '"Pickleherring" and English Actors in Germany', pp. 135–47.
165. Mundy, *The Travels in Europe and Asia*, IV, p. 181.
166. It seems that even much earlier some Continental companies styled themselves as 'English' to win the favour of local authorities. A curious incident occurred in 1602 in Nuremberg, when on 31 May an unidentified company was recorded as 'Nid[er]ländische comedians', and two days later the same players styled themselves as 'Englische Comoediant[en]'. See Junkers, *Niederländische Schauspieler und niederländisches Schauspiel*, p. 62.

1 Gdańsk

1. All the arguments for the visit of 1587 are based on indirect pieces of evidence. In 1591 a play written by Philip Waimer, entitled *Elisa*, was published in Gdańsk. This drama may be treated as the earliest play written in German with which English players may be associated, for *Elisa*, otherwise called *Edward III*, is similar to the anonymous English play, *The Reign of King Edward the Third*. Since the latter was printed in London in 1596, i.e. five years after its Gdańsk version, it is assumed that Waimer had seen the play on stage sometime before 1591. See Bolte, *Das Danziger Theater*, pp. 22–7.
2. Gdańsk was in fact the largest city in Central Europe, with a population of over seventy thousand inhabitants in the first half of the seventeenth century.
3. In *Das Danziger Theater*.
4. The very fact that the German players were not allowed to enter the city implies that they were treated by the town authorities as mere beggars and vagabonds against whom laws were exceptionally severe. See E. Cieślak and Cz. Biernat, *Dzieje Gdańska* (Gdańsk, 1975), pp. 188–9.
5. 'Dewile idt jo denn Engelschenn ist so lange tidt her ist vorgunnet wordenn hir tho spielenn, vnde noch van tage zu tage lenger spielenn . . . wir sindt auch Erbotich, ann Euwere E.H.W. eine oder zwee, oder so viell alse Euwere E.H.W. begherenn sindt, Comediam vnde Tragediam zu agirenn, Dewile Euwere E.H.W. Der Engelschenn ihre kunst habenn augesehen, das Euwere E.H.W. ock sehen mochtenn, das wir Dudesschenn noch so woll was gelhernet hettenn, gelick alse de Engelschenn' (quoted in Bolte, *Das Danziger Theater*, pp. 31–2). Note: in the case of applications to town authorities, the date given always denotes the time when an application was read at a Council, and not when it was written, or submitted.
6. Ibid, p. 31.
7. Herz, *Englische Schauspieler*, p. 63.
8. Ibid., pp. 17–18.
9. For the most recent account of Browne's association with Sackville see Schrickx, 'English Actors at the Courts of Wolfenbüttel, Brussels and Graz', pp. 153–6, 160.

10. 'Den Churfursten Christian von Brandenburg Comedianten vnd Musikanten verehret 20 Thaler = 37 Mark' (quoted in Bolte, *Das Danziger Theatre*, p. 33).
11. Herz, *Englische Schauspieler*, pp. 38–9.
12. It may be added that Browne was associated with Webster as early as 1596, and both of these players were attached for some time to the ducal court at Hesse (see Creizenach, *Die Schauspiele der englischen Komödianten*, pp. v–vi; see also Herz, *Englische Schauspieler*, p. 14). It is worth mentioning that there were in fact two actors named Webster active on the Continent, one George and the other John. It seems highly unlikely that any of these two was any relation to John Webster, the dramatist.
13. More recent studies have proved beyond doubt that Spencer had become the manager of the Elector's company by 1604 (see, for instance, Riewald, 'New Light on the English Actors in the Netherlands', pp. 75–6).
14. Hagen, *Geschichte des Theaters in Preussen*, pp. 47, 53.
15. Schrickx, 'English Actors at the Courts of Wolfenbüttel, Brussels and Graz', pp. 156 and 162. Nothing is known of Green's London career, if he ever had one. It is not certain whether he can be linked with one Robert Green, a player active on the Continent since the early 1590s (see Riewald, 'New Light on the English Actors in the Netherlands', p. 73; see also Trautmann, 'Englische Komödianten in Nürnberg', p. 115; and Schrickx, 'English Actors' Names', p. 157.
16. *Henslowe's Diary*, ed. Greg, p. 164.
17. *Henslowe Papers*, ed. Greg, p. 63.
18. Hagen, *Geschichte des Theaters in Preussen*, p. 53; see also chapter 2.
19. Bolte, *Das Danziger Theater*, p. 36; see also Gross, *Das Danziger Theater*, p. 39. That the players did in fact travel from Stettin is apparent from the Elector's letter of recommendation of 1609; see chapters 3 and 4.
20. Both the applications were first published by Bolte, *Das Danziger Theater*, pp. 38–40.
21. '. . . vermerckende aber, das sich wenigk spectatores noch zur zeit gefunden . . . Wann ich mir dann furgeschreiben bis zu dem zukohmmenden Sontage zu agiren vnd . . . hernacher mich nach Konigsbergk zu belegen, aldar so lange zu bleiben; biss wils Gott zu dem zunahenden Dominick, alss dann ich mich wiederumb anhero begeben wolte' (quoted in Bolte, *Das Danziger Theater*, p. 38).
22. The *New Comedy* mentioned here may have been staged in a temporary indoor theatre located in a building belonging to St George's Brotherhood of merchants. The edifice, built in the High Gothic style, is one of the finest relics of the past in Gdańsk today. J. Bolte (in *Das Danziger Theater*, pp. 37–8) has identified the *New Comedy* as George Peele's *The Turkish Mahomet and Hyrin the fair Greek* (1594), which was presented by the same company at Königsberg (see chapter 3).
23. Satori-Neumann, *Dreihundert Jahre berufständisches Theater in Elbing*, p. 21; see also chapter 2.
24. Reproduced by Bolte, *Das Danziger Theater*, pp. 42–3. See also discussion below.
25. Hagen, *Geschichte des Theaters in Preussen*, pp. 53–7; see chapter 3.
26. A letter, dated 16 November 1609, written by J. Beaulieu to William Trumbull, English envoy at the Brussels court, includes the following lines: 'I send you a note of my Lord Deny for the finding of a certain youth of his, who hath been debauched from him by certain players and is now with them at Brussels' (quoted in Schrickx, 'English Actors at the Courts of Wolfenbüttel, Brussels and Graz', p. 167). Schrickx has noted that 'two further letters between the same correspondents disclose the respective identity of the youth and of the actors' leader' (ibid.). Both of these documents, dated 31 January and 8 March respectively, mention Green the player by name. See also Hoppe 'English Acting Companies at the Court of Brussels', pp. 26–33.

27. In 'English Actors at the Courts of Wolfenbüttel, Brussels and Graz', p. 167, Schrickx argues that the letter in question 'being so nearly contemporaneous with the Beaulieu reference, almost certainly bears on the Green troupe'.

28. 'Es werden sich groszgünstiege Herren E.E.Herl. zu erinnern wiszen, wie Sie füren jahre den Engelschen Comoedianten alhir in dieser Stadt frey zu agiren günstiglichen vegünnet, wofür Sie auch E.E.Herl. zum unterdienstlichsten danck sagen. Weil dan grosz günstiege Herren, selbte Comaedianten, als der Johan Grin, mit einer anstehenlichenn compagnia wiederumb auf dem herwege, vnd bennen kurzen vieleicht damit sie einem bequemen ort in derzeit zu ihren gelegenheit bekommen möchten, E.E.Herrl. supplicando zu ersuchen' (in the collection of the State Archives in Gdańsk, catalogue number: 300, 36/67, fos. 87–90).

29. Herz, *Englische Schauspieler*, p. 27.

30. All the records for 1615 have been reproduced by Bolte, *Das Danziger Theater*, pp. 42–7.

31. 'Demnach vnser Gnedigster Churfürst vnndt Herr, Ihr Churf. G. zu Brandenburgk, welchen wier jungst verloffenen winter mit vnsern Actionibus Comicis gehorsahmist (vermög beigelegten von dero Gn. vns gnedigst mitgetheilteen patent) aufgewartett, Allss hatt sie vns in gnaden vergönstiget, diesen instehenden Sommer anderer örtter vns ferner zu begebenn vndt vnser Actiones zu praesentiren' (quoted in Bolte, *Das Danziger Theater*, p. 42).

32. Cohn, *Shakespeare in Germany*, p. LXXXVIII. For the activity of the Peadle brothers see Bentley, *The Jacobean and Caroline Stage*, II, pp. 521–3.

33. Cohn, ibid., p. LXXXVIII.

34. Reproduced by Bolte, *Das Danziger Theater*, pp. 44–5.

35. *Henslowe's Diary*, ed Greg, vol. 2, p. 232.

36. All the three applications have been reproduced by Bolte, *Das Danziger Theater*, pp. 45–7.

37. Among the expenses, 100 marks were paid for the benches, galleries and other 'indispensable things', which may lead us to suspect that Green's company did not perform in the Fencing-School, but in the hall of St George's Brotherhood. This would be congruous with one of the earlier applications of the Brandenburg company, in which the players expressed their anguish about the fact that in the near future the theatre, i.e. the Fencing-School, would be occupied by fencers. In addition to these expenses, Green had to pay two ducats daily for the Town Hall, which indicates that a form of taxation was introduced by 1615.

38. Green's presence was recorded at Wolfenbüttel in May 1615 (Bolte, *Das Danziger Theater*, p. 47).

39. *Henslowe Papers*, ed. Greg, p. 33.

40. All the three applications of this company were reproduced by Bolte, *Das Danziger Theater*, pp. 48–51.

41. 'Nun ist gewis, das der Lauf der welt nicht künstlicher kan abgebildet sein als in Comoedien vnd Tragoedien, die gleich wie im spiegel aller Menschen leben vnd wesen, guttes und böses repraesentiren vnd fürstellen, darin ein ieder sich selbst magk sehen und erkennen, Welche kunst bey den Alten Griecher vnd Römern vber alle masse weert, hoch vnd ansehenlich gehalten ist vnd wol tawren wird, so lang die welt stehett, vnd wird auch zu itzigen Zeiten von allen weltweisen geliebet vnd geehret, das sie in Mancherley Zungen vnd Manieren für sich genett vnd bestehet' (quoted in Bolte, ibid., p. 48).

42. Bentley, *The Jacobean and Caroline Stage*, 2, p. 543.

43. Quoted in Cohn, *Shakespeare in Germany*, p. XCVIII.

44. See Tittman, *Die Schauspiele der Englischen Komödianten in Deutschland*, where most of the texts are reproduced, including one 'Pickleherring play'.

45. Creizenach, *Die Schauspiele der englischen Komödianten*, p. LXXVI.
46. State Archives in Gdańsk: 300, 36/67, fos. 103–6. See Appendix I, item 1.
47. Ibid. For the full text see Appendix I.
48. In 'New Light on the English Actors in the Netherlands', pp. 89–90.
49. See Herz, *Englische Schauspieler*, pp. 47–51.
50. Reproduced by Bolte, *Das Danziger Theater*, p. 52.
51. Spencer was still enjoying the Electoral patronage in 1620 (see Cohn, *Shakespeare in Germany*, p. XCII and Hagen, *Geschichte des Theaters in Preussen*, pp. 59–60).
52. See Trautmann, 'Englische Komoedianten in Nürnberg', p. 131.
53. All of these were reproduced by Bolte, *Das Danziger Theater*. pp. 53–5.
54. See Bolte, *Das Danziger Theater*, p. 54 and Herz, *Englische Schauspieler*, p. 98.
55. Chambers, *The Elizabethan Stage*, 2, p. 284.
56. It may be argued, of course, that John Spencer also performed in Gdańsk before 1619; it has to be stressed, however, that Spencer's patron, the Elector of Brandenburg, was a Calvinist and this was a sufficient reason for Lutheran councillors not to show any favour to the Elector's servants.
57. Cohn (*Shakespeare in Germany*, p. CIX) identified this play with *Hester and Assuerus*, which may be found in Henslowe's Diary: in 1594 the play was staged by a joint company of the Lord Chamberlain's and the Lord Admiral's men (*Henslowe's Diary*, ed. Greg, p. 17).
58. An anonymous play from the repertory of Queen Anne's company (*Henslowe's Diary*, ed. Greg, vol. 2, p. 230).
59. This is a prose version of a play entitled *Amantes Amentes*, written in 1609 by Gabriel Rollenhagen; see Chambers, *The Elizabethan Stage*, 2, p. 230.
60. The last two plays are undoubtedly William Shakespeare's *Two Gentlemen of Verona* and *The Tragedy of Titus Andronicus*.
61. The full list of Green's repertory in 1608 and 1626 (when he performed at Dresden) was published by Hertz, *Englische Schauspieler*, pp. 66–7.
62. Ibid., p. 31.
63. Ibid., p. 42.
64. Reproduced by Bolte, *Das Danziger Theater*, pp. 58–9.
65. Creizenach (*Die Schauspiele der englischen Komödianten*, p. XIX) identifies this company as English, but provides no further proof for his claim.
66. Reproduced by Bolte, *Das Danziger Theater*, pp. 63–5.
67. 'Nachdem Wir Englische Comoedianten nach absterben hochlöblichster gedechtnis des Koniges Sigismundi Tertij, dero wir viele Jahr gedienet haben, enturlaubet waren vnd darsieder vns in Holland, bey dem Könige in Denmarken, bey dem Fursten in Holstein, wie auch hier zu lande in Konigsbergk mit vnser kunst vnd agiren aufgehalten vnd nunmehr iezigen Maiestet aus der Wilde eines Königlichen schreibens vnd allergnedigsten resolution alhier erwarten, wo wir vns hinwenden sollen zu ihrer Königlichen Maiestat Dinsten, ob es etwan nach der Wilde oder nach Warschaw soll gemeinet sein: vnd gerne, weil der Dominiks markt alhier gar for der thuere ist, mit vnserem Comoedien etwas zum Viatico verdienen wolten.' (quoted in Bolte, *Das Danziger Theater*, pp. 63–4).
68. 'Derowegen gelanget an einen Ehrenfesten, Hochweisen Rahtt als hochlöbliche, Weltweise vnd Weitberuhmete Regenten vnd aller Kunste Fautoren, vnsere groszgunstige Herren, vnsere ganz hochfleiszige bitte, ihren gunstigen Consens disfals vns nicht zu uorweigern' (quoted in Bolte, *Das Danziger Theater*, p. 64).
69. Herz, *Englische Schauspieler*, p. 31.
70. Riewald, 'New Light on the English Actors in the Netherlands', pp. 83–4; Herz, ibid., pp. 54–5.
71. For Reynolds' visit to Amsterdam see Riewald, ibid., p. 84.

72. The basis for this assumption was the fact that Archer is mentioned together with Reynolds and Pudsey in a patent of 1640 given to the players by the Elector of Brandenburg (the patent was first published by Bolte, *Das Danziger Theater*, p. 69).
73. State Archives in Gdańsk: 300, 36/68, fos. 45–8. For the original see Appendix 1, item 2.
74. State Archives in Gdańsk: 300, 36/68, fos. 49–52. For the original see Appendix 1, item 3.
75. Bolte, *Das Danziger Theater*, p. 68; Herz, *Englische Schauspieler*, p. 56.
76. The Electoral company stayed at Königsberg until July 1640, and could not be the same as that which reached Gdańsk in May 1640.
77. Satori-Neumann, *Dreihundert Jahre berufständisches Theater in Elbing*, p. 11.
78. See Chapter 6.
79. Bolte, *Das Danziger Theater*, p. 70.
80. State Archives in Gdańsk: 300, 36/68, fos. 57–60. For the original see Appendix 1, item 4.
81. 'Pisze mi też ze Gdańsk a biskup kujawski że w gospodzie swej gdańszczanom i ich żonom i dzieciom sprawował w mięsopusty komedię angielską' (quoted in Witczak, *Teatr i dramat staropolski w Gdańsku*, p. 65).
82. State Archives in Gdańsk: 300, 36/68, fos. 61–4. For the original see Appendix 1, item 5.
83. Riewald, 'New Light on the English Actors in the Netherlands', p. 86.
84. Herz, *Englische Schauspieler*, p. 56.
85. Riewald, 'New Light on the English Actors in the Netherlands', pp. 85, 87–8.
86. State Archives in Gdańsk: 300, 36/68, fos. 67–70. For the original see Appendix 1, item 6.
87. Creizenach, *Die Schauspiele der englischen Komödianten*, p. XII.
88. For the full list see Herz, *Englische Schauspieler*, p. 67.
89. State Archives in Gdańsk: 300, 36/68, fos. 71–4. For the original see Appendix 1, item 7.
90. Riewald, 'New Light on the English Actors in the Netherlands', pp. 88–9.
91. *The Commonwealth and Restoration Stage*, pp. 167–9.
92. Hotson, ibid., pp. 167–8.
93. Bentley, *The Jacobean and Caroline Stage*, 2, pp. 483–4.
94. Hotson, *The Commonwealth and Restoration Stage*, p. 167.
95. See, for instance, ibid., pp. 167–96.
96. Ibid., p. 170.
97. 'dasz mir diese tage schreiben von einer Compagnie Englischer Comedianten Zukommen, darrinen mir vermaldet wird, dz [= das] sie unterweges waren, anhero kegenst vorstehenden Dominicks Marckt sich Zubegeben, vnd Zur Ergezlichkeit der Bürgerschafft mit schönen Comedien vnd Tragedien hören Zu lassen ... Wan nun diese Compagnie, auszehalb einer oder Zweyer personen dieses ohrts nie agiret hatt, vnd eine, von des Seelig Königes Vornembsten compagnien gewesen, auch in Schweden bey Jh.K.Mayest, vnd vornembsten Herren gunst vnd guttes Lob sol eingeleget haben.' (State Archives in Gdańsk: 300, 36/68, fos. 75–8.)
98. I am grateful to Dr Gunilla Dahlberg of Göteborg for providing me with these details.
99. See Kjellberg, *Kungliga musiker i Sverige under Stormarktstiden*, pp. 263–5.
100. These were first published by Alexander, 'George Jolly', pp. 33–5. Not knowing of Alexander's article I have reproduced the same in a recent essay in *Pamiętnik Teatralny*. There are, however, subtle differences in Alexander's transcription of the originals and that of my own, with the most conspicuous being Alexander's inaccurate reading of 'Voszawen' for 'Roszawen'.
101. Bolte, *Das Danziger Theater*, p. 93.

102. State Archives in Gdańsk: 300, 36/68, fos. 99–102. For the original see Appendix 1, item 8.
103. State Archives in Gdańsk: 300, 36/68, fos. 103–106. Translated by Dr Jeremy Adler. For the original see Appendix 1, item 9.
104. See Bolte, *Das Danziger Theater*, p. 125.

2. Elbing

1. See Marian Malicki, 'Old Polish Books in Swedish Research (A Review of Major Publications on the Subject up to 1939)', Charisteria Cracoviensia Universitati Regiae Uppsaliensi Quinta Sacra Saecularia Ab Universitate Iagellonica Cracoviensi Oblata, *Zeszyty Naukowe Uniwersytetu Jagiellońskiego*, DVIII, Prace Historyczne, Zeszyt 61 (Warsaw and Kraków, 1979), pp. 123–36.
2. 'Ist beliebet den englischen Comödianten wegen dessen, dass sie vorgestern einen Erb. Rath zu Gefallen agiret 20 Thlr. zur Verehrung zukommen zu lassen. Daneben aber auch ihnen zu untersagen, dass sie nunmehr zu agiren aufhören sollen in Anmerkung sie gestern in der Comödie schandbare sachen fürgebracht' (quoted in Hagen, *Geschichte des Theaters in Preussen*, p. 53).
3. The second town was of course Gdańsk. In other towns of Central Europe public performances were usually connected with a given company's attachment to a particular court in the region.
4. 'Engländische Comödianten halten heftig an, etiam intercedente Brakel deputato, ihnen zu gestatten zu ihre Spiele. Weil es aber eine Schatzung der Bürgerschaft ist und die jetzigen traurigen Läufte solches nicht zugeben wollen, hat ein Erb. Rath beschlossen, ihnen es abzuschlagen. Don wofern der Herr Deputat oder jemand anders ihres Spiels privatim begehren würde in seinem Hause, könne es gestattet werden' (quoted in Hagen, *Geschichte des Theaters in Preussen*, p. 53).
5. Satori-Neumann, *Dreihundert Jahre berufständisches Theater in Elbing*, pp. 7–8.
6. 'In den Jahrmerkten werden Comoedien oder andere Spiel darin praesentiret' (quoted in ibid., p. 8).
7. Ibid.
8. '90 Mark Sein vf gnedigen Befehl Ihr. Churfürstl. Gnaden einem Stockfischen welchen Ihr Churfürst. G. nachm Elbing Comoedien [Commödianten] von dannen anhero zu bringen abgefertigt haben an 50 Thalern zu 36 Gr. gezahlt. 17. March' (quoted in Hagen, *Geschichte des Theaters in Preussen*, p. 59).
9. A Polish florin or guilder was valued 1½ Prussian marks, i.e. 30 groschen.
10. 'An die Oberräthe des Herzogthums Preussen Von Gottes Gnaden Johann Sigismund etc. Wir haben den Comoedianten, welche wie euch bewust, zu vnterschiedenen mahlen, vf vnter gnedigstes Begehren, in vnserm Gemache zu Königsberg vnd Balge agiret, für ihre gehapte muhe, eins vor alles, zwei Hundert gulden Polnisch bewilliget, Befehlen euch demnach hiermit gnedigst, Ihr wollet ihnen solche 200 gulden, aus Unser Renthkammer also vort entrichten lassen etc. Datum Elbing den 20. Jun 1619' (quoted in Hagen, *Geschichte des Theaters in Preussen*, p. 59).
11. '150 Mark. 18 Englischen Commedianten welche vor Ihr Churfürstl. Gnd. etzliche Commedien, agiret, gezahlt den 22 Junn' (quoted in Hagen, ibid., p. 59).
12. See *Dzieje Pomorza Nadwiślańskiego* (Gdańsk, 1978), p. 162.
13. Ibid., p. 166.
14. See *Dreihundert Jahre berufständisches Theater in Elbing*, p. 22.
15. 'demnach wir Englische Comaedianten disz Jahr aber mit agirung unserer Comaedien in Rüege vndt Königsberg zugebracht, vndt nunmehr zu Elbing angelanget, Auch ferner entschlossen, vnsere Reise nach dieser löblichen Stadt

Danzigk zu nehmen . . .' (this application is in the collection of the State Archives in Gdańsk: 300, 36/68, fos. 61–4; for the full text see Appendix 1, item 5).

3. Königsberg

1. For a detailed study of this period see Carsten, *The Origins of Prussia*; Gause, *Die Geschichte der Stadt Königsberg*, especially vol. 1; Vetulani, *Władztwo Polski w Prusiech Zakonnych i Książęcych*, and by the same author 'Prawny stosunek Prus Książęcych do Polski 1466–1657', pp. 7–41.

2. '75 Mark vff begehren Meiner gst. Fürstin und Frawen etc. der Herzogin in Preussen etzlichen Englischen Comedianten, welche vor Ihr fürstl. Gnd. agiret, zweimal getanzet und mit einer lieblichen Musica ufgewartet. gezahlt den 3ten October 1605' (quoted in Hagen, *Geschichte des Theaters in Preussen*, p. 53).

3. See Riewald, 'New Light on the English Actors in the Netherlands', pp. 75–6.

4. See Herz, *Englische Schauspieler*, pp. 38–9.

5. Ibid.

6. Ibid.

7. '1609. 14. Julij dat: Königsberg. Churfurst von Brandenburg empfiehlt an den Churfürsten zu Sachsen Johann Spencer, einen englischen Musikum, den Herzog Franz von Stettin empfohlen, der eine Zeitlang am Hofe sich aufgehalten, und dessen Musica dem Churfürsten ziemlichermassen wohlgefallen' (quoted in Bolte, *Das Danziger Theater*, p. 36).

8. '7 Mark. 57 gr. vor 53 Stück Tecturen den Churfürstlichen Commedianten und Musici 1611' (quoted in Hagen, *Geschichte des Theaters in Preussen*, p. 54).

9. '30 Mark den Englischen Commedianten welche für unserm gnedigsten Fürsten und Herrn HEn. Albrecht Friederischen etc. eine Commediam agiret und getanzet, zur Verehrung gezahlt den 23ten July' (quoted in ibid., pp. 53–4).

10. '150 Mark den Englischen Commedianten als dieselbe nach Ortelsburg verreiset uf Rechnung den 7 October 1611' (quoted in ibid., p. 54).

11. 'Aldieweil wir gegen bevorstehender Lehens empfahung deren wir uns dann noch genzlich versehen, gerne unsere Instrumentalisten und Commoedianten gekleidet sehen möchten, So ist unser gnedigstes Begehren, mit Befehl, ihr wollet nach beigefügter designation beider Zettel; uff [uss?] gemein weiss englisch tuch, und schwarzen seidenen Schnuren, zu Mantel Hosen und Wammes einen uberschlag machen lassen, und nicht allein, soviel gemein Englisch weiss Tuch und die schwarze seidene Schnure, mittel arth, nebenst aller anderer Zubehör an futter, samt gestrickten weissen Strümpfen als sichs uf vorzeichnete Personen erstrecht, aber fünf oder sechs Personen ubermaass zu solcher behuf ungeseumbt anhero schicken . . .' (quoted in ibid., p. 54).

12. 'einem Rüstwagen zu socher Kleidung an Tuch, Leinwant, strümpfen seiden Knöpfen und Borten zu, Inmassen solchs inliegenge verzeichniss vermog . . .' – quoted in ibid., pp. 54–5.

13. '979¾ elen weis Kirsey an 32 ganzen stücken und an sieben stücken so angeschnitten. – 492 elen futtertuch an 17 ganzen stücken und 16 ellen. – 287 elen flechsene leimet. – 41 paar strimpfe weis. – 2 Pfd. Nehe- und 1 Pfd. Stepseide. – 123 Dutzet eyerne Knopfe. – 883 ellen seidene borten, der rest als 2397 elen werden gemacht sollen ufs allererste nachgeschicht werden' (quoted in ibid., p. 55).

14. See Gause, *Die Geschichte der Stadt Königsberg*, p. 379.

15. '720 Mark den Englischen Commedianten uf Rechnung der Bestallung an 400 Thaler zu 36 gr. den 30. November 1611' (quoted in Hagen, *Geschichte des Theaters in Preussen*, p. 54).

16. '1080 Mark Johann Spencern Commedianten an 600 Thaler zu 36 gr. so ihm noch uf

von Ihr Churfürstl. Gnaden getroffenen Contract restiret, empfing er selbst 4. Februar 1612' (quoted in ibid., p. 56).

17. '1229 Mark 24 sh. Johann Spenszern Commoedianten an Seiden-Waaren von Heinrich Klehe ausgenommen an 683 Thaler a 36 Gr. welches ihm zu Berlin an seiner Befsoldung soll gekürzet werden' (quoted in ibid., p. 58).

18. See Cohn, *Shakespeare in Germany*, p. XCII, and also discussion below.

19. Ibid., p. XCV.

20. '26 Mark 9 sh. Anslösung Ihr Churfürstl. Gnaden Comediant Johann Spencer welcher vom 28 October bis uf den 8 November 1612 bei Christoph Hertlein gelagen. 1 Woche. 47 Mark 48 sh. Anslösung der Churfürstl. Comödianten welche Anno 1612 bei Hans Jacob gelegen worauf in der 4ten und 5ten Woche 47 Mark 16 Gr. und jetzt der Rest gezahlt. 13 März' (quoted in Hagen, *Geschichte des Theaters in Preussen*, p. 57).

21. A question mark indicates that an entry is not dated, but immediately precedes or follows another bearing a date.

22. Quoted in Hagen, *Geschichte des Theaters in Preussen*, pp. 56–7.

23. See Lahrs, *Das Königsberger Schloss*, pp. 79–81.

24. See Southern, *The Staging of Plays Before Shakespeare*, passim.

25. Quoted in Hagen, *Geschichte des Theaters in Preussen*, pp. 56–7.

26. See Herz, *Englische Schauspieler*, pp. 72–4.

27. '1613. Sontag den 27. Junij, vnd etlich Tage hernach aufs Eines Erbarn Raths grossgünstigen erlaubniss, haben sess Churfürsten zu Brandenburg Diener vnd Englische Comoedianten schöne Comedien vnd Tragödien von Philole vnd Mariane, Item von Celide vnd Sedea, Auch von Zerstörung der Stätte Troia vnd Constantinopel, vonn Türcken vnd andere Historien mehr, neben zierlichen täntzen, lieblicher Musica, vnd anderer Lustbarkeit, im Halssbrunner Hof allhie, in guter teaucher Sprach in köstlicher Mascarada vnd Kleidungen agirt vnd gehalten.' (quoted in Cohn, *Shakespeare in Germany*, p. LXXXVII).

28. See Creizenach, *Die Schauspiele der englischen Komödienten*, p. XLVIII; see also Chambers, *The Elizabethan Stage*, II, p. 289, note 6.

29. Both of these have been reproduced by Bolte, *Das Danziger Theater*, pp. 171–279.

30. See Grabau, 'Englische Komödianten in Deutschland', p. 311.

31. See note 17 above.

32. Quoted in Cohn, *Shakespeare in Germany*, p. LXXXVII.

33. See Mentzel, *Geschichte der Schauspielkunst in Frankfurt a.M.*, p. 54.

34. '112 Mark 30 sh. den Englischen Comoedianten zur Verehrung. 7. November. – 112 Mark 30 sh. haben Ihr. Churfürstl. Dchl. etc. den Englischen Comoedianten zu den vorhin empfangenen 50 Reichsthalern nochmals zur Verehrung zu geben gst. beuohlen, welche sie empfangen den 8ten November' (quoted in Hagen, *Geschichte des Theaters in Preussen*, p. 58).

35. See Brachvogel, *Geschichte des Königlichen Theaters zu Berlin*, p. 19.

36. See Cohn, *Shakespeare in Germany*, p. XCII and Herz, *Englische Schauspieler vnd englisches Schauspiel*, pp. 51–2.

37. In the Nuremberg entry of 1623 Spencer is mentioned together with, apparently, a German player, one Thomas Sebastian Schadleutner; see Trautmann, 'Englische Komoedianten in Nürnberg', p. 131.

38. See Riewald, 'New Light on the English Actors in the Netherlands', p. 82.

39. See Gause, *Die Geschichte der Stadt Königsberg*, p. 403.

40. '69 Mark Fracht von etlichen papagi [bagage], wie auch der Commedianten, Trabanten, Trompeter und bergleichen Sachen und Völker von hier über Wasser bis nach Brandenburg ins Churfürstl. Ablager mit 2 Schmakken zu führen. Durch Reinholt Klein gezahlt. 18. October. – 675 Mark Herrn Secr. Dietern an 150 Rthlr. zu

Auszahlung der Englischen Commedianten welche Reinholdt Klein vorgestreckt und von den Holzgeldern wieder gut gamacht sein, gezahlt d. 5. December' (quoted in Hagen, *Geschichte des Theaters in Preussen*, p. 60).

41. 'Wir Georg Willhelm, von Gottes gnaden, Margraff vndt Churfürst zu Brandenb. geben hiemit menniglichen, vndt sonderlich denen daran gelegen, vndt es zuwissen von nöhten, zuvernehmen, Nachdem Sich Vorzeiger Englische Comoedianten, Robertt Rennols, Aaron Asken, Willhelm Roe, Joannes Weyd, Eduard Pudey vndt Willhelm Wedwer, im nechstvergangenen iahr, bey vns, vnd vnserm Churfl. Hause einige Comoedien agieren möchten, in vnterthenigkeitt angelangett vnd gebeten, Wir ihen auch solches in gnaden verstattett, das Sie sich also erwiesen, vndt in ihrer Kunst vnd geschickligkeitt der massen vndt also bestanden . . . Nachdem Sie denn nunmehr willens, sich von hinnen weiter zu begeben, vndt ihre gelernte Kunst, auch in vnsern andern Erblanden zubeweisen, vndt vnsern gnedigsten Consensum deshalben demütigst implorirt vndt gebeten, So haben wir diessem ihrem vnrthenigsten Suchen nicht entgegen sein' (quoted in Bolte, *Das Danziger Theater*, p. 69).

42. Bolte, *Das Danziger Theater*, p. 77.

43. As we learn from this company's application submitted in 1647 to the councillors of Gdańsk.

44. See Cohn, *Shakespeare in Germany*, pp. CXVIII–CXIX; Herz, *Englische Schauspieler*, pp. 57–8; and also Prölss, *Geschichte des Hoftheaters zu Dresden*, p. 69. It may be added here that when in 1648 Roe emerged at Cologne, his repertory included, among other plays, *A History of St Ursula* and *A History of St Dorothea*; see Cohn, 'Englische Komödianten in Köln', p. 269. It seems plausible that these plays were also performed at Königsberg in 1647.

4. Pomerania

1. For a meticulous study of Pomerania's history in the period under discussion see Boras, *Książęta Pomorza Zachodniego*, who also provides full bibliography of the subject, and Carsten, *The Origins of Prussia*.

2. See Meyer, 'Englische Komödianten am Hofe des Herzogs Philip Julius', pp. 196–211.

3. See Chambers, *The Elizabethan Stage*, 2, pp. 46–7.

4. 'dasz die von E.F.G. bestellte Comedianten sich haben gelüsten lassen, gesteriges tags in die F. Schloszkirchen allhie zu Lötz zu mausen, vnd deselbst einen marckt oder palast zu Irem spielen, springen, agiren und anderem Wesen aufzuschlagen . . . das dieselbe E.F.G. auslandische Diener, in den Haus Gottes, welches en Bethaus ist, Ire possen, steckerey, tantz, lider vnd fantasey vorhaben vnd treiben vnd also ein Spielhaus, ein Tantzplatz, ein Possenkram vnd Nerrenmarckt davon machen' (quoted in Meyer, 'Englische Komödianten am Hofe des Herzogs Philip Julius', pp. 200–1).

5. 'da die Calvinischen vnd Bebtischen Auslender die tauben Irer Fantasey vnd Comedien feyl bieten vnd verkauffen, vnd die vntüchtige verbottene müntz Ihrer possen, steckerey, lieder, tantz vnd gaukeley (vmb die es eigentlich zu thum ist) mit heilligen Historien vom Isaac vnd anderen auswexeln vnd durchstecken, vnd alsz Gottes nam vnd wort zum Schanddeckel Irer leichtfertigkeit vnd thorheit (die sie ex professio treiben) verkehren vnd miszbrauchen wollen . . . So wirdt es hergegen müszen Vnrechet sein das wir izt auf neüe manier durch auslendische Comedien vnd Calvinische Spieler vnd Tantzer, Gottes Wort vnd Historien d. H. Schrifft vns in der kirchen wollen lassen vorpredigen' (quoted in ibid., p. 202).

6. 'Weil Ire Comedien in vnbekannter sprach geschrieben sindt vnd agirt werden, das man nicht weis, were der Meister vnd Dichter derselben, was darinnen neben den Historien selbsten tractirt vnd eingebracht wirdt, ob es Gottes Wort, dem

Christlichen Glauben, vnserer reiner Evangelischen Religion, der gottesfurcht, zucht vnd erbarkeit gemes sey oder nicht' (quoted in ibid., pp. 203–4).

7. This was first published by Fredén in his *Friedrich Menius*, pp. 492–4.

8. The passport was first reproduced by Fredén, ibid., p. 495.

9. Both of these documents were first reproduced by Fredén, ibid., p. 496.

10. 'Vnsere gnedige Furstinn vndtt Fraw wil hiemit vndtt in crafft dieses dem Schulzen zu Negendthin befohlen haben das Er angesichts dieses J.F.G. hern Sohns Diener vngeseumet mit fuhre als vndt 3 wagen nacher Wolgast zuuerschaffen, vnd nichts daran behindern zu laszen' (quoted in ibid., p. 496).

11. This was first reproduced by Fredén, ibid., p. 497.

12. The letter was first reproduced by Fredén, ibid., p. 498.

13. Herz, *Englische Schauspieler*, p. 44.

14. Ibid.

15. Trautmann, 'Englische Komoedianten in Ulm', p. 320.

16. Mentzel, *Geschichte der Schauspielkunst in Franckfurt a.M.*, p. 53.

17. See Herz, *Englische Schauspieler*, pp. 36–7, and also Zimmerman, 'Englische Komödianten am Hofe zu Wolfenbüttel', pp. 37–45, 53–7.

18. See Boras, *Ksiazeta Pomorza Zachodniego*, p. 225.

19. Ibid., p. 224.

20. This was first reproduced by Fredén, *Friedrich Menius*, p. 498–9.

21. 'Darauff dan wier alssbalt entschlossen gewessenn, anhero in diese Kon. See Stadt vor allen andern vnss zuuorfüegen . . . E.Hochw. vnndt Gunsten vndt anderen dero löblichen einwohnern vnser New Historische [Comoedien] . . . zu exhibiren, vnter dessen aber von Ihr F.G. Hertzogk Philippen zu Stettin vnd Hertzogk Frantzen zu Cösslin vermöge beygelegten dero testimonien ein geraume zeitt vber gnedigst auffgehalten worden' (quoted in Bolte, *Das Danziger Theater*, pp. 42–3).

22. The application of this company to the councillors in Gdańsk was first reproduced by Bolte, ibid., pp. 42–5.

23. See Nordström, 'Friedrich Menius', pp. 42–91.

24. See Fredén, *Friedrich Menius*, passim.

25. See Price, *English Literature in Germany*, pp. 20–1.

26. In *Englische Komödianten am Hofe des Herzogs Philip Julius*, p. 209.

27. 'E.F.G. erinnern sich gnedig was maszen dieselbe uns hiebevohr auff ein Jahr in bestallung genommen, wir auch in unterthenigkeit mit unser Music dermaszen auffgewartet, das verhoffentlich E.F.G. in gnadem mit uns content sein werden, Weil denn nunmehr solch Jahr vorfloszen, und wir aus bewegenden ursachen uns wiederumb in Engellandt zu begeben entschloszen.' (quoted in Meyer, ibid., p. 209).

28. See Poulton, *John Dowland*, p. 88. Robert succeeded his father as a leading court musician in London in 1625.

29. 'E.F.G. ist wiszens dasz ich fürm Jhar von E.F.G. bin abgezogen, die Ursache aber worumb ist diese, dasz Jürgen mein Landtman den mich domahlen ausz Engelandt geschrieben ich solte man meinen abscheidt von E.F.G. nehmen undt in Engelandt kommen, alda wolte mir der Printz so viele geben, dasz ich die Zeit meines Lebens dimit hin kommen konte, welches ich nunmehr erfahren dasz es alles erlogen dinck sey, als bin ich wieder ahnhero gekommen undt langer bei E.F.G. Lust undt Liebe zu dienen habe, undt weil ich ein alter Man undt des Reisens möde bin, als ist undt gelangett ahn E.F.G. meiner begehren, wieder in seinem Dienst nehmen, ich wil mich hinferner aller Treuw undt fleiszes bei' (quoted in Meyer, *Englische Komödianten am Hofe des Herzogs Philip Julius*, pp. 209–10).

30. Prince Vladislaus of Poland cannot be taken into consideration, because from both the applications it is apparent that Jones went to England in 1623 and returned in 1624.

31. There was another Englishman employed at the Wolgast court in 1625: among the

'Instrumentalisten und Musicanten' who were paid for performances in May, we find one Richard Farnaby, the son of Giles Farnaby, one of the well known English composers of the period (see Fredén, *Friedrich Menius*, p. 499). We know that Richard was a composer himself (See *Grove's Dictionary of Music and Musicians*, vol. 3, pp. 32–3).

32. See Riewald, 'Some Later Elizabethan and Early Stuart Actors and Musicians', p. 36.
33. Bentley, *The Jacobean and Caroline Stage*, II, pp. 485–7.

5. Livonia

1. This is how Livonia was described by the author of *A Relation of the State of Polonia and the United Provinces Anno 1598*: 'Livonia along the sea is 4000 stadia, the breadth 2300. Some saye the length is 90 Germance miles, others 400 Italian, and the breadth 50 German, or 240 Italian. Eastward it is divided from the Moscovitish Russia by the ryver Narva . . . and by the lake Pelbas, which is 48 Italian mile longe . . . Southward it butts uppon Lithuania Samogitia and Prussia. On the west it hath the sea, and Northward the Goulfe and continent of Fynland. The auncient inhabitants different in language and customes are the Eastlanders, Leiflanders and Curlanders, which dwell not in cittie but in townes, and villages, only following husbandry. The others comme in by conquest, and trade, are first the Germans, whose nation and language swayes most by reason of theire greate traffique, and the Dutch Orders long possessing of it; the other longe after, broughte in by severall lordes are the Swedens, Danes, Poles, Lithuanians, and some relickes of the moscovitish colonyes' ((pp. 19–20). In C.H. Talbot, ed., *Elementa and Fontium Editiones*, XIII (Rome, 1965).
2. See Wedgwood, *The Thirty Years War*, pp. 381–2, 424.
3. Ibid., p. 468.
4. Bolte, *Das Danziger Theater*, p. 70, note 1.
5. 'Wir Englische Comaedianten disz Jahr aber mit agirung unserer Comaedien in Rüege vndt Königsberg zugebracht, vndt nunmehr zu Elbing angelanget, Auch ferner entschlossen, vnsere Reise nach dieser löblichen Stadt Danzigk zu nehmen' (State Archives in Gdańsk: 300, 36/68, fos. 61–4; for the full text see Chapter 1 above, and Appendix 1, item 5).
6. Herz, *Englische Schauspieler*, p. 56.
7. See Cohn, *Shakespeare in Germany*, p. XCIX.
8. The source is provided in note 5 above.
9. See Chapter 1 above.
10. Both of these have been reproduced by Bolte, *Das Danziger Theater*, pp. 77–8.
11. 'wir die Englischen Comoedianten, welche vor 4 Jahren durch günstiges zulaszen E.H.E.H. allhir agiret allhie angelanget, im willens hiwiederümb vnser Comoedien, Tragoedien, Historien etc. offentlich zu praesentiren. Gelanget derwegen an E.W.E.H. vnser gesambtes demütiges bitten, Sie wollen ihnen vnbeschweret zu gemüte füren, mit was groszen Vnkosten wir solch einen weiten weg (nemlich von Dantzig vndt Königsberg, woselbst wir letztes mal agiret) über landt hieher gereiset, vnserm vorhaben platz vergönnen vndt, gleich in Dantzig vndt Königsberg' (quoted in ibid., p. 77).
12. 'im Nahmen des königlichen Herren Burggrafen der Hausschlieszer vns angesagt, das wir nicht weiter solten agiren . . . Jetziger Zeit aber solche reise zu vollen ziehen ist vnmüglich; es mögen vielleicht E.E.H. gedencken, als wen wir grosze gelder erhascheten, haben aber noch zur Zeit wie schon erwehnet die Vnkosten nicht erholet, viel weniger einen Zehrpfennig, weiter zu reisen, erworben . . . Es ist ietzund in solcher Zeit, das wir nicht füglich anders wohin vns begeben können. Vber waszer zu reisen ist vnmüglich, vber land in die hah bey gelegenen Städte, mühsam, kostet viel

vndt ist der mühe vndt vnkosten nicht wert. Es pflegt vns ja auch umb diese Zeit vom Jahre an keinem orte gewegert werden . . . vndt gleich wie vergangen E.E.H. vns die Ehre genieszen laszen, als eine geringschätzige Comoedi anzuschawen, als gelanget anietzo an E.E.H. vnser gleichmäsziges gitten, sie wollen zum andern mal ihre Hocherwünschete gegenwart in einer Tragoedia (von der Märterin Dorotheâ) vns geniszen laszen' (quoted in ibid., pp. 77–8).

13. Bolte, *Das Danziger Theater*, p. 76.

6. Warsaw

1. This is the case in particular of German scholarship in the field. The theatrical activity of the English in Warsaw has attracted some attention by Polish scholars; see, for instance, Windakiewicz, *Teatr Polski*, Borowy, 'Angielscy Komedianci', pp. 757–9, Bernacki, 'Komedyanci angielscy', pp. 267–76, Raszewski, 'Jeszcze o teatrze zawodowym', pp. 153–6, and Limon, 'Komedianci angielscy w Warszawie', pp. 469–77. This chapter, however, remains the fullest account of the subject.

2. Raszewski, ibid., pp. 153–6. This view is also shared by Gause in his *Die Geschichte der Stadt Königsberg*, I, p. 435, and also by Kindermann in *Theatergeschichte Europas*, vol. III, p. 599.

3. *Elementa ad Fontium Editiones*, published by C.H. Talbot, VI (Rome, 1962), p. 113.

4. Sigismund III was not only a learned man, but also a great admirer of almost all the arts. He was interested in painting and sculpture, knew a lot about goldsmithery and metal engraving, loved music and theatre, and, strangely enough, was an ardent footballer. See Lechicki, *Mecenat Zygmunta III*.

5. *Elementa ad Fontium Editiones*, VI (Rome, 1962), p. 124.

6. See Targosz-Kretowa, *Teatr dworski Władysława IV* p. 301.

7. Although Sigismund III lost his succession war over his legal rights to the Swedish throne, he kept the title of the King of Sweden to stress that the ruling monarch in Sweden was a usurper.

8. 'Es ist uns aber wegen I.K. Matt. zu Polen und Schweden angemüttet, noch etwas abzuwarten auf gnedigste Resolutie, ob I.K. Matt. vnsers Dinstes möchte begerende sein. Wan dan damit etzliche tage hinlaufen, ehe wir gnedigsten bescheid erlangen vnd vnser gelegenheit nicht leiden wil, in mittels hie am schweren ortt ohn verdinst zu zehren, da vns auch sonst grosse vnkosten sein aufgegangen, die wir nicht eingenommen, weil wir hie agiret haben, Als gelanget an E.Edle H. vnser hohes bitten, Sie geruhen I.K.Matt. höchstgemelt zu besondern Ehren vns zu indulgiren, das wir dero gnedigsten willen abzuwarten vnd zu verhüttung vnsers praesent schadens in mitler Zeit mit vnsern Actionibus Comoedicis vnd Tragoedicis verfahren vnd die Zehrungs vnkosten erschwinden mögen. Das gereicht I.K.Matt. zu gnedigstem wolgefallen, vnd wir weind es bey deroselben gantz vnterthänig zu rühmen vnd auch anderweit E.Edle H. grossen fäuor vnd freundlischste Affection bey Potentaten vnd landen zu euulgiren vnd commendiren schuldig vnd erböttig' (quoted in Bolte, *Das Danziger Theater*, pp. 50–1).

9. Quoted in Cohn, *Shakespeare in Germany*, pp. XCIII–XCIV. The original letter is in Brno in the Bocek collection.

10. One of the courtiers accompanying the Prince, S.Pac, wrote a diary of the voyage [See *Obraz dworów europejskich*], in which it is mentioned that when, for instance, Vladislaus visited the Archduke Charles at Nysa, music was played during the evening meals (ibid., p. 14); Vladislaus also visited Cardinal von Dietrichstein, at whose court at Nikolsburg he listened to a concert performed by five Franciscan friars (ibid., p. 21); and in Vienna, at the Emperor's court, a 'comedy in singing' was presented by the Imperial players (ibid., p. 25). It is not unlikely that this comedy in

singing ('komedyja w śpiewaniu') was actually a jig – a form popularised by the English players.

11. The first of these documents was first noticed by Riewald in 'New Light on the English Actors in the Netherlands', pp. 89–90; the second one was first analysed by Schrickx in 'Pickleherring', p. 140.

12. *Acts of the Privy Council*, vol. 35, p. 257.

13. *Acts of the Privy Council*, vol. 36, p. 247.

14. See Schrickx, 'Pickleherring', p. 139.

15. Jones' first Continental visit was relatively short, and he was back in London by January 1593, when he appeared as a witness there; see *Henslowe's Diary*, ed. Greg, vol. I, F.3/14/.

16. Greg dated this entry 7–13 January 1602; see *Henslowe's Diary*, vol. II, p. 288.

17. See Riewald, 'New Light on the English Actors in the Netherlands', p. 90.

18. See Bolte, *Die Singspiele der englischen Komödianten*, p. 3.

19. A number of scholars have treated the English players' presence at Warsaw as incidental, as if the players stopped there on the way from Gdańsk to Prague.

20. Although a company of English 'instrumentalists' was brought directly from London to Nyköping in Sweden in 1591, it is not certain whether this was an acting company. See Wikland, *Elizabethan Players in Sweden*, *passim*.

21. 'Demenach Vnsere Compagnia Welche sich vf eine Zeit bey kön: Maytt: in polen Verhalten, auch gegen den Winter wiederumb dachinn begeben wirdt' (State Archives in Gdańsk: 300, 36/67, fos. 103–6; for the full text see chapter on Gdańsk and the Appendix 1, item 1).

22. Quoted in *Henslowe Papers* ed. Greg, pp. 94–5.

23. The same conclusion is reached independently by Schrickx in 'Pickleherring', p. 145.

24. See Niessen, *Dramatische Darstellungen*, p. 89.

25. 'Nachdem Wir Englische Comoedianten nach absterben hochlöblichster gedechtnis des Koniges Sigismundi Tertij, dero wir viele Jahr gedienet haben' (quoted in Bolte, *Das Danziger Theater*, p. 63).

26. See Herz, *Englische Schauspieler*, p. 31.

27. As identified by Riewald in 'Some Later Elizabethan and Early Stuart Actors', pp. 34–5.

28. See Herz, *Englische Schauspieler*, p. 54.

29. Ibid., p. 54.

30. Apart from the English company, Italian musicians were also kept at Sigismund's court. Two names of the latter were, for instance, mentioned in a letter written in 1626 by an Italian poet Jacopo Cicognini to Prince Vladislaus – Pellegrino Muzi and Michelangelo Gelsomini; see Targosz-Kretowa, *Teatr dworski Władysława IV*, pp. 63–4.

31. Tomkiewicz, 'Widowiska dworskie w okresie renesansu', pp. 94–5.

32. Ibid.

33. 'Nach der Zeit haben wir uns bei I.K.Mtt. zu Warschau aufgehalten, vnd deroselben nach behagen vnd begeren auffgewartet, auch auf eine zeit dimizion erhalten, doch mit dem verschprechen, das in gewiszer Zeit wir uns wieder daselbst einstellen sollen. (State Archives in Gdańsk: 300, 36/68, fos. 45–8). The full text is in Appendix 1, item 2.

34. The full text of the patent was originally published by Bolte, *Das Danziger Theater*, p. 69. See also Chapter 3.

35. See Riewald, 'Some Later Elizabethan and Early Stuart Actors', 1960, p. 84.

36. Mundy, *The Travels in Europe and Asia*, vol. IV, pp. 181–2. The quoted passage was first noticed by Borowy in 'What was known in Old Poland of English literature and English theatre', p. 3.

37. Riewald has uncovered some interesting documents relating to the subsequent fortunes of Reynolds' wife; see 'Some later Elizabethan and Early Stuart Actors', p. 86.
38. See Chapter 1.
39. See Chapter 1.
40. Targosz-Kretowa, *Teatr dworski Władysława IV*.

7. Bohemia

1. 'Das unns jegenwertige unsere Comoedianten Undertheniglich angelanget unndt gebetten, wir ihnenn gnediglich erleubenn woltenn, Damit sie auch an andere ortter Verreisen unndt etzliche Comoedias agiren mochtenn, wann wir nun solchem ihrem suchenn raumb unndt stadt gebenn, Alsts ist ann auch unser gnedigs begehrenn, Im fall bemelte Unsere Comoedianten uff solcher ihrer Reise sich auch naher Prag begebenn, unndt des orts etzliche Comoedias agiren würdenn, Ihr ihnenn alssdann soviel müglich güte beforderung anzeigenn wollet' (quoted in Hartleb, *Deutschlands erster Theaterbau*, p. 26). This letter was first referred to by Rommel in his *Neuere Geschichte von Hessen*, p. 402, note 122, but owing to what presumably was a printer's error the letter was wrongly dated 1595 – a mistake recurring in the literature on the subject.
2. See Herz, *Englische Schauspieler*, p. 13.
3. Ibid; see also Schrickx, 'English Actors at the Courts of Wolfenbüttel, Brussels and Graz', pp. 157–9.
4. Herz, *Englische Schauspieler*, p. 13. See also Trautmann, 'Englische Komoedianten in Nürnberg', p. 117.
5. Hartleb, *Deutschlands erster Theaterbau*, p. 28.
6. See Mentzel, *Geschichte der Schauspielkunst in Frankfurt a.M.*, pp. 23–6; Schrickx, 'English Actors at the Courts of Wolfenbüttel, Brussels and Graz', p. 156.
7. See Witkowski's review of *Englische Schauspieler*, by E. Herz in: *Zeitschrift für deutsche Philologie*, pp. 262–4; see also Weilen, *Geschichte des Wiener Theaterwesens*, p. 52.
8. See Herz, *Englische Schauspieler*, p. 41 and Meissner, *Die Englischen Comoedianten*, pp. 45–6.
9. Herz, ibid., pp. 11–13.
10. Meissner, ibid., p. 45.
11. Ibid., pp. 45–6.
12. The most recent account of Silesia's history in the period under discussion is Boras' *Związki Śląska i Pomorza Zachodniego z Polską w XVI wieku*, esp. pp. 178–216.
13. Ibid., p. 181.
14. See Hartleb, *Deutschlands erster Theaterbau*, pp. 58–62.
15. Ibid., p. 58.
16. Quoted in Cohn, *Shakespeare in Germany*, p. LXXXIII.
17. Herz, *Englische Schauspieler*, p. 41.
18. Ibid., p. 38–42; Mentzel in *Geschichte der Schauspielkunst in Frankfurt a.M.* adds one more name to the list: John Hull, who was recorded with Webster and Machin at Frankfurt in 1600.
19. Mentzel, ibid., p. 52.
20. Herz, *Englische Schauspieler*, p. 41.
21. See Mentzel, *Geschichte der Schauspielkunst in Frankfurt a.M.*, p. 55.
22. 'Nach abgelegten unserm f'rstlichen Beilager, haben wier die von E.L. unss zugeschichte Engellendische Comedianten wiederumb Abfertigenn lassenn, Undt thun unss Zue förderst gegen E.L. . . . dass Sie sich hierinn so bearbeitet und unss

selbige zugeschickt . . . ganz freundlichen bedanckenn'. (quoted in Hartleb, *Deutschland erster Theaterbau*, p. 62).

23. Ibid., p. 72.
24. See Herz, *Englische Schauspieler*, pp. 41–2.
25. Quoted in Cohn, *Shakespeare in Germany*, pp. XCIII–IV.
26. See Leszczyński, 'Zarys dziejów miasta do roku 1740', p. 49.
27. Ibid., p. 50.
28. See Kębłowski, *Nysa*, pp. 212–229.
29. See Wedgwood, *The Thirty Years War*, pp. 71–7.
30. See Meissner, *Die englischen Comoedianten*, p. 52; Meissner rightly identifies Archer with 'Rueprecht Ertzer' who appears in the entry he quoted (pp. 55–6).
31. See Elze, 'John Spencer in Regensburg', p. 362; see also Meissner, ibid., pp. 52–3.
32. 'dieser Comödiant [i.e. John Spencer] viele herrliche Comödien selbst vor den Kaiser Mathias aufgeführt' (quoted in Meissner, ibid., p. 53).
33. This patent has not been preserved, but it was mentioned by Spencer himself in his application to the councillors at Frankfurt, dated 5 September 1615; see Mentzel, *Geschichte der Schauspielkunst in Frankfurt a.M.*, pp. 57–9.
34. Both of these are reproduced by Meissner, *Die englischen Comoedianten*, p. 58.
35. See Meissner, ibid., p. 58.
36. Schmidt was paid 100 florins on the last day of July 1617; see ibid., p. 59.
37. Quoted in Cohn, *Shakespeare in Germany*, p. LXXXI.
38. See Herz, *Englische Schauspieler*, p. 49.
39. See Meissner, *Die englischen Comoedianten*, pp. 59–61.
40. Ibid., p. 61.
41. Herz wrongly conjectures (in *Englische Schauspieler*, p. 29) that Green's company went from Prague to Warsaw, because the company active at that time in Poland's capital was that of Richard Jones (see chapter on Warsaw).
42. See Herz, ibid., pp. 21–2.
43. For a detailed account of the events see Wedgwood, *The Thirty Years War*, pp. 69–80 and also Vajda, *Felix Austria*, pp. 282–96.
44. See Trautmann, 'Englische Komoedianten in Nürnberg', p. 129.
45. See Crüger, 'Englische Komoedianten in Strassburg', p. 120.
46. See Trautmann, 'Englische Komoedianten in Nürnberg', p. 130.
47. See Mentzel, *Geschichte der Schauspielkunst in Frankfurt a.M.*, p. 61. And John Green was recorded as the manager of a company in April 1620 at Cologne (see Wolter, 'Chronologie des Theaters der Reichstadt Köln', p. 97). We cannot, however, be certain that Green went together with Browne to Prague in 1619.
48. 'neve schöne Nationen-Däntz edle Musica und ganz neve schöne Comedien' (quoted in Meissner, *Die englischen Comoedianten*, p. 65).
49. See ibid., pp. 65–6.
50. See Herz, *Englische Schauspieler*, p. 57.
51. See ibid., p. 57.
52. *Archív mesta Bratislavy, účtovná kniha z roku 1649*. I would like to express my gratitude to Dr Milena Cesnaková-Michalcová of Bratislava who provided me with this piece of information.
53. See Cohn, *Shakespeare in Germany*, p. CII.
54. The full list is provided by Herz, *Englische Schauspieler*, pp. 67–8.
55. Quoted from Cohn, *Shakespeare in Germany*, p. CII. Cohn does not quote the German original.
56. See Bolte, *Das Danziger Theater*, pp. 92–3.
57. See Cohn, *Shakespeare in Germany*, p. CII.
58. The original text was published by Meissner in 'Die englischen Komödianten in

Oesterreich', pp. 144–5.

59. See František Černý (ed.), *Dějiny Českého Divadla*, part I: *Od počótku do sklonku osmnástého století*, (Praha, 1968), p. 197; the original source was first published by Menčík in *Příspěvky k dějinám českého divadla*, pp. 91 and 109.

60. The diary was first published by Hippe, 'Aus dem Tagebuch eines Breslauer Schulmannes', pp. 159–192.

61. 'Augusti 22: Advenae quidam histriones Anglicani in aedibus transolanis aurea aquila insignibus tragoediam nescio quam egere. Augusti 23: Histrionum Anglicanorum secunda actio. Augusti 24: Tertia actio Anglicanorum histrionum' – quoted in ibid., p. 190.

8. Austria

1. 'Wir haben dem Jenig Engelländischen Comedianten, welche auf Unser gnedigsten Begern hieher khumen Und Ihre Comedian Zu Unserem gndsten gefallen etlich mallen gehalten auss gnaden Und zu einer Verehrung 300 Reichstaller gnedigst Verordnet' (quoted in Meissner, *Die englischen Comoedianten*, p. 74).

2. 'die engellender haben heut Zu der Lötz wider ein comedi geholten, von ein khinig auss engelandt, der ist in eins goltschmitt weib verliebet gewest' (quoted from Meissner, ibid., p. 74).

3. See discussion below.

4. Irene Morris, 'A Hapsburg Letter', pp. 13–14: 'miesz E.L. gleich auch schreiben, was die Engellender für Comedi gehabt haben, alsz erstlich wie sy sein am mitwoch nach liehtmesen her khommen, haben sy am pfingstag Donnerstag auszgerast, am freitag nacher haben sy die Comedi von dem verlornen sohn gehabt, wie zu Passau; amb samstag von einer frommen fraween von Antorf, ist gewiss gar fein und zuchtig gewest; am sontag haben sy gehabt von dem dockhtor Faustus; am Montag von ein herzog von florenz, der sich in eines Edelmanns tochter verliebt hat; am Erchtag Dienstag haben sy gehabt von des fortunatus peitl und Wünschhietel, ist auċ gar schön gewest; am pfingstag haben sy die von dem Juden gehalten, die sy auch zu Passau gehalten haben . . . am faschung sontag haben die khöch ihr hochzeit gehabt, darnach haben mir umb 5 gessen und zu nachts nach dem essen haben die Engellender wider ein Comedi gehalten von den 2 priedern Chünig ludwig und khünig friderich von ungern, ist ein erschröckhliche Comedi gewest, ein und so hats der khünig friderick alsz erstochen und ermördt; am unsinigen Montag haben sy wider ein Comedi gehalten von ein Chünig von Chipern und ein herzog von venedig, ist auch gar schön gewest . . . umb 5 sein mir nacher wider zu dem essen gangen und haben die Engellender wider ein Comedi gehalten von dem reichen mann und von dem Lazarusz: ich khon E.L. nit schreiben, wie schön sy gewest ist, dann khein pissen von puellerey darin gewest ist, sy hat vnns recht bewegt, so woll haben sy aggiert; sy sein gewisz woll zu passieren für guete Comedianten.'

5. For the full list of plays see Herz, *Englische Schauspieler*, pp. 66–7. For a recent detailed discussion see Murad, *The English Comedians*, passim.

6. For a general study of the Landgrave's patronage see Dunckcr, 'Landgraf Moritz von Hessen', pp. 260–75; see also the Introduction. For a meticulous, though not always precise, account of Green's fortunes on the Continent see Herz, *Englische Schauspieler*, pp. 24–32.

7. See Meissner, *Die englischen Comoedianten*, pp. 67–8. The players appeared for the first time together in 1603 at Cologne (see Schrickx, 'English Actors at the Courts of Wolfenbüttel, Brussels and Graz', p. 162).

8. Meissner, ibid., pp. 70–1.

9. Quoted in Cohn, *Shakespeare in Germany*, pp. XCIII–XCIV.

10. It is interesting to note that the Archduchess did not know the name of the actor; obviously, these were not times when nobility found pleasure in socialising with artists.

11. See Morris, 'A Hapsburg letter', p. 20. Incidents of the kind described by Maria Magdalena, involving English players, were not uncommon. A contemporary account tells us that in 1603 an English player was engaged in a brawl in Paris, and that he 'drewe out his dagger and broke the poore man's heade' (see Yates, 'English Actors in Paris', p. 400). And in 1655 another English actor, George Jolly, struck and wounded a German player Christoph Blümels, who thereupon sued him for damages (see Hotson, *The Commonwealth and Restoration Stage*, p. 170).

12. See Morris, 'A Hapsburg Letter'.

13. See Bischoff, 'Niemand und Jemand in Graz', p. 139, where the dedication is reproduced. The dedication was signed by 'Studiosissimus Joannes Grün Nob. Anglus'. See also Murad, *The English Comedians*, pp. 52–3.

14. See Meissner, *Die englischen Comoedianten*, pp. 4–10.

15. 'Dergleichen schaw- und hörspiel seyn der zeit im Teuschland zufinden / vnd dern Comoedianten / wie ich selbst gesehen auss den Nider- vnd Engelländischen Stätten / so von eim ort zum andern herumb ziehen / vnd jre lächrige bossen vnd gauckelspiel / doch ohne ungebür / umb dass gelt denen / so es zusehen vnnd hörn begeren / zimlicher massen / soviel man in Teuscher Sprach vnd geberden zuwegen bringen kan / verrichten' (quoted in Meissner, ibid., p. 6).

16. In his 'English Acting Companies at the Court of Brussels', pp. 26–33.

17. Schrickx, 'English Actors at the Courts of Wolfenbüttel, Brussels and Graz', p. 167.

18. See Meissner, *Die englischen Comoedianten*, pp. 72–3.

19. See Trautmann, 'Englische Komoedianten in Nürnberg', pp. 125–6.

20. Meissner, *Die englischen Comoedianten*, p. 50.

21. The entry in the book of Royal expenses is very short indeed: 'Skoczkom na drogę do Wiednia'. This was uncovered by Zbigniew Raszewski among the Royal receipts in the *Archiwum Główne Akt Dawnych* in Warsaw, Rachunki Królewskie, 349, k.244.

22. See Crüger, 'Englische Komoedianten in Strassburg', p. 121.

23. Quoted in Cohn, 'Englische Komödianten in Köln', p. 273.

24. See Weilen, *Geschichte des Wiener Theaterwesens*, p. 53.

25. Quoted in Cohn, *Shakespeare in Germany*, pp. C–CI.

26. Weilen, *Geschichte des Wiener Theaterwesens*, p. 53.

27. See Herz, *Englische Schauspieler*, pp. 57–8.

28. The full list of players' names is provided in the introduction.

29. See Prölss, *Geschichte des Hoftheaters zu Dresden*, p. 69.

30. For an account of Jolly's fortunes on the Continent see Hotson, *The Commonwealth and Restoration Stage*, pp. 167–76. Actually, George Bentley was the last great English stroller.

31. See Herz, *Englische Schauspieler*, pp. 60, 62.

32. See Alexander, 'George Jolly', pp. 35–6.

33. Alexander's identification, ibid., p. 36. For the original see Faber du Faur, *German Baroque Literature*, p. 104.

34. See Ludvik, 'Zur Chronologie und Topographie', p. 63, note 78.

35. See Hotson, *The Commonwealth and Restoration Stage*, p. 175.

36. Quoted in Cohn, *Shakespeare in Germany*, p. CIII.

37. See Ludvik, 'Zur Chronologie und Topographie', p. 63, note 76.

9. The Gdańsk Fencing-School

1. This chapter is a revised version of my essay, 'Pictorial Evidence for a Possible Replica

of the London Fortune Theatre in Gdańsk', and of a paper I presented at the annual meeting of the Shakespeare Association of America in 1979.

2. *Der Stadt Danzig historische Beschreibung.*

3. The only other fact known about Heidemann is that he was a student of the Academic Gymnasium in Gdańsk in the 1590s (see *Ksiega wpisów uczniów Gimnazjum Gdańskiego 1580–1814*, ed. Z. Nowak and P. Szafran (Warsaw and Poznań, 1974) p. 62).

4. Bolte, *Das Danziger Theater*, p. 42.

5. In an application to the City Council in Gdańsk of 20 July 1615, a company of Brandenburg players asked for leave to play in the 'fechtschullen', where their 'antecessor vor dreyen Jahren' had also given performances, i.e. in 1612. In an article I wrote for *Shakespeare Survey*, referred to above in note 1, I noted that 'at present it is not possible to identify the English company that visited Gdańsk in 1612 and as the first one (at least according to the sources) which performed in the "Fencing-School"'. But in the course of subsequent research in the State Archives in Gdańsk, I have uncovered an interesting document, discussed above in Part I, which leaves no doubt that this company was John Green's.

6. A German scholar, W. Krause, was the first one to identify the 'Fencing-School' in Willer's engraving as the actual theatre. In his *Das Danziger Theater* he also noticed its general similarity to the contemporary London theatres, but thought of the Globe rather than of the Fortune, which in fact he did not even mention. See my article 'Przypuszczalne związki między teatrem w gdańskiej "Szkole Fechtunku" a teatrem "Fortune" w Londynie', pp. 29–38.

7. Early seventeenth-century panoramas of Gdańsk were made by I. Dickmann (1617) and his copyists; Peter van der Keere (1618); Claesz Jansz Visscher (1620); and M. Meriam (1640). An English copy of Dickmann's panorama was published by J. Fielding in the 1780s (entitled *Dantzig in Polish Prussia*).

8. This was suggested to me by Professor Marian Szarmach of the Toruń University.

9. For a meticulous account of this event see Witczak, *Teatr i dramat staropolski w Gdańsku*, pp. 65–85.

10. *Relation du voyage de la Royne de Pologne*, p. 157. It may be noted here that the Queen was very impressed by the performance, and she described it to Cardinal Mazarin in the following terms: 'My mind is so full of a comedy which I just saw that I can't write to you about anything else. I have never seen anything so beautiful before and it was only with difficulty that I would decide to watch the usual French and Italian presentations. This pleasure lasted five hours which seemed to pass in an instant. The music was excellent and the stage effects so astounding that I was really captivated.' For the original see Targosz-Kretowa, *Teatr dworski Władysława IV*, p. 296 (the English version of the letter was translated by Mr David Evans).

11. In a private letter.

12. See Bolte, *Das Danziger Theater*, p. 168.

13. Now in the collection of the National Museum in Poznań: Mp. 2256.

14. For an iconographical analysis of the painting see Iwanoyko, 'Model świata i społeczeństwa gdańskiego', pp. 44–64.

15. The numerous German prose versions of English plays, even if performed in Gdańsk by the English players, cannot be taken into consideration in our analysis of stage conditions in the Gdańsk theatre, simply because these plays were not written for that particular stage.

16. In the collection of the PAN Library in Gdańsk: MS 2429.

17. See Bolte, *Das Danziger Theater*, pp. 41–78.

18. An unpublished Latin manuscript in the collection of the PAN Library in Gdańsk: MS 1654, pp. 1–36.

19. *Henslowe's Diary*, ed. Greg, II, p. 197.
20. See Holinshed, *Chronicles of England, Scotland and Ireland*, vol. 4, pp. 505–7; Camden, *Annales rerum Anglicarum*, p. 389.
21. *Henslowe's Diary*, ed. Greg, II, p. 173.
22. *A Particular Description of the City of Dantzick*, p. 20.
23. Documentary evidence is provided by Krause, *Das Danziger Theater*, pp. 11–13.

10. The Royal Theatre in Warsaw

1. See Windakiewicz, *Teatr polski*, p. 24.
2. We learn about this event from a letter of nuncio A. Santa Croce to Cardinal F. Barberini, dated 8 March 1628. The nuncio mentioned in his letter that a 'musical drama' had been staged a week before, and that it was about Galatea; in addition, he observed that an engineer from Mantua was hired for this purpose. For the original see Targosz-Kretowa, *Teatr dworski Władysława IV*, p. 255. It may be noted here that *Galatea* was one of the first opera productions north of the Alps. Earlier examples may be found in Salzburg (1618–19) and at Hartenfels near Torgau (1627).
3. 'Na górze zaś nad tymi wschodami idzie sala wzdłuż, do której drzwi porządne z dobrym zamkiem i oknami całymi, jak przedtem. W tejże sali komedialnia przeforstowana, wszystka wcale, z ławami, chórami, perspektywami, niebiosami, kolumnami i sufitem nad theatrum, jak i przedtem było' (quoted in Tomkiewicz, 'Dwie lustracje Zamku Warszawskiego', pp. 302–3). The hall in question is marked as number 12 in illustration 2 in Tomkiewicz's article.
4. See Schüpli, *Kurtze Beschreibung*, p. 3.
5. See Lileyko, *A Companion Guide to the Royal Castle in Warsaw*, p. 43.
6. This figure was given to us by a contemporary biographer of Vladislaus IV, Everhart Wassenberg, in his *Gestorum gloriosissimi ac invictissimi Vladislai*, II, p. 251.
7. See Miks-Rudkowska, 'Niektóre projekty dekoracji', pp. 19–20.
8.   A pod wierzchem niebo własne,

                Z obłokami, zda sie jasne,

                Słońce, miesiąc i z gwiazdami,

                Niebieskimi planetami

   (quoted from Jarzębski, *Gościniec*, lines 873–6); The similarity between Gisleni's design and Jarzębski's description of the theatre's ceiling was first noticed by Miks-Rudkowska, ibid.
9. 'Z tyłu, i po bokach senatorowie i wojewodowie, którzy są przy dworze, oraz wybrane damy zasiadali na ławach pokrytych czerwonym płótnem, inne damy i szlachta oglądali balet stojąc.' (quoted in Lewański, 'Świadkowie i śsiadectwa opery władysławowskiej', p. 45.
10. See Windakiewicz, *Teatr Władysława IV*, p. 10. In Jarzębski's description of the theatre, 'double windows' are mentioned ('Dwoiste ma okna . . .'). This peculiar use of 'windows' was not unknown in Italy. For instance, Joseph Furttenbach (1591–1667) in his famous *On the Construction of Theatres* recalls a Florentine theatre in which one could look into the theatre interior through windows.
11. See Targosz-Kretowa, *Teatr dworski Władysława IV*, pp. 274–288.
12. 'tkaninę rozpiętą od samej góry sceny aż do podłogi z obrazem lasu, malowanym ściále wedle wymagań perspektywy, a podobnie na drugiej ścianie wszystkie będą miały wymalowane w perspektywie chmury, na trzeciej ogień, na czwartej pałace i budynki, wszystkie zaś dadzą sie obrócić w jednej chwili na jeden i ten sam bok' (quoted in Król-Kaczorowska, *Teatr dawnej Polski*, p. 100).
13.   'Jedne kunszty na dół schodzą,

                       Wagami do góry wchodzą'

   (quoted from Jarzebski, *Gościniec*, p. 33).

14. 'Qui apertosi il prospetto della scena apparve nell' ultima parte di essa mare' (quoted in Targosz-Kretowa, *Teatr dworski Władysława IV*, p. 276).
15. This particular libretto was published by Puccitelli in *Pamiętnik Teatralny*, XVIII, no. 4 (1969), pp. 511–27.
16. Wassenberg, *Gestorum gloriosissimi ac invictissimi Vladislai*, p. 251.
17. Puccitelli, *La Maga Sdegnata*, lines 178–9.

Bibliography

Acts of the Privy Council, ed. J.V. Lyle, vols. 35, 36 (1927, 1929).

Alexander, R.J., 'George Jolly [Joris Joliphus] der wandernde Player und Manager. Neues zu seiner Tätigkeit in Deutschland 1648–1660', *Kleine Schriften der Gesellschaft für Theatergeschichte*, Helt. 29/30 (1978), pp. 31–48.

Baesecke, A., *Das Schauspiel der englischen Komödianten in Deutschland. Seine dramatische Form und seine Entwicklung* (Halle, 1935).

Bentley, G.E., *The Jacobean and Caroline Stage*, vols. 1–6 (Oxford, 1941–68).

Bernacki, L., 'Komedyanci angielscy w XVII wieku', *Pamiętnik Literacki*, 9 (1910), pp. 267–76.

Bischoff, F., 'Niemand und Jemand in Graz im Jahre 1608', *Mittheilungen des historischen Vereines für Steiermark*, XLVII (1899), pp. 127–92.

Bolte, J., 'Englische Komödianten in Dänemark und Schweden', *Jahrbuch der Deutschen Shakespeare-Gesellschaft*, 23 (1888), pp. 99–106.

Die Singspiele der englischen Komödianten und ihrer Nachfolger in Deutschland, Holland und Scandinavien, (Hamburg and Leipzig, 1893).

Das Danziger Theater im 16. und 17. Jahrhundert (Hamburg and Leipzig, 1895).

'Englische Komödianten in Münster und Ulm', *Jahrbuch der Deutschen Shakespeare-Gesellschaft*, 36 (1900), pp. 273–6.

Boras, Z., *Książęta Pomorza Zachodniego* (Poznań and Słupsk, 1968).

Zwiazki Slaska i Pomorza Zachodniego z Polska w XVI wieku (Poznań, 1981).

Borowy, W., 'What Was Known in Old Poland of English Literature and English Theatre', *The Warsaw Weekly* (6 November 1937), p. 3.

'Angielscy Komedianci w Polsce', *Scena Polska*, vol. XV, no. 4 (1938), pp. 757–9.

Brachvogel, A.E., *Geschichte des Königlichen Theaters zu Berlin*, Erster Band: *Das alte Berliner Theaterwesen* (Berlin, 1877).

Brennecke, E., *Shakespeare in Germany 1590–1700* (Chicago, 1964).

Camden, W., *Annales rerum Anglicarum et Hibernicarum regnante Elizabeth* (Amstelodami, 1677).

Carsten, F.L., *The Origins of Prussia* (Oxford, 1954).

Chambers, E.K., *The Elizabethan Stage*, I–IV (Oxford, 1923).

Cohn, A., *Shakespeare in Germany in the Sixteenth and the Seventeenth Centuries: an Account of English Actors in Germany and the Netherlands and of the Plays Performed by Them During the Same Period* (London and Berlin, 1865).

'Englische Komödianten in Köln (1592–1656)', *Jahrbuch der Deutschen Shakespeare-Gesellschaft*, 21 (1886), pp. 245–76.

Creizenach, W., *Die Schauspiele der englischen Komödianten* (Berlin and Stuttgart, 1889).

Crüger, J. 'Englische Komoedianten in Strassburg in Elsass', *Archiv für Litteraturgeschichte*, XV (1887), pp. 113–25.

Curicke, R., *Der Stadt Danzig historische Beschreibung* (Amsterdam and Gdańsk, 1687).

Czapliński, W., Galos, A., Korta, W., *Historia Niemiec* (Wrocław, Warsaw, Kraków and Gdańsk, 1981).

Dejiny Ceského Divadla, ed. by Frantisek Cerný, Part I: *Od počátku do sklonku osmnástého stoleti* (Praha, 1968).

BIBLIOGRAPHY

Descriptio Urbis Londini in Anglia, an anonymous manuscript in the collection of the PAN Library in Gdańsk: MS 1654, pp. 1–36.

Dessoff, A., 'Über englische, italienische und spanische Dramen in den Spielverzeichnissen deutscher Wandertruppen', *Studien zur vergleichenden Litteraturgeschichte*, 1 (Berlin, 1901), pp. 420–44.

Duncker, A., 'Landgraf Moritz von Hessen und die englischen Komödianten', *Deutsche Rundschau*, XLVIII (Berlin, 1886), pp. 260–275.

Elze, Th., 'John Spencer in Regensburg', *Jahrbuch der Deutschen Shakespeare-Gesellschaft*, 14 (1879), p. 362.

Enziger, M., *Die Entwicklung des Wiener Theaters vom 16. zum 19. Jahrhundert (Stoffe und Motive)*, 1 (Berlin, 1918); volume 28–9 of *Schriften der Gesellschaft für Theatergeschichte*.

Faber du Faur, Curt von, *German Baroque Literature. A Catalogue of the Collection in the Yale University Library* (New Haven, Conn., 1958).

Flemming, W., 'Englische Komödianten', *Reallexikon der deutschen Literaturgeschichte*, ed. P. Merker and W. Stammler, 1 (Berlin, 1925–6), pp. 271–9.

Das Schauspiel der Wanderbühne, (Leipzig, 1931); volume 3 of *Deutsche Literatur Reihe Barock: Barock-drama*.

Fredén, G., *Friedrich Menius und das Repertoire der englischen Komödianten in Deutschland* (Stockholm, 1939).

Frenzel, H.A., *Brandenburg-Preussische Schlosstheater*, vol. 59 of *Schriften der Gesellschaft für Theatergeschichte* (Berlin, 1959).

Fürstenau, M., *Zur Geschichte der Music und des Theaters am Hofe zu Dresden* (Dresden, 1861).

Gause, F., *Die Geschichte der Stadt Königsberg* (Köln and Graz, 1965).

Gierszewski, S., *Elbląg. Przeszłość i ternaźniejszość* (Gdańsk, 1970).

Grabau, C., 'Englische Komödianten in Deutschland', *Jahrbuch der Deutschen Shakespeare-Gesellschaft*, 45 (1909), pp. 311–12.

Greg, W.W., ed, *Henslowe's Diary*, vols. 1–2 (London, 1904).

Henslowe Papers (London, 1907).

Gross, G., *Das Danziger Theater in der ersten Hälfte des 17. Jahrhunderts* (Leipzig, 1939).

Grove's Dictionary of Music and Musicians, ed. Eric Blom (London, 1954), fifth edition.

Hagen, E.A., *Geschichte des Theaters in Preussen, vornämlich der Bühnen in Königsberg und Danzig* (Königsberg, 1854).

Hammerich, A., 'Musical Relations between England and Denmark in the Seventeenth Century', *Sammelbände der Internationalen Musikgesellschaft*, XIII (1912), pp. 114–19.

Harris, Ch., 'The English Comedians in Germany Before the Thirty Years' War: The Financial Side', *PMLA*, 22 (1907), pp. 446–64.

Hartleb, H., *Deutschlands erster Theaterbau* (Berlin and Leipzig, 1936).

Heck, R., Orzechowski, M., *Historia Czechosłowacji* (Wrocław, Warsaw and Kraków, 1969).

Herz, E., *Englische Schauspieler und englisches Schauspiel zur Zeit Shakespeares in Deutschland* (Hamburg and Leipzig, 1903).

Hippe, M., 'Aus dem Tagebuch eines Breslauer Schulmannes im siebzehnten Jahrhundert', *Breslauer Studien. Zeitschrift des Vereins für Geschichte und Alterthum Schlesiens*, XXXVI (1901), pp. 159–92.

Holinshed, R., *Chronicles of England, Scotland and Ireland*, 6 vols. (London, 1808).

Hoppe, H.R., 'English Actors at Ghent in the Seventeenth Century', *Review of English Studies*, XXV (1949), pp. 305–21.

'George Jolly at Bruges, 1948', *Review of English Studies*, new series V (1954), pp. 265–8.

BIBLIOGRAPHY

'English Acting Companies at the Court of Brussels in the Seventeenth Century', *Review of English Studies*, new series VI (1955), pp. 26–33.

Hotson, L., *The Commonwealth and Restoration Stage*, (London, 1962).

Hysel, F.E., *Das Theater in Nürnberg von 1612 bis 1863 nebst einem Anhange über das Theater in Fürth* (Nuremberg, 1863).

Iwanoyko, E., 'Model świata i społeczeństwa gdańskiego w trzech obrazach z początku XVII wieku w Muzeum Narodowym w Poznaniu', *Studia Muzealne*, 11 (1975), pp. 44–64.

Jarzębski, A., *Gościniec albo opisanie Warszawy r.1643* (Warsaw, 1643).

Junkers, H., *Niederländische Schauspieler und niederländisches Schauspiel im 17. und 18. Jahrhundert in Deutschland* (Haag, 1935).

Kębłowski, J., *Nysa* (Wrocław, 1972).

Kindermann, H., *Theatergeschichte Europas*, 10 vols. (Salzburg, 1957–74).

Kjellberg, E., 'Kungliga musiker i Sverige under stormarktstiden. Studier kring deras organisation, verksamheter och status ca 1620–c. 1720' [unpublished dissertation], (Uppsala, 1979).

Köhler, R., 'Einige Bemerkungen und Nachträge zu Albert Cohns "Shakespeare in Germany"', *Jahrbuch der Deutschen Shakespeare-Gesellschaft*, 1 (1865), pp. 406–17.

Konarski, K., *Warszawa w pierwszym jej stołecznym okresie* (Warsaw, 1970).

Könnecke, G., *Bilderatlas zur Geschichte der deutschen Nationalliteratur* (Marburg, 1895 ?).

Deutscher Literaturatlas von Gustav Könnecke. Mit einer Einführung von Christian Muff (Marburg, 1909).

Krause, W., *Das Danziger Theater und sein Erbauer Carl Samuel Held* (Gdańsk, 1936).

Król-Kaczorowska, B., 'Jeszcze o teatrze Władysława IV na Zamku Królewskim w Warszawie', *Pamiętnik Teatralny*, XX (1971), pp. 211–22.

Teatr dawnej Polski. Budynki–Dekoracje–Kostiumy (Warsaw, 1971).

Laboureur, J.Le, *Histoire et Relation du Voyage de la Royne de Pologne* (Paris, 1647).

Lahrs, F., *Königsberger Schloss* (Stuttgart, 1956).

Lechicki, Cz., *Mecenat Zygmunta III i życie umysłowe na jego dworze* (Warsaw, 1932).

Lewański, J., 'Świadkowie i świadectwa opery władysławowskiej', *Opera w dawnej Polsce na dworze Władysława IV i królów saskich* (Wrocław, Warsaw, Kraków and Gdańsk, 1973), pp. 25–60.

Leszczyński, J., 'Zarys dziejów miasta do roku 1740', *Miasto Nysa. Szkice monograficzne* (Wrocław, 1970).

Lileyko, J., 'Theatrum Jana III a sale teatralne Wettinów na Zamku Królewskim w Warszawie', *Pamiętnik Teatralny*, XX (1970), pp. 51–9.

A Companion Guide to the Royal Castle in Warsaw (Warsaw, 1980).

Limon, J., 'Przypuszczalne związki między teatrem w gdańskiej "Szkole Fechtunku" a teatrem "Fortune" w Londynie', *Pamiętnik Teatralny*, XXVI (1977), pp. 29–38.

'Komedianci angielscy w Warszawie. Przegląd źródeł', *Pamiętnik Teatralny*, XXVIII (1979), pp. 469–77.

'Pictorial Evidence for a Possible Replica of the London Fortune Theatre in Gdańsk', *Shakespeare Survey* 32 (1979), pp. 189–99.

'New Evidence for the Activity of English Players in the Netherlands in the Second Quarter of the Seventeenth Century', *English Studies*, 62 (1981), pp. 115–19.

Linthicum, M.Ch., *Costume in the Drama of Shakespeare and his Contemporaries* (Oxford, 1936).

Ludvik, D., 'Zur Chronologie und Topographie der 'alten' und 'späten' englischen Komödianten in Deutschland', *Acta Neophilologica*, VIII (1975), pp. 47–65.

BIBLIOGRAPHY

Massner, K., *Die Kostümaustellung im K.K. Österreichischen Museum 1891*, (Vienna, 1892–3).

Meissner, 'Die englischen Komödianten in Oesterreich', *Jahrbuch der Deutschen Shakespeare-Gesellschaft*, 19 (1884), pp. 113–54.

Die englischen Comoedianten zur Zeit Shakespeares in Oesterreich (Vienna, 1884).

Mencík, F., *Příspévky k dějinám českého divadla* (Prague, 1865).

Mentzel, E., *Geschichte der Schauspielkunst in Frankfurt a.M.*, (Frankfurt, 1882).

Meyer, C.F., 'Englische Komödianten am Hofe des Herzogs Philip Julius von Pommern-Wolgast', *Jahrbuch der Deutschen Shakespeare-Gesellschaft*, 38 (1902), pp. 196–211.

Miks, N., 'Zbiór rysunków G.B. Gisleniego architekta XVII w. w Sir John Soan's Museum w Londynie', *Biuletyn Historii Sztuki*, XXIV (1962), pp. 328–39.

Miks-Rudkowska, N., 'Niektóre projekty dekoracji scenograficznych Giovanniego Battisty Gisleniego na dworze Wazów', *Opera w dawnej Polsce na dworze Władysława IV i królów saskich*, (Wrocław, Warsaw, Kraków and Gdańsk, 1973), pp. 9–24.

Morris, I., 'A Hapsburg Letter', *Modern Language Review*, 69 (1974), pp. 12–22.

Mundy, P., *The Travels . . . in Europe and Asia, 1608–1667* ed. R.C. Temple, 5 vols. [in six] (London, 1907–36) (Hakluyt Society Publications, Second Series, vols. 17, 35, 45, 46, 55, 78).

Murad, O., *The English Comedians at the Court in Graz 1607–1608, Elizabethan and Renaissance Studies*, 81 (Salzburg, 1978).

Niedecken-Gebhart, H., 'Neues Aktenmaterial über die Englischen Komödianten in Deutschland', *Euphorion*, 21 (1914) pp. 72–85.

Nieseen, C., *Dramatische Darstellungen in Köln von 1526–1700* (Cologne, 1917).

Nordström, J., 'Friedrich Menius, enavertyrlig Dorpatprofessor och hans glömda insats i det engelska komediant-dramatis historia', *Samlaren*, II (1922), pp. 42–91.

Nungezer, E., *A Dictionary of Actors* (New Haven, 1929).

Obraz dworów europejskich na początku XVII w. przedstawiony w dzienniku podróży królewicza Władysława syna Zygmunta III do Niemiec, Austrii, Belgii, Szwajcarii i Włoch w roku 1624–1625 (Wrocław, 1854).

A Particular Description of the City of Dantzick (London, 1734).

Poulton, D., *John Dowland* (London, 1982).

Price, L.M., *English > German Literary Influences*, University of California Publications in Modern Philology, vol. 9, no. 2 (1920).

English Literature in Germany, University of California Publications in Modern Philology, vol. 37 (1953).

Prölss, R., *Geschichte des Hoftheaters zu Dresden. Von seinen Anfängen bis zum Jahre 1862* (Dresden, 1878).

Puccitelli, V., 'La Maga Sdegnata (1640)', *Pamiętnik Teatralny*, XVIII, no. 4 (1969), pp 511–27.

Raszewski, Z., 'Jeszcze o teatrze zawodowym w dawnej Polsce', *Pamiętnik Teatralny*, 4 (1955), pp. 150–5.

Z tradycji teatralnych Pomorza, Wielkopolski i Śląska (Wrocław, 1955).

Krótka historia teatru polskiego (Warsaw, 1977).

Ravn, V.C., 'English Instrumentalists at the Danish Court in the Time of Shakespeare', *Sammelbände der Internationalen Musikgesellschaft*, VII (1905), pp. 550–63.

Relacje Nuncjuszów Apostolskich i innych osób o Polsce od roku 1548 do 1690, 2 vols., (Berlin and Poznań, 1864).

Riewald, J.G., 'Some Later Elizabethan and Early Stuart Actors and Musicians', *English Studies*, 40 (1959), pp. 33–41.

'New Light on the English Actors in the Netherlands, c. 1590–c. 1660', *English Studies*, 41 (1960), pp. 65–92.

Rommel, Ch.v., *Neuere Geschichte von Hessen* (Cassel, 1837).

Rub, O., *Die Dramatische Kunst in Danzig von 1615–1893* (Gdańsk, 1894).

Sarbiewski, M.K., 'O poezji doskonałej czyli Wegiliusz i Homer', *Pamiętnik Teatralny*, 3 (1953), pp. 21–39 (with an introduction by Z. Raszewski).

Satori-Neumann, B.Th., *Dreihundert Jahre berufständisches Theater in Elbing* (Gdańsk, 1936).

Scanlan, E.G., 'Notes on George Jolly's Stage in Frankfurt-on-Main, 1648–1658', *Theatre Notebook*, 7 (1952–3), pp. 17–18.

Schrickx, W., 'English Actors at the Courts of Wolfenbüttel, Brussels and Graz During the Lifetime of Shakespeare', *Shakespeare Survey*, 33 (1980), pp. 153–68.

'English Actors' Names in German Archives and Elizabethan Theatre History', *Jahrbuch der Deutschen Shakespeare-Gesellschaft* (1982), pp. 146–57.

'"Pickleherring" and English Actors in Germany', *Shakespeare Survey*, 36 (1983), pp. 135–47.

Schüpli, H., *Kurtze Beschreibung, was sich verlofnen Jahr bey Abholung Caecilliae Renatae etc. zugetragen* (Vienna, 1638).

Southern, R., *The Staging of Plays Before Shakespeare* (London, 1973).

Stahl, E.L., *Shakespeare und das deutsche Theater* (Stuttgart, 1947).

Stiehl, C., *Geschichte des Theaters in Lübeck* (Lübeck, 1902).

Stochholm, J.M., 'Introduction' to *The Great Duke of Florence by Philip Massinger* (Baltimore, 1933), pp. I–xxv.

Stopes, C.C., 'Dramatic Records from the Privy Council Register. James I and Charles I', *Jahrbuch der Deutschen Shakespeare-Gesellschaft*, 48 (1912), pp. 103–15.

Szumska, U., *Anglia a Polska w epoce humanizmu i reformacji. Związki kulturalne* Lwów, 1938).

Targosz-Kretowa, K., *Teatr dworski Władysława IV* (Kraków, 1965).

Teksty Zródłowe do Historii Teatru i Dramatu, ed. by Z. Raszewski, II (Wrocław, 1958).

Thaler, A., 'Travelling Players in Shakspere's England', *Modern Philology*, XVII, no. 9 (1920), pp. 489–514.

Thoms, J., 'English Actors in Germany', *Notes and Queries*, 2nd series, VIII (1859), pp. 21–2.

Tittmann, J., *Die Schauspiele der englischen Komödianten in Deutschland* (Leipzig, 1880).

Tomkiewicz, W., 'Widowiska dworskie w okresie renesansu', *Pamiętnik Teatralny*, 3 (1953), pp. 80–109.

'Dwie lustracje Zamku Warszawskiego', *Biuletyn Historii Sztuki*, XVI (1954), 3, pp. 295–314.

Z dziejów polskiego mecenatu artystycznego w XVIIw., (Wrocław, 1952).

Tragedia o bogaczu y Łazarzu, anonymous manuscript, dated 1643, in the collection of the PAN Library in Gdańsk: MS 2429.

Trautmann, K., 'Englische Komoedianten in München 1597, 1600, 1607', *Archiv für Litteraturgeschichte*, XII (1884), pp. 319–20.

'Englische Komoedianten in Ulm (1594–1657)', *Archiv für Litteraturgeschichte*, XIII (1885), pp. 315–24.

'Englische Komoedianten in Nürnberg bis zum Schlusse des Dreissigjährigen Krieges (1593–1648)', *Archiv für Litteraturgeschichte*, XIV (1886), pp. 113–36.

'Englische Komoedianten in Ulm (1602)', *Archiv für Litteraturgeschichte*, XV (1887), pp. 216–17.

'Englische Komoedianten in Stuttgart (1600, 1609, 1613–1614) und Tübingen (1597)', *Archiv für Litteraturgeschichte*, XV (1887), pp. 211–16.

BIBLIOGRAPHY

'Englische Komödianten in Rothenburg of der Tauber', *Zeitschrift für vergleichende Litteraturgeschichte*, 7 (1894), pp. 60–7.

Vajda, S., *Felix Austria. Eine Geschichte Österreichs* (Vienna and Heidelberg, 1980).

Vetulani, A., *Władztwo Polski w Prusiech Zakonnych i Książecych* (Wrocław, 1953). 'Prawny stosunek Prus Książecych do Polski 1466–1657', *Czasopismo Prawno-Historyczne*, VI (1954), pp. 7–41.

Vydra, B., *Teatr czeski od czasów czeskiego odrodzenia*, (Warsaw, 1926).

Wassenberg, E., *Gestorum gloriosissimi ac invictissimi Vladislai Poloniae et Sueciae Regis pars prima (et secunda)* (Gedani, 1641).

Wedgwood, C.V., *The Thirty Years War* (New York, 1961).

Weilen, A. von, *Geschichte des Wiener Theaterwesens von den ältesten Zeiten bis zu den Anfängen der Hoftheater*, vol. 1 of *Die Theater Wiens* (Vienna, 1899).

Wereszycki, H., *Historia Austrii*, (Wrocław, Warsaw, Kraków and Gdańsk, 1972).

Wikland, E., *Elizabethan Players in Sweden 1591–92. Facts and Problems* (Stockholm, Göteborg and Uppsala, 1962).

Wiley, W.L., *The Early Public Theatre in France* (Harvard and Cambridge, 1960).

Windakiewicz, S., *Teatr Władysława IV 1633–1648* (Kraków, 1893).
Teatr polski przed powstaniem sceny narodowej (Kraków, 1921).

Witczak, T., *Teatr i dramat staropolski w Gdańsku* (Gdańsk, 1959).

Witkowski, G., review of E. Herz's *Englische Schauspieler und englisches Schauspiel*, in: *Zeitschrift für deutsche Philologie*, XXXVI (1904), pp. 562–4.
'Englische Komödianten in Leipzig', *Euphorion*, XV (1908), pp. 441–4.

Wolter, J., 'Chronologie des Theaters der Reichstadt Köln', *Zeitschrift des Bergischen Geschichtsvereins*, 32 (1896), pp. 85–115.

Wormstall, A., 'Das Schauspiel zu Münster im 16. und 17. Jahrhundert', *Zeitschrift für vaterländische Geschichte und Alterthumskunde Westfalens*, LVI (1898), pp. 75–85.

Yates, F.A., 'English Actors in Paris During the Lifetime of Shakespeare', *Review of English Studies*, I (1925), pp. 392–403.

Zbierski, H., *Shakespeare and the 'War of the Theatres'* (Poznań, 1957).

Zimmerman, P., 'Englische Komödianten am Hofe zu Wolfenbüttel', *Braunschweigisches Magazin*, 4 (April 1902), pp. 37–45, 53–7.

Zins, H., *England and the Baltic in the Elizabethan Era* (Manchester, 1972).

Index

INDEX

INDEX

INDEX